This book offers a detailed study of political argument in early eighteenth-century England, a time in which the politics of virtue were vigorously pursued – and just as vigorously challenged. In tracing the emergence of a privately oriented conception of civic virtue from the period's public discourse, this book not only challenges the received notions of the fortunes of virtue in the early modern era but provides a promising critical perspective on the question of what sort of politics of virtue is possible or desirable today.

Virtue Transformed

Virtue Transformed

Political Argument in England, 1688–1740

Shelley Burtt

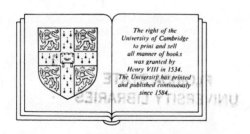

The right of the
University of Cambridge
to print and sell
all manner of books
was granted by
Henry VIII in 1534.
The University has printed
and published continuously
since 1584.

CAMBRIDGE UNIVERSITY PRESS
Cambridge
New York   Port Chester   Melbourne   Sydney

JA
79
B86
1991

Published by the Press Syndicate of the University of Cambridge
The Pitt Building, Trumpington Street, Cambridge CB2 1RP
40 West 20th Street, New York, NY 10011, USA
10 Stamford Road, Oakleigh, Melbourne 3166, Australia

First published 1992

Printed in the United States of America

Library of Congress Cataloging-in-Publication Data
Burtt, Shelley G.
Virtue transformed : political argument in England, 1688–1740 /
Shelley Burtt.
p.   cm.
Includes bibliographical references (p.   ) and index.
ISBN 0-521-37528-2 (hardcover)
1. Political ethics – Great Britain – History – 17th century.
2. Political ethics – Great Britain – History – 18th century.
3. Political science – Great Britain – History – 17th century.
4. Political science – Great Britain – History – 18th century.
I. Title.
JA79.B86   1991
172'.0941 – dc20   91-27095
CIP

A catalog record of this book is available from the British Library.

ISBN 0-521-37528-2 hardback

This book was published with the assistance of the Frederick
W. Hilles Publications Fund of Yale University.

For Donald, of course

Contents

Acknowledgements

In the long and satisfying process of nursing a first book into print, I have benefited immensely from the gifts of friends, family, and teachers. I must thank first of all my parents, for making my graduate education possible, and Judith Shklar, a demanding and dedicated adviser, for making it worthwhile. Others at Harvard, Cambridge and Yale who offered comments and encouragement at various stages of my academic travels and of this manuscript's development include Bruce Ackerman, John Brewer, John Dunn, Stephen Holmes, Istvan Hont, Tanya Luhrmann, Suzanne Marilley, Michael Sandel, Simon Schama, Ian Shapiro, George Shulman, Quentin Skinner, Rogers Smith and Steven Smith. Julia and Constance Meltzer, now four and two, deserve a special tribute for putting up with their mother's absences as gracefully as they did. Finally, this book is dedicated to Donald Meltzer, husband and friend, whose enthusiasm and unwavering support for my intellectual and academic endeavors have illumined the past decade. To all you who inspired and advised, thank you.

1

◁══▷

Introduction

After staking so much for so long on the effective operation of self-interest rightly understood, political scientists, political theorists, politicians themselves have begun to call for a renewed appreciation of the place of virtue in the citizenry's moral and political life. The roles virtue is invited to play are manifold, and the politics that underlies this renewed interest in such virtue is diverse. The cultivation of virtue – moral virtue, civic virtue, private virtue, public virtue – is praised both as an intrinsic good that might animate the citizen's public and private endeavors and as a means to the better securing of the most basic political end: "the preservation of the community and its way of life."[1] Some of those striving to bring virtue back into political argument have only minimal quarrels with the status quo, adapting their proposals to a modern polity understood to function primarily on the basis of self-interest and the satisfaction of material desires.[2] Others, however, espouse a more transformative politics of virtue – one that would recall the modern polity to Aristotelian principles of government – or at the very least, to a political program in which the cultivation of the virtues, public or private, moral or civic, would play a far greater role than the one accorded it in the current Western incarnations of liberal democracy.[3]

1 William A. Galston, "Liberal Virtues," *American Political Science Review* 82 (1988), 1280.
2 The case for the pursuit of political virtues already practiced by or easily cultivated within liberal democratic citizens is made by, among others, Bruce A. Ackerman, "The Storrs Lectures: Discovering the Constitution," *Yale Law Journal* 93 (1984): 1013–72; Rogers Smith, *Liberalism and American Constitutional Law* (Cambridge: Harvard University Press, 1985); Stephen L. Elkin, *City and Regime in the American Republic* (Chicago: University of Chicago Press, 1987); Stephen Macedo, *Liberal Virtues: Citizenship, Virtue, and Community in Liberal Constitutionalism* (Oxford: Oxford University Press), 1990.
3 Alasdair MacIntyre's moral philosophy implicitly supports an Aristotelian politics of virtue; see especially *After Virtue: A Study in Moral Theory* (Notre Dame: University of Notre Dame Press, 1981). Explicit advocacy of such a politics can be found in, among others, J.

The possibility and desirability of implementing any of these agendas is rightly a matter of some debate, mostly within the academy, but also, in attenuated tones, without. Two issues figure most prominently in this discussion. The first concerns the compatibility of wealth and virtue. What sort of virtues can be expected of the citizens of commercial liberal society, their private lives bursting with claims on their time and energy, their public, political lives strangely stunted?[4] Although it is possible to consider this question solely in terms of the political culture of late twentieth-century capitalism, most recent work has focused on a related historical inquiry. To what extent did the rise of commercial society and its attendant ideology of liberalism make the practice of civic virtue impossible? J. G. A. Pocock has framed his account of the last generations of the republican tradition in terms of this antinomy between virtue and commerce, and much of the continuing controversy surrounding the principles of the American founding places this question at its center.[5] The issue of the compatibility of wealth and virtue is thus historical as well as contemporary: not just whether we twentieth-century Americans (and Europeans) are handicapped

Budziszewski, *The Resurrection of Nature: Political Theory and the Human Character* (Ithaca: Cornell University Press, 1986); *The Nearest Coast of Darkness: A Vindication of the Politics of Virtues* (Ithaca: Cornell University Press, 1988) and Stephen Salkever, *Finding the Mean: Theory and Practice in Aristotelian Political Philosophy* (Princeton: Princeton University Press, 1990).

   Other works not explicitly Aristotelian, but still committed to a strong politics of virtue include George Will, *Statecraft as Soulcraft: What Government Does* (New York: Simon and Schuster, 1983); Clarke Cochran, *Character, Community, and Politics* (University: University of Alabama Press, 1982); William Sullivan, *Reconstructing Public Philosophy* (Berkeley: University of California Press, 1986) and from a religious perspective, Stanley Hauerwas, *A Community of Character: Toward a Constructive Christian Social Ethic* (Notre Dame: University of Notre Dame Press, 1981).

4 For an early effort to grapple with this problem, see Fred Hirsch, *Social Limits to Growth* (Cambridge: Harvard University Press, 1976) and more recently Robert N. Bellah et al., *Habits of the Heart* (Berkeley: University of California Press, 1985).

5 For Pocock's account, see especially "Virtue and Commerce in the Eighteenth Century," *Journal of Interdisciplinary History* 3 (1972): 119–34; "Early Modern Capitalism: The Augustan Perception," in Eugene Kamenka and R.S. Neale, eds., *Feudalism, Capitalism and Beyond* (Canberra: Australian National University Press, 1975); *The Machiavellian Moment: Florentine Political Thought and the Atlantic Republican Tradition* (Princeton: Princeton University Press, 1975), chapters 14 and 15 and *Virtue, Commerce, and History: Essays on Political Thought and History, Chiefly in the Eighteenth Century* (Cambridge University Press, 1985).

   On the American debate, see besides Pocock, Gordon S. Wood, *The Creation of the American Republic, 1776–1787* (New York: W.W. Norton and Company, 1969) and the slew of books and articles that followed its publication, ably summarized in the articles of Robert E. Shalhope, "Toward a Republican Synthesis: The Emergence of an Understanding of Republicanism in American Historiography," *William and Mary Quarterly*, 3d series, 29 (1972): 49–80; "Republicanism and Early American Historiography," *ibid.* 39 (1982): 334–56 and Peter S. Onuf, "Reflections on the Founding: Constitutional Historiography in Bicentennial Perspective," *ibid.* 46 (1989): 341–75.

in the pursuit of virtue by commercial society, but whether at the founding of their new republic, Americans took a turn away from virtue that continues to plague (or bless) their polity today.

The second question central to the debate on civic virtue raises issues equally as far-reaching. Is it possible to institute a politics of virtue in which the freedoms of liberalism would coexist with a greater commitment to a common morality and the public good? Most participants in what has come to be called the "republican revival" assure us that we may have the best of both worlds, a modern pluralistic society converted into a "community of the good" without endangering the personal liberties that remain the distinctive achievement of liberal democracies.[6] Critics of such republican communitarianism dispute this assertion, arguing that the practice of political virtue called for in such proposals necessarily entails the type of homogeneous, close-knit, overbearing community lauded by theorists like Harrington and Rousseau but rarely found palatable in practice. Calls for the renewal of virtue, these critics point out, retain their appeal by avoiding the question of what precisely the renewal of virtue would mean politically, what procedures and institutions would be used to call forth the virtue desired.[7]

How then are we to decide whether a politics of virtue is fit for the modern world or not? One possibility, little explored in the literature, is to consider the lessons of history. Ours is certainly not the first generation to entertain the idea of bettering society through increasing the virtue of its members. However, the fact that we are once again debating the uses to which a greater civic virtue could be put is ample evidence that none of the previous experiments in a politics of virtue was lastingly effective. Perhaps by examining the problems encountered by an earlier effort to impose a

6 Explicit assurances to this effect can be found in Frank Michelman, "Law's Republic," *The Yale Law Journal* 97 (1988): 1493–538 and Cass Sunstein, "Beyond the Republican Revival," *ibid.:* 1539–90. See also Clarke Cochran, *Character, Community, and Politics,* esp. chapters 7 and 8; Benjamin R. Barber, *Strong Democracy: Participatory Politics for a New Age* (Berkeley: University of California Press, 1984) and Michael J. Sandel, "Morality and the Liberal Ideal," *The New Republic,* May 7, 1984.

7 A particularly damning indictment of republican vagueness can be found in John R. Wallach, "Liberals, Communitarians and the Tasks of Political Theory," *Political Theory* 15 (1987): 581–611. For the potential dangers implicit in contemporary proposals for a politics of virtue, see Amy Gutmann, "Communitarian Critics of Liberalism," *Philosophy and Public Affairs* 14 (1985): 308–22; Don Herzog, "Some Questions for Republicans," *Political Theory* 14 (1986): 473–93; H. N. Hirsch, "The Threnody of Liberalism: Constitutional Liberty and the Renewal of Community," *ibid.:* 423–50; Stephen Holmes, "The Permanent Structure of Antiliberal Thought," in Nancy L. Rosenblum, ed., *Liberalism and the Moral Life* (Cambridge: Harvard University Press, 1989) and George Kateb, "Democratic Individuality and the Meaning of Rights," in *ibid.* A far more sympathetic consideration of the strengths as well as the weaknesses of communitarian ideals can be found in Christopher J. Berry, *The Idea of a Democratic Community* (New York: St. Martin's Press, 1989).

4 *Virtue Transformed*

politics of virtue, we can learn more about the prospects for such an under-
taking today. Were the problems encountered by the advocates of civic
virtue unique to that period or are they likely to surface again today? Were
these problems directly linked to the rise of commercial society? Or was the
gradual eclipse of virtue the result of contingent factors that would not
trouble a renewal of virtue today? Did this earlier debate on the importance
and possibility of civic virtue produce any conceptions of the good citizen
upon which we now could draw? Or are all forms of civic virtue tied to
political and social structures no longer available to modern polities? None
of these questions has been systematically addressed by either proponents
or critics of the revival of virtue. Yet an understanding of how and why
various politics of virtue once lost their force could help us decide if it is
appropriate or possible again to pursue politics of this sort in the contemporary political arena.

This study then looks backwards in time to the beginning of the modern
era, to the first years of the eighteenth century in England, a time in which
the politics of virtue were vigorously pursued – and just as vigorously challenged. By investigating the factors that led in this period to the transformation of virtue, to the discrediting of publicly oriented ideas of civic virtue
and the emergence of privately oriented ones, I hope to provide a promising
critical perspective on the question of what sort of politics of virtue are
possible or desirable today.

In tackling this question, I begin with the vexing problem of definitions. I
have just written of public virtue and civic virtue, of publicly oriented civic
virtue and privately oriented civic virtue. Because my argument is not one
that sits easily with the generally accepted account of political thought in
this period, I want to clarify here what I mean by these terms.

The term "civic virtue" as applied to eighteenth-century political thought
is an anachronism. Augustan writers consumed with the problem of the
place of virtue in their polity spoke of public virtue, private virtue, public
spirit, politick virtues, patriotism, but not of civic virtue nor even of political
virtue.[8] J. G. A. Pocock, however, among others, has made a forceful case that
at least some Augustans worried about something that we can now call civic
virtue even if the eighteenth-century authors gave this praiseworthy citizenly disposition other names, and I agree with him. The question then

8 These terms come, in order, from Charles Davenant, *An Essay on the Probable Methods of
Making the People Gainers in the Balance of Trade* (1699) in *The Political and Commercial Works* (London, 1771), II, 338; John Trenchard and Thomas Gordon, *Cato's Letters*, 4 v.,
3d ed., facsimile reprint in 2 v. (New York: Russell and Russell, [1733] 1969), II, 11; *ibid.*, I,
6–7; *The Spectator*, 4 v. (London: J.M. Dent and Sons, 1957), no. 93; *ibid.*, no. 248; Henry St.
John, Viscount Bolingbroke, *Letter on the Spirit of Patriotism*, in *Works*, 4 v. (London: Henry
Bohn, 1844; reprint New York: A.M. Kelley, 1967).

arises of what we take the term "civic virtue" to mean both in general and as it is applied to the thought of eighteenth-century Englishmen.[9]

In thinking about this question it is helpful to observe that the virtues can be defined both substantively (through a descriptive list of what counts as human virtues) and formally (by means of a definition abstract enough to accommodate the various members of the substantive list). Considerations of virtue in moral philosophy typically proceed along these lines. Thus Edmund Pincoffs defines the moral virtues as "forms of regard . . . for the interests of others" and provides a listing of them which includes honesty, loyalty, benevolence, selflessness, reliability, helpfulness.[10] Josef Pieper speaks of those excellences which "can enable man to attain the furthest potentialities of his nature" and focuses on four in particular, the cardinal virtues of prudence, justice, fortitude and temperance.[11]

This mode of understanding the moral virtues may be extended by analogy to the political virtues. We tend, for example, to define political virtue with a list of the citizenly dispositions favored by the classical republican tradition: public spirit, patriotism, love of country, love of equality, the willingness to subordinate private to public good. But republican authors consider these character traits politically virtuous because, given republican ideals of the good community, they render the citizen the best possible member of the polity. Just as the moral virtues "make an individual a good human being" so the political virtues, formally understood, are those that make the individual a good citizen.[12] Joseph Raz's account captures this approach when he describes the political virtues as "mark[ing] the quality of people as citizens. They are forms of individual excellence which are manifested in public attitudes and actions."[13]

9 I use the word "Englishmen" advisedly. Although a few women entered the lists of Augustan political controversy (Mary Astell, for example, in favor of the ultraconservative High Church cause), the writers on political virtue are overwhelmingly male. On Astell, see Ruth Perry, *The Celebrated Mary Astell: An Early English Feminist* (Chicago: University of Chicago Press, 1986). There remains the more difficult issue of whether the virtues argued for by these men are understood to be desirable properties of men alone or of English men and women. This issue was never confronted in the contemporary literature and, by keeping most references to citizens plural, my analysis generally reflects this ambiguity. In fact, of the works discussed below, only Bolingbroke's account of a virtuous "spirit of patriotism" is on its face exclusively masculine for it assumes that patriots will be members of parliament, an office barred to women at this time. The other understandings of citizen virtue I examine here see it issuing in public actions available, at least in theory, to both men and women.

10 Edmund L. Pincoffs, *Quandaries and Virtues: Against Reductivism in Ethics* (Lawrence: University Press of Kansas, 1986), 89, 85.

11 Josef Pieper, *The Four Cardinal Virtues: Prudence, Justice, Fortitude, and Temperance* (Notre Dame: University of Notre Dame Press, [1954] 1966), xii.

12 James D. Wallace, *Virtues and Vices* (Ithaca: Cornell University Press, 1978), 41.

13 Joseph Raz, "Facing Diversity: The Case of Epistemic Abstinence," *Philosophy and Public Affairs* 19 (1990), 22. The philosophical literature on the virtues contains a certain amount

Different understandings of what constitutes and sustains the good state will thus produce different understandings of what constitutes political virtue. There are certain political virtues that fit liberal society, others that fit republican; Christian philosophies will offer one sort of vision of the good citizen, secular theories another. This pluralistic approach to political virtue reflects Aristotle's view that while there might be one best regime, political virtue cannot be said to exist only in that polity. Rather, "the excellence of the citizen must be an excellence relative to the constitution."[14]

A very few modern commentators regard "civic virtue" as synonymous with "political virtue." They treat it as a term that stands simply for "the moral and political qualities that make a good citizen," whatever the regime within which the citizen finds him- or herself.[15] Thus Richard Sinopoli contends, "Civic virtue can be defined formally as a disposition among citizens to engage in activities which support and maintain a just political order." He adds specifically, "This definition is neutral with regard to the particular plan of justice the citizen supports."[16] This conflation has the advantage of simplicity, yet it slights the particularly charged meaning "civic," as opposed to "political," has acquired in recent years. For most people interested in the matter, to say that individuals have civic virtue is to say something very definite about the regime in which these virtuous individuals live, the qualities they possess and the activities in the public realm which these qualities support or dispose to. For this reason, it makes sense to treat "civic" as a separate, narrower category than "political," and to designate civic virtue as a specific sort of political virtue, one particularly appropriate to and manifested in a political regime that allows for a civic mode of life.

What we need now is a concrete sense of what is meant by a civic mode of life. Following much of the recent work on this question, I would describe a civic mode of life as one that is grounded in "participatory self-rule." It is bounded on one side by despotism and on the other by extreme forms of

---

of debate on the question of how to characterize the virtues: as "dispositions to act in certain ways," "skills," "habits," "qualities," "excellences," "properties of the person," "character traits," etc. For these alternatives in particular, see Gilbert C. Meilaender, *The Theory and Practice of Virtue* (Notre Dame: University of Notre Dame Press, 1984), chapter 1; Budziszewski, *Resurrection of Nature*, 95; Pincoffs, *Quandaries and Virtues*, chapter 5. Without slighting what is at stake in making these distinctions, I use "dispositions," "character traits," "excellences," and "qualities," interchangeably to describe the nature of the political and civic virtues with which I am concerned.

14 Aristotle, *The Politics*, 1276b:11–31.

15 Michael Walzer, *Radical Principles: Reflections of an Unreconstructed Democrat* (New York: Basic Books, 1980), 55.

16 Richard C. Sinopoli, "Liberalism, Republicanism and the Constitution," *Polity* 19 (1987), 344.

"procedural liberalism."[17] Between these poles lie a variety of regimes in which individuals participate, to a greater or lesser extent, in the shaping of their collective destiny. Here I think is the key to an appropriately expansive definition of civic virtue. Civic virtue names those dispositions of the individual that make him or her a good citizen of this sort of regime – that is, that lead him or her to engage in the sort of public (and private) behavior that enable a civic mode of life both to survive and to flourish.

Some might object that this approach frames the definition of civic virtue too broadly. For them, the distinguishing feature of a civic regime is the priority it places on political activism – either as "the very substance of the good life," or as the only way to stave off despotism.[18] The qualities or dispositions that make an individual an enthusiastic and effective participant in such a demanding public life are the only ones that, in this reading, should count as civic virtue. Regimes that do not require or expect a thorough engagement in public affairs cannot be homes to *civic* virtue, although their inhabitants may exhibit political virtue of some other sort.

But this objection unduly narrows the scope of the civic, ruling out of hand its presence in free societies that have a somewhat less demanding sense of the nature of and requirements for "participatory self-rule." A correct understanding of the virtues that sustain a free society must include some that dispose the citizen to political action on a fairly regular basis. However, it is possible to imagine and proper to leave room for an account of the qualities that keep people free that does not depend on their immersing themselves in the public realm, and I shall attempt to make the case for one at the conclusion of this study.

Of course, most students of the classical republican tradition describe its conception of civic virtue in a way that would seem to be at odds with the definition I have just defended. Thus Isaac Kramnick writes, "The meaning of virtue in the language of civic humanism is clear. It is the privileging of the public over the private." Gordon Wood describes "what the eighteenth century termed public virtue" as the "willingness of the individual to sacrifice his private interest for the good of the community." And Anthony Pagden observes, "For most classical republicans, liberty could only be achieved by each man's willingness to renounce his purely private concerns for the greater good of the community."[19] But the evident gap between my

17 Charles Taylor, "Cross-Purposes: The Liberal-Communitarian Debate," in Nancy L. Rosenblum, ed., *Liberalism and the Moral Life* (Cambridge: Harvard University Press, 1989), 178, 172.
18 Budziszewski, *Resurrection of Nature,* 109. For a classic formulation of this view, see Hannah Arendt, "What is Freedom?" in Hannah Arendt, *Between Past and Future: Eight Exercises in Political Thought* (New York: Penguin Books, 1954).
19 Isaac Kramnick, "The 'Great National Discussion': The Discourse of Politics in 1787," *William and Mary Quarterly,* 3d ser. 45 (1988), 15; Wood, *Creation of the American Repub-*

definition and theirs does not necessarily mean that the accounts conflict. Their definitions correctly characterize the particular answer given consistently throughout the republican tradition to the question, "What citizen excellences are necessary to preserve a free and flourishing society?" What is particularly interesting about the eighteenth century – and what the following case studies seek to underscore – is that for perhaps the first time in history, new answers to this question emerged, answers that affirmed the importance and possibility of civic virtue while refashioning its content.

Up until this point in history, those speculating about the conditions for a free society argued that its inhabitants must possess a strongly public virtue, one understood, says J. G. A. Pocock, in an "austerely civic, Roman and Arendtian sense."[20] (Not all inhabitants need possess this virtue – just those men with sufficient property to qualify them for the franchise or, more restrictively, for service in parliament.) In this view, the character traits that made such a citizen virtuous, that made him an effective defender of civic liberty and a judicious deliberator on the public good, were those that disposed him to give priority to the realm of politics, to find personal fulfillment in public service.

Pocock has vividly evoked the various political and economic pressures which led some writers in early eighteenth-century England to fear for the survival of such virtue and in consequence propose strategies by which society might remain free and stable without recourse to political virtues at all.[21] As Pocock describes it, those Augustan authors who interpreted the circumstances of England's post-revolutionary polity as undermining the English citizen's capacity for virtue faced a stark alternative. They could pursue a traditional politics of public virtue in the hopes that such virtue "might be reaffirmed independently of social conditions" (perhaps "by means of legislation or educative example"). Or they could "admit that government was an affair of managing the passions" and seek to develop an account of the good polity that dispensed with an ideal of citizen excellence altogether.[22]

This account, although a powerful rendering of certain aspects of eighteenth-century thought, overlooks a third path, an important alternative to these extremes in which civic virtue is not abandoned but transformed. I have tried to capture the nature of this transformation by distinguishing

---

lic, 68; Anthony Pagden, "Introduction," in Anthony Pagden, ed., *The Languages of Political Theory in Early Modern Europe* (Cambridge University Press, 1987), 10.

20 Pocock, *Virtue, Commerce, and History,* 48.
21 See especially Pocock, *Machiavellian Moment,* 446–60, "Early Modern Capitalism," and *Virtue, Commerce, and History,* chapter 6.
22 Pocock, *Machiavellian Moment,* 459.

between a publicly oriented civic virtue (what we now usually call civic virtue or public virtue) and a privately oriented one, arguing that as the case for publicly oriented virtue faltered in eighteenth-century English political argument, the idea of a civic virtue more privately oriented emerged.

To call a civic virtue "privately oriented" might strike one as a contradiction in terms; let me say a little here about how I use the term and why I think the term makes sense of a particular development in Augustan political thought.

The accounts of civic virtue with which we are most familiar are ones that posit a stark divide between public and private, arguing that the good citizen is one who privileges the public, political realm over private, personal wants, desires, ambitions.[23] Civic virtue conceived in this manner is often called "public virtue." Thus Carter Braxton, writing during the American Revolution contrasted public virtue, "a disinterested attachment to the public good, exclusive and independent of all private and selfish interest," with private virtue, in which man "acts for himself, and with a view of promoting his own particular welfare."[24] Public virtue retains a similar meaning today: a recent account described "the elements of public virtue" as "dedication to the well-being of one's political community and willingness to sacrifice for it."[25] In describing the virtuous citizen as imbued with "love of one's country" or "public spirit," the classical republican tradition embraces this publicly oriented conception of civic virtue as well.

In all these examples, the qualities that make a citizen virtuous, while variously described, hinge on a mindset in which the goods of the public realm, the world of political action and deliberation, are given priority over private goods – whether from a rational decision to set aside "private interests" or from an intense emotional engagement with the public and its goods (liberty, national honor, political action itself.)[26] I call conceptions of political or civic virtue grounded in such a mindset "publicly oriented."

Political virtues in general and civic virtues in particular may also be privately oriented. That is, individuals can serve the public, engage in behavior that advances the stability, freedom and flourishing of their polity without possessing the passionate attachment to the polity and its needs that

23 For the various meanings the words "public" and "private" can take on in political argument, see Hanna Pitkin, "Justice: On Relating Public to Private," *Political Theory* 9 (1981): 327–52. I use public here in a strongly political sense, to refer to the goods and concerns of the *res publica* as considered separately from both the personal and the broadly social.
24 Carter Braxton, *Address to the Convention of...Virginia; on the Subject of Government* (Williamsburg, 1776) as quoted in Wood, *Creation of the American Republic*, 96.
25 Smith, *Liberalism and American Constitutional Law*, 52.
26 For a further discussion of these alternatives see Shelley Burtt, "The Good Citizen's Psyche: On the Psychology of Civic Virtue," *Polity* 23 (1990): 23–38.

grounds the more familiar sort of publicly oriented political virtue described above. This is not to say that such individuals have suddenly become
"perfect privatists," inhabitants of a liberal state that asks nothing from them
but that they treat others and others' life goals with equal concern and
respect.[27] Rather, these are individuals who are exemplary citizens, energeti-
cally defending the ideals of their polity in public, political action, but who
are disposed to these endeavors by concerns or character traits that lie
outside of or do not directly engage the public realm.

Consider for example the account of the good citizen offered by Court
Whig journalists, whose business it was to defend the prime minister Robert
Walpole from opposition attacks in the 1730s. The opposition argued that
only an unswerving devotion to the principles of the balanced constitution
could gird individuals to defend the independence of parliament against the
corrupting force of ministerial influence. Court Whigs took an opposing
view, arguing that the dispositions which contributed most importantly to
the preservation of public liberty were personal honesty, industry, frugality
in one's personal affairs. By preventing one from becoming so needy as to
succumb to ministerial blandishments these qualities grounded the responsible public deliberation that was the mark of the good citizen.[28] It would be
hard to characterize this Court Whig conception of citizen virtue as publicly
oriented: the citizens' actions are not grounded in the "disinterested attachment to the public good" or "dedication to the well-being of one's political
community" that both eighteenth-century and modern accounts describe as
central to public virtue.[29] But neither is it correct to say that the Court
Whigs have given up on civic virtue altogether. Their ideal citizens behave
in precisely the same way as the opposition's, acting in public to defend the
nation's liberty against pernicious usurpers. In the Court Whig account,
however, the character traits that ground this service to the public are
personal virtues of honest and frugal household management. For this reason it is appropriate to describe the Court Whigs as advocating a privately
oriented civic virtue, i.e., a quality that disposes to behavior beneficial to the
public but not for publicly oriented reasons.[30]

Cato's Letters, the work of two critics of Walpole's administration writing
in the 1720s, also advances a conception of civic virtue that is best understood as privately oriented. The letters, first published in the wake of the

27 The phrase "perfect privatist" is Bruce Ackerman's, used with somewhat different connota-
   tions in "The Storrs Lectures," 1033.
28 These contrasting accounts of civic virtue are further discussed in chapters 5 and 6.
29 See notes 24 and 25 of this chapter.
30 One can grant that the Court Whigs articulate a privately oriented conception of civic
   virtue without implying that it is a particularly persuasive one. See chapter 8.

South Sea Bubble, are concerned to urge an unduly complacent citizenry to defend good government and liberty against the corrupt and tyrannical schemes of those in power. Cato however expects such behavior to stem not from an abstract public spirit or love of one's country but from the most visceral personal concern for one's individual safety and happiness.[31] Because the citizens of Cato's imagination act publicly to defend traditional English liberties against tyrannous usurpers, they are virtuous, not just morally but politically. But because they enter the public arena out of concern for their own well-being rather than from a devotion to the public good, understood as separate and distinct from private advantage, their virtue is best characterized as privately oriented.

One final example should give a sense of the distinction to be made between publicly and privately oriented political virtue. Ever since Locke, we readily place tolerance among the pantheon of liberal virtues. Now, if one undertook to be publicly tolerant out of dedication to all that a liberal regime stands for, if one set aside personal distastes, or explictly renounced religious enthusiasms, because one believed such personal preferences must be subordinated to the public good of the liberal polity, we could and should describe this character trait as a publicly oriented political virtue. Tolerance of different beliefs and lifestyles might also come from more self-interested motives, perhaps a calculation that a tolerant disposition towards others' life choices was the best way to secure the pursuit of one's own goals. In this circumstance, one would still possess a political virtue valued by the liberal regime. But it would be a virtue properly characterized as privately rather than publicly oriented, arising from concerns that did not engage the community as a whole.[32]

It might seem paradoxical to admit to the existence of privately oriented civic virtues. Because a civic mode of life is usually thought to glorify public actions (whether bellicose military adventurism or sober public deliberation) at the expense of mundane, personal, private concerns, it is also thought to require citizens devoted to the public realm, willing to subordinate or sacrifice private interests to the public good. Civic virtue, in this vision, must be publicly oriented. But to insist on this connection grants the classical republican tradition a monopoly of insight into the qualities necessary to sustain a free, self-governing polity. My argument, pursued in the

---

31 See the discussion in chapter 4.
32 Two recent and helpful considerations of tolerance as a liberal political virtue are Joseph Raz, "Autonomy, toleration, and the harm principle," in Susan Mendus, ed., *Justifying Toleration: Conceptual and Historical Perspectives* (Cambridge University Press, 1988) and Susan Mendus, *Toleration and the Limits of Liberalism* (Atlantic Highlands, NJ: Humanities Press International, 1989), chapter 5.

chapters that follow, is that eighteenth-century English authors offered no uniform response to the question of what qualities best sustained a civic mode of life, what dispositions of the citizenry best enhanced the possibilities of self-government and protected against despotism. Some affirmed the necessity of a virtue best described as publicly oriented; others proposed to rely on a civic virtue that was, in one way or another, privately oriented. It may turn out, as one examines the alternatives, that the classical republican tradition is uniquely persuasive about the virtues required to uphold a civic regime; that fact does not however justify dismissing all other comers out of hand.[33]

This distinction between political virtues that are publicly and privately oriented is an important one for the purposes of this study on two counts. First, it alerts us to the varieties of virtue in eighteenth-century political argument. In so doing, it underscores the fact that the questions of what happened to the politics of public virtue in the post-revolutionary polity and why should not simply be converted into the question of what happened to the classical republican ideal of civic virtue between 1688 and 1740. There are more understandings of political virtue present in Augustan political argument than the republican one alone. But I have used the phrase "politics of *public* virtue" advisedly. The conceptions of political virtue most prominent in the early eighteenth century were publicly oriented ones – ideals that saw a citizen's virtue, civic and otherwise, as directed towards public ends and cultivated by public means. To document the decline of such conceptions of virtue is not to exhaust the possibilities for political virtue. Distinguishing between publicly and privately oriented conceptions of political virtue thus allows a more precise characterization of the accounts of political virtue flourishing in this period – and a first hint of what, in the end, might have caused their difficulties.

The question then arises of whether Augustan political argument provided any alternatives to the politics of public virtue once these various politics began to founder. Here too the distinction between publicly and privately oriented sorts of political virtue plays an important role. J. G. A. Pocock has recently argued that as a publicly conceived civic virtue was seen to slip from the reach of modern citizens, the favored political alternative became the ethos of politeness; moralists and philosophers argued that

---

33 It is important to remember in assessing this argument that "civic virtue" is not a term indigenous to the eighteenth century. It is a term used by twentieth-century scholars to identify those qualities and character traits, called in the eighteenth century by other names, that are seen as necessary to the safeguarding and flourishing of a civic mode of life. The term is generally limited in application to the account of these qualities provided by the classical republican tradition, although I argue here that it need not be.

manners might substitute for virtue in making the political world run smoothly.[34] Or one might argue simply that Adam Smith's invisible hand emerged to do the job; enlightened self-interest replaced civic virtue in modern liberal democracies.[35] Both these proposals capture aspects of eighteenth-century political argument. The school of political journalists associated most notably with Addison and Steele can indeed be read as offering in the ideal of politeness a way to ground society without resort to political virtue; Adam Smith and the Scottish political economists are usually seen as favoring market mechanisms to accomplish this same task.[36] But these accounts overlook a third alternative, one more immediately the child of early eighteenth-century English debate about the possibility of civic virtue than the other two. This alternative reserves a place for virtuous citizens in the modern polity but does not ground their virtue in an attachment to or affinity for public life. Rather, good citizens come to serve their country and preserve its liberty for reasons rooted in personal interests and commitments, private concerns that also dispose to virtuous public action.

Most historical studies graphing the trajectory of civic virtue portray its fate in all or nothing terms: a society passes directly from a republican politics based on an all-encompassing emotional engagement with the *polis* to a liberal society peopled by economically active, politically passive interest-maximizers. In fact, there are ways of conceiving of civic virtue, ways I have subsumed under the category "privately oriented civic virtue," which do not demand of citizens the intense public orientation so often held to epitomize the civically virtuous individual but which do preserve the potential for public-regarding action in the life of the citizen. This approach to the understanding of civic virtue emerged in the early eighteenth century

---

34 Pocock, *Virtue, Commerce, and History,* 48–9; 235–7.
35 The classic argument here is Alexis de Tocqueville, *Democracy in America,* ed. J.P. Mayer (New York: Doubleday, 1969), 525–8 (v. 2, part 2, chapter 8).
36 For Addison's contribution, see Edward A. Bloom and Lillian D. Bloom, *Joseph Addison's Sociable Animal in the Market Place, on the Hustings, in the Pulpit* (Providence: Brown University Press, 1971) and J. G. A. Pocock, "The Problem of Political Thought in the Eighteenth Century: Patriotism and Politeness," *Theoretische Geschiedenis* 9 (1982): 14–17. On the Scottish Enlightenment, see especially Nicholas Phillipson, "The Scottish Enlightenment," in Roy Porter and Mikulas Teich, eds., *The Enlightenment in National Context* (Cambridge University Press, 1981), 36 and for an account that links Addison to the Scottish Enlightenment, Nicholas Phillipson, "Adam Smith as Civic Moralist," in Istvan Hont and Michael Ignatieff, eds., *Wealth and Virtue: The Shaping of Political Economy in the Scottish Enlightenment* (Cambridge University Press, 1983), 197–201. See also, in the same volume, John Robertson, "The Scottish Enlightenment at The Limits of the Civic Tradition" and Frank D. Balog, "The Scottish Enlightenment and the Liberal Political Tradition," in Allan Bloom, ed., *Confronting the Constitution* (Washington, DC: American Enterprise Institute, 1990). As the different arguments of these authors indicate, there is as yet no agreement on how precisely Scottish writers reconstituted or replaced the classical principles of civic virtue.

in England as one alternative to the various and variously unsatisfactory politics of public virtue that characterized the period.

Focusing on this aspect of political argument in Augustan England thus illuminates a part of the history of political thought that is usually in shadow. Although we know a great deal about the ideology of public virtue as put forward in classical republican thought and a good deal about the more or less liberal philosophies that, from the Scottish Enlightenment on, began to replace it, we have much less knowledge of the processes that paved the way for the transition from one to the other. At times this transition is even pictured as the triumph of an alien ideology (liberalism) over an aging competitor, a tired republicanism thrust aside by the forces of history.[37] In tracing the emergence of a privately oriented conception of civic virtue from the contentious debates over the prospects for a publicly oriented one, this book deliberately relimns this confrontational image. Instead of a showdown between hostile alternatives I make the case for a gradual development of political possibilities spun out from within the politics of virtue themselves. The task that then faces the historian of political thought – and forms the focus of the following chapters – is not to document and explain the eclipse of virtue, but to trace its *transformation.*

37 Isaac Kramnick, *Bolingbroke and His Circle: The Politics of Nostalgia in the Age of Walpole* (Cambridge: Harvard University Press, 1968), 6, 234. Although Pocock's account is far more nuanced, it too can suggest this image as, for example, in *Virtue, Commerce, and History,* 234–9.

2

The politics of virtue in Augustan England

February 1689, just over three months since William of Orange's army had landed at Torbay. James II was in France, having fled the country in late December. William was in London, the most likely candidate to fill the vacancy that James had created. A newly elected Convention Parliament was attempting to draft a "settlement" that would bring a new monarch to the throne under conditions set by the people of England. The parliament met for the first time on January 22. A Declaration of Rights was passed February 12; a formal invitation to William and Mary made on the thirteenth.[1]

In three short weeks, English elites had successfully and on the whole peaceably overhauled the political foundations of their nation, exchanging an essentially absolutist system for the relative freedoms of a limited monarchy. But how best to consolidate the gains so miraculously obtained? For some the answer was a comprehensive "reformation of manners," the sooner the better. The "inundation of immorality and irreligion" that had plagued the country under James II's reign had to be stanched if the health and stability of the new regime were to be secured.[2] In fact, the firmly protestant regime ushered in by the Revolution appeared to many Englishmen ideally suited to the revival of a politics of public virtue made difficult by the religious and political commitments of the Stuarts. As one of the leaders of the Country opposition wrote of this time, "we expected virtue and honesty should have succeeded better than ever."[3]

1 J. R. Jones, *The Revolution of 1688 in England* (New York: W. W. Norton and Company, 1972), chapters 10 and 11.
2 *Reflexions upon the Moral State of the Nation* (London, 1701), 4. See also [Francis Grant, Lord Cullen], *A Brief Account of the Nature, Rise, and Progress of the Societies for Reformation of Manners, &c,* (Edinburgh, 1700).
3 The first Earl of Shaftesbury, quoted in E. L. Ellis, "William III and the Politicians," in Geoffrey Holmes, ed. *Britain after the Glorious Revolution* (London: Macmillan, 1969), 118.

Such sentiments were unfortunately mistaken, in part because so many people had precisely the same hope. It is one thing to call for the renewal of moral and political virtue from under the looming shadows of popery and arbitrary rule. It is quite another to step into the sunlight and fashion from such aspirations a concrete politics of virtue, particularly one which can win the support of a parliamentary majority. The importance of civic virtue to the good state had been a comfortable commonplace of Restoration political thought. Because little could be done concretely to advance such virtue, a consensus on its importance was relatively easy to obtain. But now that reformation of one sort or another was an actual possibility, this consensus had begun to unravel. There were just too many ways in which what had once seemed a harmless platitude could be politically instantiated. The first years following the Revolution thus saw not only a revived concern with virtue, both political and moral, but significant disagreement over the qualities that constituted the good citizen and the lengths to which government should go to cultivate them. There was not one politics of virtue on offer at this time, but several.

Against this view, some may object that only one group of political actors offered a true or "serious" politics of public virtue in early eighteenth-century England: the small but influential band of opposition politicians and journalists who cast the challenges of Augustan politics in classical republican terms.[4] But what of individuals without republican commitments who also insisted on the importance of virtue to the good state? It is neither just nor accurate to take their writings simply as evidence that republican ideals "trickled down" into the general political consciousness. In fact, Augustan political culture offered a number of competing conceptions of citizen excellence. The clerics and politicians, peers and commoners active in Augustan politics differed profoundly over what dispositions or character traits made the individual politically virtuous. The republican tradition had no monopoly on the notion of political or civic virtue.

I

At least three accounts of the good citizen figure prominently in the political debate and divisions of early eighteenth-century England, each linked to a

4 On English opposition ideology as the repository of a politics of public virtue, see J. G. A. Pocock, *Politics, Language and Time: Essays on Political Thought and History* (New York: Atheneum, 1973), chapters 3, 4; *The Machiavellian Moment: Florentine Political Thought and the Atlantic Republican Tradition* (Princeton: Princeton University Press, 1975), chapters 12–14 and also Isaac Kramnick, *Bolingbroke and His Circle: The Politics of Nostalgia in the Age of Walpole* (Cambridge: Harvard University Press, 1968), chapters 3, 8, 9.

particular politics of public virtue. One, that of the Country interest, is republican in heritage. The others, which I distinguish as High Church and Low Church, are religious. All three accounts of virtue are publicly oriented, in the sense I set out above, and all three eventually give way (some ceding ground more quickly than others) to alternative understandings of what, besides public virtue, makes society free, stable and flourishing. To modern audiences, the most familiar conception of civic virtue is undoubtedly that championed in the propaganda and programs of Country politicians.

Court and Country represented distinct and opposing affiliations in English politics from at least the middle of the seventeenth to the middle of the eighteenth century, allegiances cutting across the more formalized party lines of Whig and Tory. On one side was the small clique of men who linked their political and personal fortunes to service to the Crown (the "Court party"). From the accession of William III most, but not all, of these men were Whigs. Ranged against them were first, conservative country gentry (mostly Tory), who suspected all government policies and politicians, and second, a small group of "Old Whigs" or commonwealthmen, who affirmed the original and radical Whig principles evolved during the Exclusion Crisis against what they saw as the new Court Whigs' unfortunate betrayal of them. Joined with these "permanent backbenchers,"[5] too distrustful of government to seek any position in it, were those professional politicians temporarily in opposition who claimed to speak in the backbenchers' name. These three groups together made up the Country interest.[6]

Uniting these disparate groups were both an agenda and an ideology which together made up a recognizable politics of public virtue. One modern scholar has written that "the Country interest wished to see in England a classical populus [*sic*], a community of virtue."[7] This assessment is probably too generous, crediting a shifting and opportunistic coalition with more ideological coherence than it merits. Still, the writings and speeches produced in support of the Country program do reflect a fundamentally republican understanding of the political world in which the paramount task of

5 W. A. Speck, *Stability and Strife: England, 1714–1760* (Cambridge: Harvard University Press, 1977), 205.

6 The precise extent to which those whose politics had a Country feel about them might be said to represent a "party" and the dates during which such themes dominated English politics remain a matter of historical debate. See, for example, Colin Brooks, "The Country Persuasion and Political Responsibility in England in the 1690s," *Parliaments, Estates and Representation* 4 (1984): 135–46. Without slighting the importance of these issues for the history of eighteenth-century politics, I use the phrases "Country interest," "Country sympathizers," "Country party," and "Country opposition" interchangeably to indicate individuals adhering to the Country principles discussed here.

7 H. T. Dickinson, *Liberty and Property: Political Ideology in Eighteenth-Century Britain* (New York: Holmes and Meier Publishers, 1977), 103–4.

citizenship is taken to be defense of civic and individual liberty against the corrupt encroachments of executive power. Country sympathizers understood this task to be properly the responsibility of parliament – if its members could be made virtuous enough. How to stock parliament with such virtuous citizens, individuals devoted to the public rather than the Court interest, and how to protect them and the nation against incipient tyranny were their principal preoccupations.

Given the objectionable nature of Court policies, Country writers had little question about what dispositions characterized the virtuous citizen. The virtuous citizen, the individual whose action and behavior most powerfully sustained England's civic mode of life, was the member of parliament or potential member of parliament who supported political initiatives intended to limit the Court and ministry's influence over parliament and society at large. These initiatives included the disbanding of a standing army, limits on taxation, frequent parliaments, free elections and the banning of "placemen," administrative officers and Court functionaries from parliament – in short, the historic agenda of the Country party. The good citizen, the citizen disposed to support political liberty and the public good over the forces of tyranny and corruption, would above all support and fight for these measures.[8]

Civic virtue conceived of in this way is without question publicly oriented. Broadly limned, it is a habit of responsible public deliberation grounded in a concern for, indeed passionate attachment to, English liberties. In practice, this virtue was often reduced to a disposition to support the agenda of the Country opposition, again because of one's devotion to the ideals of the English constitution. In either case, the habit of thought praised as virtuous is properly denominated publicly oriented because it requires the citizen both to distinguish public from private concerns and to subordinate the latter to the former. Charles Davenant, writing in 1699, nicely captures these expectations: "all thoughts, endeavors and designments [of the good citizen] should tend to the good and welfare of our country," he insists. And elsewhere: "The public virtue which must preserve a state . . . [is] a constant and perpetual will to do our country good."[9]

Those associated with the Country interest lost little time in transforming their vision of the good citizen into a politics of public virtue. They saw in

8 On the identity of Country politicians and the principles they espoused, see also Geoffrey Holmes, *British Politics in the Age of Anne* (London: Macmillan, 1967), 118–24; J. B. Owen, *The Eighteenth Century, 1714–1815* (New York: W. W. Norton and Company, 1974), 107–14; J.B. Owen, "The Survival of Country Attitudes in the Eighteenth-Century House of Commons," in J. S. Bromley and E. H. Kossmann, eds., *Britain and the Netherlands, Volume 4: Metropolis, Dominion and Province* (The Hague: Martinus Nijhoff, 1971).

9 Charles Davenant, *The Political and Commercial Works* (London, 1771), II, 338; II, 167. See also Bolingbroke's account of civic virtue, discussed in chapter 5.

William's succession the opportunity to achieve in one swift stroke the political measures that had languished for years under Charles II and James II. Thus, the Declaration of Rights, presented to the Commons in February 1689 as the basis of a new agreement between Crown and parliament, gave concrete expression to Country ideals, proposing a broad range of measures designed to limit executive power, protect individual liberties and secure the role of the independent landed gentry in shaping the policies of the nation.[10] The ensuing battles over disbanding the standing army, eliminating placemen from parliament, holding more frequent parliamentary elections, increasing the property qualifications for members of parliament can and should be seen as more than convenient pawns in the partisan struggle for political power. The effort to reshape British politics in this way was a politics of virtue, an attempt to secure through parliamentary legislation the conditions under which the virtuous citizen, as defined by the Country interest, might flourish.

But Country politicians were not the only set of like-minded individuals possessed of a coherent conception of public virtue at this time nor the only ones eager to see their ideas reflected in formal political arrangements. High and Low Church Anglicans also embraced particular conceptions of political virtue and lobbied vigorously for their codification and recognition in contemporary political life.

High and Low Church, familiar terms to participants in the contemporary debate, named two wings of the Anglican Church. High Church Anglicans adopted a conservative attitude to monarchical authority, preaching the doctrines of "indefeasible hereditary right" and "passive obedience" to their congregations. They denied the religious or political legitimacy of nonconformity, refusing to grant dissenters (protestants who worshiped independently of the Church of England) the right to establish separate churches or to hold political office.[11]

Low Church clergy, although reluctant to embrace "revolution principles" in all their glory, accepted William's installation as king, implicitly rejecting the principles of hereditary right and nonresistance to which the High

---

10 See Lois Schwoerer, "The Bill of Rights: Epitome of the Revolution of 1688–89," in J. G. A. Pocock, ed., *Three British Revolutions, 1641, 1688, 1776* (Princeton: Princeton University Press, 1980).

11 A typical outpouring of High Church animus for dissenters, revolutionaries and waverers within the Church is Charles Leslie, *The New Association*, parts I and II (London, 1702–3). A more temperate example is Mary Astell, *The Case of Moderation and Occasional Conformity* (London, 1705), which ably argues the High Church position. On the ideology of the High Church more generally, see J. P. Kenyon, *Revolution Principles: The Philosophy of Party, 1689–1720* (Cambridge University Press, 1977), chapters 3, 5, 6 as well as the political histories cited in note 17 of this chapter.

Church pledged allegiance. They accepted the inevitability, and even legiti-macy, of dissent and the necessity of religious toleration (at least for all orthodox protestants). Finally, they differed on the Test and Corporation Acts' requirement that local and national officeholders take communion in the Anglican church. While supporting the Acts in principle, Low Church-men accepted the practice of occasional conformity – an annual visit to the local Anglican church expressly to qualify oneself – as a way for dissenters to meet this obligation; High Churchmen did not.[12]

These disparate political commitments gave rise as well to different ideals of political virtue. To the conservative High Churchman, for whom political stability and ecclesiastical authority were the primary political goods, the distinguishing characteristic of the virtuous citizen was conformity to the established church, a conformity that he believed should be required by law. Devotion to the Church of England was the crucial mark of good citizenship for two reasons. Since the church preached the religious and political duty of "passive obedience," a duty which forbade resistance even to a tyrant, church members were safely inoculated against the revolutionary doctrines which had so disrupted the English state in the seventeenth century. Dissent-ers, of course, were the completely untrustworthy descendants of the Puri-tan revolutionaries who had repudiated the doctrine of nonresistance and murdered a king.[13] In addition, church membership reflected a commitment to the historical conception of the English people in which secular and spiritual authority had always been closely intertwined. The dissenter's re-fusal to worship in the Church of England challenged this connection and in so doing undermined the very constitution of the English state – hardly the mark of a virtuous citizen.[14]

If we take the civic virtues to be those dispositions of the individual that best fit him or her to sustain a civic mode of life, we can hardly place the High Church understanding of the good citizen in this category. Its highest

---

12 Gilbert Burnet's preface to the third edition of his *Discourse of Pastoral Care* (London, 1713) provides a sympathetic contemporary account of Low Church principles. Historical treatments include Norman Sykes, *Church and State in England in the Eighteenth Century* (Cambridge University Press, 1934) and R. N. Stromberg, *Religious Liberalism in Eighteenth-Century England* (Oxford: Oxford University Press, 1954).

13 See, for example, Joshua Barnes, *The Good Old Way: or Three Brief Discourses Tending to the Promotion of Religion* (London, 1703), 18–19; Charles Leslie, *Cassandra. (But I Hope Not) Telling What Will Come of It. Number II* (London, 1704), 41–2; *The Memorial of the Church of England* (London, 1705); *Occasional Paper Upon the Subject of Religion . . .* (London, 1735), 12–13.

14 This point is made in *Civil Security, Not Conscience, Concerned in the Bill Concerning Occasional Conformity* (London, 1702), 7–13. See also J. C. D. Clark, *English Society, 1688–1832: Ideology, Social Structure and Political Practice During the Ancien Regime* (Cambridge University Press, 1985), 136–7.

concern is not with preserving liberty or the conditions for "participatory self-rule" but with safeguarding both piety and social order. But if confessional allegiance to the Anglican church is not a civic virtue, it is a political one. Just as Country thinkers believed the public good of parliamentary independence was most reliably furthered by the citizen's embrace of a Country political agenda, so High Churchmen considered the public goods of political stability and religious orthodoxy best served by the citizen's devotion to the interests and needs of the Church of England – love of country sacralized. In both cases, the political virtue valued is publicly oriented: the virtuous citizen advances the welfare of a public entity (commonwealth or church), not incidentally, but because of a dedication to that public entity's well-being.

High Churchmen not only offered a publicly oriented account of political virtue, but a politics of public virtue as well. Whether individuals developed into good citizens (conforming Anglicans) was not a matter to be left to family education or individual choice. The government must actively promote political virtue – in this case by requiring citizens to attend the Church of England, penalizing dissenters for their schismatic ways and disqualifying them from public office.

The first steps in this direction came soon after William's installation as king, when conservatives in parliament proposed a new accommodation with dissenters. Most nonconforming protestants were to be "comprehended" within the Anglican church (through compromises on liturgy and ritual), although those dissenters, still orthodox, who insisted on worshiping in separate meeting houses would be granted a limited toleration.[15] This promising overture to nonconformists, supported not only by the High Church but by some influential moderates as well, was almost immediately derailed by William's extremely ill-timed proposal to abolish the Test and Corporation Acts altogether. In the political confusion that followed, all that was passed was the Toleration Act. A dismayed High Church clergy quickly closed ranks and began their efforts to restore "the conditions of the old establishment ... by firm political action."[16] Their primary target was the practice of occasional conformity (which allowed dissenters willing to take communion in an Anglican church to enter politics), but they also sought legislation forbidding dissenting academies (the dissenters' answer to Ox-

15 Excluded from this proposed settlement were those holding anti-Trinitarian views, the expression of which remained a crime (Clark, *English Society*, 283, 286–7).
16 G. V. Bennett, *The Tory Crisis in Church and State* (Oxford: Clarendon Press, 1975), 20. The political blunders that wrecked the opportunities for comprehension – and thus gave the Toleration Act far more significance than originally intended – are detailed in Henry Horwitz, *Parliament, Policy, and Politics in the Reign of William III* (Manchester: Manchester University Press, 1977), 21–9.

ford and Cambridge), expanding the jurisdiction and authority of ecclesiastical courts and repealing the Toleration Act.[17]

In their advocacy of these measures, High Church clergymen and their sympathizers in parliament pursued a politics of public virtue just as intense as the Country party's. The Country opposition sought to impose its conception of political virtue through measures designed to guarantee the independence of parliament. The High Church party pursued the same end through legislation designed to strengthen the established church. In both cases, the impetus for such intense activity was the Revolution of 1688. The new era signaled by the defeat of a popish and tyrannical king and the establishment of a protestant constitutional monarchy prompted both religious and republican activists to pursue contentious and contested politics of public virtue.

High Churchmen and Country politicians thus saw in the change of regime an opportunity for reform and renewal of virtue. But a new beginning in politics might mean a new beginning in morals as well. Or so at least thought the supporters of the Societies for Reformation of Manners (SRMs), a moral reform movement that brought Anglicans and dissenters together to combat public licentiousness through the stricter enforcement of already existing morals legislation. The point of this reforming work was above all religious – first, to make the targets of reformation better human beings and second, to bring society into greater conformity with the will of God. But reformers also went out of their way to detail the strictly temporal advantages of the behavior they sought to elicit. Ridding the community of the grossest offenses against public decency and order not only served God's purposes but the state's as well. These more tolerant Low Church Anglicans and their dissenting colleagues identified good citizens not by their selfless love of country nor by their pious affection for the church establishment, but by their abstention from the reigning vices of the age.

This account of political virtue as grounded in the habits of personal morality is not as publicly oriented as the conceptions embraced by the Country party and the High Church. To exhibit the characteristics of the good citizen understood in this way does not require any special engagement with or devotion to the public realm, but rather an interest in conforming to a religious conception of good moral behavior. Simply by striving to be morally good, one develops the dispositions, the habits of character, that make one a good citizen. Of course, if one cultivated the virtues of personal morality *because* of their beneficial public consequences, the virtue practiced could be considered publicly oriented in the sense I have given that

17 On the subsequent legislative battles of the High Church, see George Every, *The High Church Party, 1688–1718* (London: Society for the Promotion of Christian Knowledge, 1956) and Bennett, *Tory Crisis.*

term. But it seems unlikely that the moral reformers had this sort of motivation in mind. It remains appropriate however to speak of those Anglicans and dissenters joined in the moral reform movement as possessing a politics of virtue (if not of public virtue). In demanding the stricter enforcement of morals legislation already on the book, the Societies for Reformation of Manners sought to use governmental institutions and resources (the judiciary in particular) to enforce a particular conception not only of personal but of political virtue.[18]

For many Englishmen, then, the most fitting tribute to the success of the Glorious Revolution, in which the advocates of absolutism and popery were so resoundingly defeated, was a national reformation. If citizen virtue was indeed crucial to the public good, as almost every political tract of the period allowed, now was the time to secure this virtue through legislation and political action. This conviction, as we have seen, spawned not one but several politics of virtue. High Churchmen looked forward to a return to orthodoxy and uniformity under a staunchly protestant king, Low Churchmen to undoing the licentiousness and disorder brooked by his Catholic predecessors. The Country interest, having drawn on republican themes in its criticism of Charles and James, sought to restructure political life in accordance with these values.

Each of these groups proposed specific legislative reforms designed to further their ideals of the good citizen. Country politicians wanted citizens actively involved in legislative politics, choosing their representatives and deliberating on public policy independent from Crown influence. Only in this way, they believed, could England preserve its freedom and prevent any return to arbitrary rule. Churchmen believed that the state's prosperity and stability required citizens whose devotional energies were focused exclusively on the Anglican church. And moral reformers proposed their own understanding of the good citizen as the individual, of whatever denomination, who refrained from personal and public immorality, whose pious behavior upheld the order of the Augustan state.

There was no consensus, then, on the qualities that would transform Englishmen into virtuous citizens. But there was also little disagreement that some sort of political virtue was necessary and that parliament must take the lead in creating the conditions under which it might flourish. Within a generation, this striking consensus had collapsed. The shared concern for public virtue as the ground of the good state, so prominent in the religious and republican views of politics in the years following the Glorious Revolution, did not survive mid-century. By 1740, the idea of a public virtue as

18 For more on the Societies for Reformation of Manners, see chapter 3.

crucial to the well-being of the state or excellence of the citizen simply did not figure prominently in either political argument or practice. This striking defeat frames the central question of the following chapters. What happened to the politics of public virtue? Why within the space of thirty or forty years did the whole idea of a publicly oriented political virtue, of whatever form, cease to exercise a compelling hold on the English political imagination?

II

Any account of how and why traditional understandings of political virtue faltered in Augustan England must begin with the stark fact of political defeat: not one of the competing politics of public virtue managed to secure parliamentary or ministerial support for its program. This failure is the first of a number of problems that pushed both religious and republican understandings of public virtue from the center to the sidelines of political debate.

Moral reformers were perhaps the most unfortunate in this regard. Absolutely convinced that they had found the key to both the spiritual and temporal flourishing of the English nation, supporters of the Societies for Reformation of Manners found their plans for a more vigorous enforcement of personal morality condemned from within and without the Church. High Church clergy were both appalled at the reformers' willingness to work with dissenters (thus lending legitimacy to nonconformist worship) and dismayed with their decision to use civil rather than ecclesiastical courts for the correction of moral offenses. The problems complained of by the Societies—drunkenness, blasphemy, profaning the Sabbath, etc. – were best dealt with by strengthening the Church against the assaults of deists and dissenters, not by hauling petty transgressors in front of justices of the peace.[19] Secular critics complained just as vehemently about a different set of problems: the Societies' exclusive focus on the offenses of the poor and middling sort (both unjust and ineffective if one's aim was national reformation), their use of often unscrupulous informers, and the threat to individual liberties posed by prosecuting citizens for minor morals offenses.[20] The

19 Henry Sacheverell's sermon, *The Communication of Sin. A Sermon Preach'd at the Assizes held at Derby* (London, 1709), is the most notorious example of this sort of attack; see also the High Church complaints catalogued in William Bisset, *Plain English: A Sermon Preach'd to the Societies for Reformation of Manners* (London, 1704), 42; Dudley Bahlman, *The Moral Revolution of 1688* (New Haven: Yale University Press, 1957), 86–97; Horwitz, *Parliament, Policy, and Politics*, 238.

20 Representative complaints can be found in Matthew Hole, *The True Reformation of Manners; or the Nature and Qualifications of True Zeal* (Oxford, 1699), i; *Reflexions upon the Moral State of the Nation* (London, 1701); Thomas Newman, *Reformation, or Mockery . . . A Sermon Preach'd to the Societies for Reformation of Manners at Salter's Hall* (London, 1729), 28. See also Horwitz, *Parliament, Policy, and Politics*, 256.

Societies for Reformation of Manners were not completely at a loss for allies; their literature proudly lists those "spiritual and temporal Lords" who had publicly endorsed their plans.[21] However, their goals offended too many laymen and clergy ever to attract sustained political support. Victims of secular suspicion and Church resentment, they found their efforts marginalized almost from the start and by the 1730s most activities of the SRMs had lapsed.

The attempts of Country politicians to guarantee and nurture a virtuous citizenry met a similar fate. Bills relating to at least one or another of the items on the Country agenda surfaced in almost every parliamentary session from 1690 through the 1730s. There were occasional legislative successes but no ministry adopted the Country program as its own. In fact, since the entire thrust of Country politics was precisely to impose limits on executive power, to undermine the various strategies by which the Court secured its parliamentary majorities, a government committed to a Country program was more or less a contradiction in terms. From time to time the most fervent supporters of Country ideals (backbenchers with little interest in political office) allied themselves with more ambitious politicians ready to champion their cause. But when such individuals gained power (as they did in 1710), they "failed to fulfill their promises that they would effect an improvement in the quality of administration," doing nothing to curb the power of Whig financiers or limit the reach of patronage.[22] The Country politics of public virtue thus operated under a double handicap: it was an

21 Such lists can be found in [Grant], *Brief Account* and Josiah Woodward, *The Judgement of the Rev. Dr. Henry Sacheverell, concerning the Societies for Reformation of Manners...* (London, 1711). John Tutchin, *England's Happiness Consider'd* (London, 1705) lists sessions orders that "encouraged good Christians or good citizens, to give Information to the Magistrate against Prophane and Vicious Persons." William III's addresses to parliament in 1698, 1699 and 1700 also asked parliament to consider legislation for the "further discouraging of vice and profaneness." But this concern with the "depravation of manners" related not only to the immorality complained of by moral reformers but also to the publication, following the lapsing of the Licensing Act in 1695, of heterodox (anti-Trinitarian) theology (Horwitz, *Parliament, Policy, and Politics,* 249, 234).

22 On the all-important issue of "placemen" (individuals employed by the Crown seeking seats in parliament), the legislative record was mixed. Bills banning certain categories of placemen from parliament passed in 1694, 1700, 1701, 1716 and 1742, but none eliminated them completely. Bills directed at this end failed four times between December 1692 and early 1700. The Act of Settlement banned all officeholders from the Commons, but the provision was repealed in the Regency Act of 1705 (Jennifer Carter, "The Revolution and the Constitution," in Holmes, ed., *Britain after the Glorious Revolution,* 45; Owen, *Eighteenth Century,* 100). Similarly, it took four tries (1696, 1697, 1703, 1711) to secure a bill requiring landed property of all members of parliament, and even this bill was a "dead letter" within a few years (Holmes, *British Politics,* 182). On the Country's equally unsuccessful effort to disband England's "standing" or professional army, see Lois Schwoerer, *"No Standing Armies!" The Antiarmy Ideology in Seventeenth-Century England* (Baltimore: The Johns Hopkins University Press, 1974), chapters 8 and 9.

ideology almost necessarily condemned to opposition, and the actual opposition with which it was associated often deployed it opportunistically. These
two conditions combined to assure that, despite a well-developed theory of
what it meant to be civically virtuous, Country politicians were never able
to instantiate their vision of political virtue in the nation's lawbooks.[23]

Despite widespread support for its cause in the nation at large, the High
Church found parliament and the Crown at least as unresponsive to its
program as they were to the Country party's. Except for a brief moment in
1714, the Toleration Act, which publicly mocked the High Church's cherished ideal of uniformity, was never in doubt. Similarly, the practice of
occasional conformity (by which dissenters nominally conformed to the
requirements of the Test and Corporation Acts) flourished throughout the
period, despite repeated Tory efforts for its proscription. And from 1718 on,
almost annual indemnification acts protected dissenters holding local offices
from the penal provisions of the Corporation Act.[24] Even the much anticipated benefits of Anne's staunchly Anglican sympathies failed to materialize
as "the High Church agitation had to develop as an opposition to the moderate and conciliatory policies of the Queen and her ministers."[25]

Three factors, in particular, explain the failure of the High Church to
reap what it saw as the promise of the Revolution: Whig hostility to the
High Church agenda, Whig control of parliament throughout this period,
and the unacceptably factious politics of the High Church party itself.
Given their domination of virtually every post-revolutionary parliament,
the Whigs' historic commitment to religious freedom, if not to dissent per
se, spelled disaster for the clergy's ideals. Even when the Commons rallied
to the cry of "Church in Danger," Whigs could count on the House of
Lords to support the government line. Thus while occasional conformity
bills passed the Commons between 1702 and 1704, all were rejected in
the upper house.[26]

High Church Tories might well be increasingly resentful that Whigs, who
so clearly "represented only a minority of the political nation," retained
sufficient majorities in parliament to frustrate their pious designs.[27] But

23 J. R. Jones, *Country and Court in England, 1658–1714* (Cambridge: Harvard University
   Press, 1978), 340.
24 On the single threat to the Toleration Act, see Holmes, *British Politics,* 103–4. Only one bill
   banning occasional conformity passed parliament, in 1711 when Opposition Whigs traded
   their votes on this issue for Tory votes against a peace treaty. The bill was repealed in 1718.
   On the annual indemnity acts, see K. R. M. Short, "The English Indemnity Acts, 1726–1867,"
   Church History 42 (1973): 366–76.
25 Bennett, *Tory Crisis,* 167.
26 Jones, *Country and Court,* 322–4.
27 *Ibid.,* 355.

they could do little beyond continual sparring in parliament to show their displeasure. Ironically, this bitter partisanship also told against High Church politics of public virtue. No monarch appreciated the factious manner in which the Church often pressed its proposals, and even ministers sympathetic to the High Church worked to moderate its demands rather than indulge them.[28]

As a politics of public virtue, the High Church agenda proved more resilient than the moral reformers' or Country party's platform. Despite the increasingly organized protests of dissenters, the Test and Corporation Acts remained in force until well into the nineteenth century, officially preserving the Anglican monopoly on office. Nor was Anglicanism's status as the state religion ever seriously in doubt. Still, the Church's cherished desire to preserve the absolute identity of citizen and congregant came to nought. Whigs remained too powerful and too committed to a religiously pluralistic polity to give the notion of the good citizen as conforming Anglican full legislative sanction. In this sense, the High Church's politics of public virtue failed just as decisively as the moral reformers' bid to enforce a virtue of personal morality and the Country's call for legislation to stem public corruption.

Those who pursued the politics of public virtue thus had many political defeats and few political successes. But political defeat alone cannot account for the English public's rapid disillusionment with the claims for public virtue. By 1740, political argument had ceased to grant the idea of a politics of public virtue an important place in public dialogue. It is hard to sustain in the public mind a compelling vision of the benefits to be secured by a politics of public virtue when that vision is consistently denigrated and denied by those in power – hard but not impossible. What prevented the various religious and republican conceptions of public virtue from persisting, without official sanction, as powerful alternative views of what the good state needed? Why, rejected by those in power, did they not live on as robust opposition ideologies?

One possibility is that the Court Whigs offered a sustained practical rebuff to the contentions of their opponents. Those who called for the cultivation of public virtue consistently warned of the terrible consequences that would follow upon not resisting vice or corruption. But a nation's Jeremiahs can warn of the imminent dangers of decadence, instability and tyranny for only so long. With the nation remaining fairly prosperous, peaceful and free, with dissenters proving reliable subjects, drunkards failing to undermine public stability, placemen not ushering in tyranny, the argument that the

28 Kenyon, *Revolution Principles,* 96–101.

nation must cultivate public virtue to combat these dangers inevitably loses its force. So, by governing successfully for two generations and four monarchs without paying much attention to politics of public virtue, Court Whigs undercut the opposition's complaints.

But this explanation misses the ideological force of the various politics of public virtue. To understand Walpole's government as able, despite its shortcomings, to provide freedom, peace and prosperity for the country would be to employ an understanding of how these goods are achieved completely foreign to any of these politics of public virtue. To the High Churchman who wanted to preserve the traditional Church-state alliance, any concession to dissenters would necessarily appear as a disastrous departure from the English constitution, whatever its actual effects. Similarly, no amount of economic prosperity or political stability could convince a Country sympathizer that the political arrangements he deplored were safe ones. Without a citizenry devoted to a balanced constitution, tyranny lurked just around the corner. My point is this: to interpret Walpole's record as evidence that a genuinely free and stable government might exist independently of public virtue, one would first have to abandon the conviction that only public virtue could provide for the nation's well-being. But this is precisely the development for which we are trying to account. Thus the political successes of Walpole's government cannot in themselves explain the demise of public virtue. These successes "proved" the dispensability of virtue only to those willing to concede its secondary importance to the polity in the first place.

One other possibility deserves consideration. Perhaps, in the process of governing so successfully for fifty-odd years, the Court Whigs developed and promulgated a convincing alternative vision of the good state, one that argued for the possibility of stability and freedom without reliance on a public virtue of either religious or republican origins. Those who see the triumph of Lockean political theory in the constitutional settlement of 1689 might advance such an explanation. Although Locke certainly did not regard virtue as superfluous to the good state, he still did not embrace a politics of public virtue in the way republicans or orthodox clerics did. If his *Second Treatise* was indeed the philosophical basis of the Whig regime, and was accepted as such by the English polity, perhaps this explains the increasingly lackluster popular response to those seeking to impose a politics of public virtue.

The problem with this argument is that there is little evidence that the Whigs developed a consistent, coherent defense of a politics independent of public virtue until the very end of the period under consideration. J. P. Kenyon makes it clear, for example, that Lockean principles played a minimal role in Whig defenses of the post-revolutionary polity.[29] J. G. A. Pocock has pointed out that Defoe, writing in support of such Whig policies as a standing army, questioned the necessity of a publicly oriented civic virtue as early as the 1690s.[30] But there is no evidence that his views persuaded his Country opponents. Nor were his arguments incorporated into any official Whig defense of Court policies.[31] Mandeville's aggressive dissociation of political flourishing from the performance of virtue offered another possible way for Whigs to defend their political choices. They did not however avail themselves of this option, and *The Fable of the Bees* was condemned by the general public and ignored by party regulars.[32] In short, before the 1730s, we find few efforts to provide a well-thought-out alternative to a politics of public virtue and none that was widely influential or accepted.

Neither the practical nor the theoretical achievements of the Whig regime, then, explain satisfactorily the decline in the fortunes of public virtue during this period. The political record of the Court Whigs could not in itself quell calls for a renewal of virtue. Nor did the Whigs develop a theory of the good state that made arguments for the necessity of public virtue seem less plausible.

Perhaps then we should look outside the political arena altogether and consider instead the dramatic social and economic changes that were remaking the world of the English citizen. Proponents of public virtue greeted the inauguration of William and Mary's reign with enthusiasm, eager to use a new political beginning to revive the nation's commitment to political virtue as well. But the foreign and domestic policies pursued successively by the ministers serving William, Anne and George I seem profoundly to have affected the prospects for a successful politics of public virtue of either the Church or Country variety.

Consider, for example, the effects of the Toleration Act. It was originally intended to relieve the consciences of a few sectarians unable to join a generous "comprehension" of dissenters within the Church of England. But

---

29 *Ibid.*, chapters 4 and 7. See also John Dunn, "The Politics of Locke in England and America in the Eighteenth Century," in John W. Yolton, ed., *John Locke, Problems and Perspectives. A Collection of New Essays* (Cambridge University Press, 1969); Martyn P. Thompson, "The Reception of Locke's *Two Treatises of Government,* 1690–1705," *Political Studies* 24 (1976): 184–91.

30 Pocock, *Virtue, Commerce, and History: Essays on Political Thought and History, Chiefly in the Eighteenth Century* (Cambridge University Press, 1985), 111, 231.

31 For example, the Whig philosophy discussed in Kenyon, *Revolution Principles,* chapters 8– 10 betrays little evidence of a Defoean perspective.

32 W. A. Speck, "Bernard Mandeville and the Middlesex Grand Jury," *Eighteenth Century Studies* 11 (1978): 362–74. For some evidence to the contrary, see J. A. W. Gunn, *Beyond Liberty and Property: The Process of Self-Recognition in Eighteenth-Century Political Thought* (Kingston and Montreal: McGill-Queen's University Press, 1983), 106–7.

such a comprehension had never come to pass. The Toleration Act thus officially permitted a wide variety of protestant worship outside the Church of England, putting the dissenting sects on a social, if not political, parity with Anglicanism. (Church membership was still required for public office.)[33] Besides the Toleration Act, Anglicans had to contend as well with the lapsing of the Licensing Act in 1695. Clergy and laymen alike were soon taken aback at the "free-thinking" literature issuing from London's presses.[34] With dissenters preaching openly and the Church's teachings ridiculed in print, it became more and more difficult for the High Church to maintain a credible case for the political virtue of Anglican uniformity. In this sense, the social change inaugurated by changes in English law did undermine a High Church politics of public virtue.

The striking growth in public credit, government bureaucracy and the professional army, all due to William's extended continental wars, posed similar difficulties for the Country's conception of political virtue. The men brought to power by such developments appeared to Country eyes as too dependent on government place and credit to deliberate impartially on the public good. How might a nation cultivate a civic virtue grounded in the possession of real property and independent political opinions when men in power were conspicuously lacking in both? But the problem was not just that corrupt individuals occupied places of political authority. By encouraging the changes from which they benefited, such men were actively transforming the political economy in a way that undermined the status and fortunes of those with the resources to remain civically virtuous. Country advocates, like the High Church faithful, saw the public space available for the practice of their version of public virtue grow smaller and smaller.[35]

Nor were these the only changes that influenced the possibilities for virtue in the English polity. Commerce and trade expanded exponentially,

33 Some of the profound impact of the Toleration Act is suggested by the worries of a country parson in a letter to Archbishop Sharp in 1706: "If ye Toleration Act be continued in force as it is, without any alteration, it seems impossible to keep up any due discipline in ye Established Church because if pastors admonish, suspend or excommunicate any ... persons ... they can herd themselves (under a pretence of conscience) amongst some of the Tolerat'd Dissenters" (Dickinson, *Liberty and Property*, 55).

34 This explosion of heterodox thought is chronicled in John Redwood, *Reason, Ridicule, and Religion: The Age of Enlightenment in England, 1660–1750* (Cambridge: Harvard University Press, 1976).

35 For a detailing of the political and economic changes that sparked so many Country worries, see P. G. M. Dickson, *The Financial Revolution in England* (London: Macmillan, 1967) and John Brewer, *The Sinews of Power: War, Money and the English State, 1688–1783* (New York: Alfred A. Knopf, 1989). For the panicked Country response, see especially J. G. A. Pocock, "Early Modern Capitalism: The Augustan Reaction," in Eugene Kamenka and R. S. Neale, eds., *Feudalism, Capitalism and Beyond* (Canberra: Australian National University Press, 1975) and *Machiavellian Moment*, chapters 13 and 14.

creating a class of newly wealthy, powerful and usually dissenting citizens, unversed in either the Anglican or Country catechisms.[36] The idea that an organized opposition might play a constructive role in political life began to undermine the traditional emphasis on a unified body politic served by individuals who shunned faction in the name of a common good.[37] The scientific vision of Newton's *Principia* suggested new accounts of God's existence and man's duties towards Him, while moral philosophy began increasingly to embrace an egoistic psychology of human nature that raised serious questions about man's aptitude for any moral or civic virtue.[38]

The early eighteenth century, then, was a turning point for the politics of public virtue, even as it encouraged their pursuit. During this time, the English polity changed in a number of ways that made the practice of publicly oriented forms of political virtue appear more difficult if not impossible.[39] But simply to point to these changes and the difficulties they raise for realizing a politics of public virtue is not to explain how or why political argument so decisively abandoned such politics by the mid-1740s. Long established social facts can indeed push the advocacy of certain political possibilities to the margin of political debate. It is partly the fact that Great Britain has for so long tolerated nonconforming congregations that would make any call for the reimposition of Anglican uniformity in the late twentieth century purely utopian, if not absurd. But the possibilities are not so circumscribed within the crucible of change itself. There, one is far more likely to argue for changing the offending circumstances – in the Augustan

36 The political views fostered in such circumstances are ably surveyed in Isaac Kramnick, *Republicanism and Bourgeois Radicalism: Political Ideology in Late Eighteenth-Century England and America* (Ithaca: Cornell University Press, 1990).

37 See the original sources collected in J. A. W. Gunn, *Factions No More: Attitudes to Party in Government and Opposition in Eighteenth-Century England. Extracts from Contemporary Sources* (London: Frank Cass, 1971) as well as the analyses provided in Archibald Foord, *His Majesty's Opposition, 1714–1830* (Oxford: Clarendon Press, 1964) and Harvey C. Mansfield, *Statesmanship and Party Government: A Study of Burke and Bolingbroke* (Chicago: University of Chicago Press, 1965).

38 On the impact of Newton, see M. C. Jacob, *The Newtonians and the English Revolution, 1688–1720* (Hassocks, Sussex: Harvester Press, 1976). Helpful overviews of the changes in moral philosophy include Norman Fiering, *Jonathan Edwards's Moral Thought and Its British Context* (Chapel Hill, NC: University of North Carolina Press, 1981), chapters 3 and 4; Redwood, *Reason, Ridicule, and Religion*; Leslie Stephen, *History of English Thought in the Eighteenth Century*, v. 1 (New York: Harcourt, Brace and World, Inc., 1962).

39 The politics of virtue promoted by the Societies for Reformation of Manners was less affected than the others by these changes. The difficulties it faced in gaining acceptance for its particular conception of political virtue were rooted in already entrenched aspects of English political life, such as the reluctance to allow government to mandate standards of personal behavior. Thus the changes noted above neither expanded nor contracted its political prospects significantly.

case, repealing toleration or restricting the market in public debt – than for abandoning the ideals which the new developments endangered.

The central question for this inquiry then is how advocates of virtue *reacted* to the new circumstances that threatened their ideals. Did the proponents of public virtue simply reject the threatening developments and insist on their systematic dismantling? If so, how did this rigidity affect their political fortunes? Or did they try to come to terms with such far-reaching social and political changes? In this case, did their efforts strengthen or weaken the appeal of their arguments and why? With what effect? In answering these questions, we can come to understand the reverses suffered by both religious and republican politics of public virtue and the origins of political alternatives to them.

III

J. G. A. Pocock, who has done much to demonstrate the vitality of civic humanist and classical republican ideals in seventeenth- and eighteenth-century England, locates the decline of the Country politics of virtue in the revolution in Britain's financial affairs that occurred in the years following the accession of William III and the divided political response to it. The problem, Pocock argues, began in the last quarter of the seventeenth century. It was at that time that the English Augustan citizen began "to envisage himself as civic individual," as a public actor capable of civic virtue. Because of "the realities of the seventeenth-century social structure," this citizen also decided that freehold property was the necessary ground of this virtue. The reason, says Pocock, was that the freehold was "founded upon real or landed property which was inheritable rather than marketable, was protected by the ancient sanctions of the common law, and brought with it membership in the related structures of the militia and the parliamentary electorate, thus guaranteeing civic virtue." For perhaps a brief moment, England's social structure conformed to this ideal community of freeholders, secure in a virtue secured by their land. But the realities of Albion's polity began to drift from this ideal image almost immediately upon its crystallization. As Pocock explains, "the advent from about 1675 of parliamentary patronage, a professional army, and a rentier class maintaining the two foregoing for its own profit, posed a threat of corruption to the whole edifice . . . pervading it with new social types whose economic substance if not property – pensions, offices, credit, funds – defined them [in the republican scheme of things] as dependent on the executive power and hence incapable of virtue."[40] The

40 Pocock, *Machiavellian Moment,* 450.

series of continental wars to which William committed England after 1688 only exacerbated this problem, confirming the suspicion, held by friends and opponents of the new regime alike, that the nation had entered a new era in which there was little room for the virtuous citizen as traditionally understood.

According to Pocock, the theoretical response to this crisis, a response that ultimately undid the Country politics of virtue, occurred in two stages. First, Defoe, Addison and other political journalists attempted to tame the many-headed monster, Credit, which had come to symbolize the corruption of the new order. Credit appeared to undermine the possibilities for virtue by giving "opinion, passion, and fantasy" power in human affairs. If it could be depicted instead as "a stabilizing, virtuous, and intelligent agency," the prospects for the expression of virtue in a credit-driven society might be restored. Thus in the works of Defoe, Davenant and Addison, "Credit is now being translated into virtue [which]... was now the cognition of social, moral and commercial reality... everything possible had been done to eliminate the element of fantasy and fiction which had seemed so subversive of property and personality." But English citizens steeped in the civic human-ist ideal simply could not grant individuals enmeshed in the gilded webs of commercial enterprise the autonomy and breadth of mind necessary for civic virtue. Pocock describes the problem this way: "Defoe and Addison... sought to validate the commercial world by appeal to conceptions of public virtue, but found themselves confronted by the paradigm of a citizen whose virtue did not rest upon a capacity for exchange."[41]

The failure of this effort to habilitate commerce and credit "left two directions in which the Augustan mind might go." It could simply reaffirm the vital importance of public virtue to "the foundations of government" and work, despite the infelicity of social conditions, to revive its practice.[42] Bolingbroke's later writings on patriotism are one example of such an effort; Andrew Fletcher's early call for a Spartan-styled militia is another.[43] "The alternative," says Pocock, "was to admit that government was an affair of managing the passions" and give up on the pursuit of public, political virtue altogether. In this schema, the virtues of sociability, in particular "the real passions of sympathy and honesty," replace those of citizenship. With a little help from attentive politicians, these "real virtues... secure the edifice of

41 *Ibid.,* 452, 454, 456, 458.
42 *Ibid.,* 458.
43 Viscount Bolingbroke, *Letter on the Spirit of Patriotism* (1736) and *The Idea of a Patriot King* (1738), in *The Works of Lord Bolingbroke,* v. 2 (London: Henry Bohn, 1844; reprint New York: A. M. Kelley, 1967). Andrew Fletcher, *A Discourse of Government with Relation to Militias* (1691), in David Daiches, ed., *Selected Political Writings and Speeches* (Edinburgh: Scottish Academic Press, 1979).

government" by bringing men's "opinions, hopes and fears" into concert with one another.[44] But the individual distinguished by these character traits is no longer a civic being; he is a private individual, a gentleman of manners, finding fulfillment in economic success and personal pursuits, not in deliberation on the public good. Pocock tells much the same story in later works, concluding that the image of "the man of commerce . . . had to fight its way to political recognition in the teeth of the 'patriot' ideal."[45]

Pocock's account, though crudely summarized here, provides a powerful synthesis of several strands of Augustan political thought. In it, polite journalists, Country ideologists and Court Whig apologists play successive parts in a compelling drama, a tragedy perhaps that ends with the republican hero laid low and *homo economicus* emerging from the wings. The arguments of the following chapters do not challenge the broad outlines of this tableau, but they do attempt to provide a different sort of explanation for how the actors came to find themselves in this position. It is an account that differs from Pocock's in three respects.

In both *The Machiavellian Moment* and his later works, Pocock divides the possible (and actual) responses to the emergence of the new political and economic order into two categories. Augustan writers either reaffirmed the vital importance of political virtue to the good polity or they did away with it altogether, relying on social virtues to "secure the edifice of government."[46] The following chapters highlight the existence of an alternative to these two extremes, a vision of active citizenship that upholds the attractiveness and viability of political virtue and of the citizen as civic being without demanding a return to the community of arms-bearing freeholders. The works that articulate this vision undercut the traditional republican or civic humanist account of civic virtue, but do not do so by defending social virtues as a plausible substitute. Rather they reject a more publicly oriented conception of civic virtue (in which the good citizen acts from and for a deep love of the common good) for a more privately oriented one (in which the good citizen serves the cause of liberty and public welfare without such a radical subordination of personal desires and interests). Civic virtue is transformed, rather than eclipsed.

Some of those who work this sort of transformation are quite conscious of

44 Pocock, *Machiavellian Moment*, 459, 460.
45 Pocock, *Virtue, Commerce, and History*, 109; for a similar account in the Scottish context, see J. G. A. Pocock, "Cambridge Paradigms and Scotch Philosophers: A Study of the Relations between the Civic Humanist and the Civil Jurisprudential Interpretation of Eighteenth-Century Social Thought," in Istvan Hont and Michael Ignatieff, eds., *Wealth and Virtue: The Shaping of Political Economy in the Scottish Enlightenment* (Cambridge University Press, 1983), 240–5.
46 Pocock, *Machiavellian Moment*, 460.

the project in which they are engaged and the stakes involved. This seems to me to be the case, for example, with the Court Whigs of Robert Walpole's era. Pocock places the work of the Court Whigs in the second of his two categories: because they are not championing a politics of public virtue (a task more than willingly assumed by their Country opponents), they are therefore grounding government independently of political virtue (the only alternative provided in Pocock's schema). In fact, Court Whigs repeatedly insist on the vital importance of civically virtuous citizens to the eighteenth-century polity. They simply define the character traits, the dispositions that constitute this civic virtue differently from their Country antagonists. The key to civic virtue, they argue, is not freehold, the possession of real property, but the responsible management of whatever property one has. Honesty, frugality, industry are the character traits that make a good citizen, that guide responsible public deliberation. This prescription may seem banal, a disappointing rejoinder to the polemical extravagances of the Country opposition. But not all conceptions of civic virtue have to be as robust as traditional republican ones. The point is that the Court Whig version of the good citizen offered an alternative to the Country politics of public virtue without dispensing with the notion of political virtue altogether.[47]

Other political thinkers of the period edged away from traditional, publicly oriented accounts of political virtue without intending to provide an explicit alternative and without defining themselves in opposition to the republican tradition. *Cato's Letters,* an opposition publication of the 1720s, calls for a vigorous public response to the financial and political scandal of the "South Sea Bubble." It urges the citizenry wronged by corrupt politicians to turn out those members of parliament tainted by ministerial scandal and insist on better government from their successors. This project assumes a reservoir of political virtue in the populace – a disposition to defend English liberties against those that threaten them. But to tap this virtue, the *Letters* rely not on the sacrifice of personal interest to the public good, but on a vigorous defense of one's personal interest against the depredations of corrupt ministers. As with the Court Whigs, *Cato's Letters* rejects the publicly oriented conceptions of virtue enshrined in traditional republican thought while affirming a privately oriented, but still political, conception as more appropriate to present-day realities.[48]

To suggest that we make room in the history of political thought for those who, in the eighteenth century, argued for the desirability and possibility of a privately oriented conception of civic virtue is not to claim for such ideas a

47 See chapter 6.
48 See chapter 4.

great deal of contemporary influence. The intellectual future, as recent accounts of the Scottish Enlightenment have made clear, lay with a more fully privatized vision of virtue, one in which the citizen was replaced by the gentleman of commerce. Yet, works like *Cato's Letters* suggest that, whatever the contemporary reception, the conceptual resources did exist in the first part of the eighteenth century in England to describe the individual as a civic being, as an active citizen defending public freedom, in terms other than the neo-Harringtonian ones favored by Pocock's authors.[49] The effort to reconceive the virtuous citizen in this way, then, represents a road not taken in the history of political thought, one that could still, perhaps, be fruitfully explored.

My account also questions the extent to which the financial innovations transforming England at this time should be credited with initiating the transformation of virtue which both Pocock and I are concerned to explain. Consider the turn towards a more privately oriented civic virtue evident in *Cato's Letters*. Fear of what the stock market might do to the citizen's capacity for virtue is not the source of this transformation (although the *Letters* do attack the fraud and speculating frenzy that fed the disastrous "South Sea Bubble"). Rather, Cato's reworking of the notion of civic virtue stems from his effort to graft an egoistic psychology onto the republican tradition, to make a case that the virtuous citizen can and will thwart corruption and advance public liberty from quite selfish motives. Consider as well the Court Whig response to the opposition charges, so brilliantly put by Bolingbroke in the *Craftsman*. Bolingbroke argues that the economic and political practices pursued by Walpole and his allies are fundamentally corrupt and corrupting, threatening to English liberties and a dangerous prelude to an age of tyranny. Court Whigs challenge Bolingbroke's account of the imminent collapse of civic virtue, articulating a different, privately oriented understanding of the good citizen grounded in personal temperance and frugality, still available to those "corrupted" in a Country sense. One should not, however, trace the genesis of this new account of virtue to England's financial revolution or to the problems the financial revolution posed to reigning paradigms in political thought. Rather, both Bolingbroke's prediction of a virtue-less polity and the Court Whigs' response to it are prompted by the interests of partisan politics, by the contention between political factions, for which Whig financial and political policies provided a convenient target.

---

49 Pocock argues for the "neo-Harringtonian" character of Country thought in *Politics, Language and Time,* chapter 4. For difficulties with this characterization, see Jesse Goodale, "Pocock's Neo-Harringtonians: A Reconsideration," *History of Political Thought* 1 (1980): 237–60.

Thus, not all political theorizing about virtue at this time revolves around the twined efforts to vindicate or limit the political damage of the political and financial innovations transforming the Augustan polity. There is instead an expansive debate, often optimistic in tone, about the sort of political virtue possible and appropriate to a limited monarchy. In this debate, the typically Country concern with the corrupting effect of recent social and political developments plays only a part, an important one, but still a part.

The final respect in which my account of the transformation of virtue differs from Pocock's concerns the role or responsibility assigned in this process to the politics of virtue themselves. Most current accounts seem to present traditional ideologies of virtue as more or less innocent victims of events unfolding beyond their control. Worthy ideals when first conceived, they find continued expression in the modern world as elegy or critique (Kramnick's and Pocock's views of Country ideology, respectively), but never as practical political possibilities. Unsuited to new social and political realities, the politics of public virtue are overtaken by developments external to them. Against this view, I propose, in the chapters that follow, an alternate vision: the ideology of public virtue not as innocent victim but as accomplice in its own demise.

Put bluntly, the politics of public virtue failed in eighteenth-century England not only or mainly because of the threats posed to its practice by the financial and political developments of the post-revolutionary polity. Rather, they failed because few besides the true believers found the proffered plans for cultivating the good citizen – or the understanding of public virtue on which they rested – very appealing. Tested in the crucible of public opinion and parliamentary deliberation, the politics of public virtue were found wanting.

In seeking, then, to understand the fortunes of virtue in the eighteenth century, we need to take seriously the politics of the politics of virtue. My focus is less on the dramatic shift in social conditions so ably chronicled by Pocock and others, than on the efforts, undertaken in the shadow of these changes, to win for particular understandings of public virtue, political success and public acceptance. It was these initiatives that in large measure prompted the decline in public commitment to public virtue and the emergence of alternatives to it.

Those theorists of virtue who sought to accommodate their account of citizen virtue to the realities of eighteenth-century politics and culture encountered a particularly cruel irony. Seeking to preserve the possibility of citizen virtue in a world radically transformed from the seventeenth century, they ended up transforming the conception of political virtue itself. Most notably, they did so in a way that encouraged what I have called a privately

oriented conception of political virtue to take hold. The gradual disintegra-
tion of the politics of public virtue, the emergence of new conceptions of
citizen excellence, the emergence of theories that dispensed with virtue
altogether – these developments constitute the "transformation of virtue" in
eighteenth-century English political argument.

The processes that fueled this transformation cannot be subsumed under
any unitary scheme of ideological change: not all politics of public virtue
failed in the same way or for the same reasons. However, if we look case by
case at the various efforts to make room for the virtuous citizen in the
Augustan polity, each, for different reasons and in different ways, ends up
undercutting the possibilities for a politics of public virtue. Each in its own
way pushes political thought one notch nearer the point at which citizen
virtue comes to seem a characteristic easily dispensed with in the effort to
construct a good polity.

The chapters that follow do not attempt a comprehensive intellectual
history of the politics of virtue in eighteenth-century England, nor do they
make a chronological survey of all the various texts that together reconstituted the understanding of political virtue in the Augustan era. Rather, they
examine particular cases and texts that might be said to exemplify the
breakdown in the politics of virtue. These chapters offer a cautionary tale of
the pressures which, in one way or another, pushed traditional, publicly
oriented understandings of political virtue to the sidelines of political debate and created the intellectual space within which a more privately oriented conception of political virtue emerged.

3

A religious politics of virtue: Low Church Anglicanism and the Societies for Reformation of Manners

In the previous chapter, I made the point that not all politics of virtue in the early eighteenth century were republican. To borrow the words of J. C. D. Clark, not all those concerned with the nature and possibility of the good citizen "spoke with a 'humanist and Machiavellian vocabulary' after 1688 [in which]... politics increasingly revolved around secular concepts of credit and commerce, virtue and corruption."[1] Equally, if not more, important to the politics of the day were the various religious understandings of political virtue, articulated in the sermons, tracts and polemical literature of the decades following the Glorious Revolution.

Anglican clerics and dissenting ministers considered themselves not only qualified but obligated to pronounce upon the dispositions that made an individual a good citizen – forays into the political realm made even more controversial by their efforts to enforce these notions in the nation's laws. Although modern scholars have provided us with political histories of the occasional conformity debate, the Test and Corporation Acts dispute and the national movement for reformation of manners, none has explicitly considered these political initiatives in the context of the debate about public virtue. Yet to Augustan citizens, the Church's competing accounts of the good citizen loomed just as large, if not larger, than the classical republican or civic humanist account put forward most articulately by writers in the Country tradition.

Anglican theology of the Augustan era actually offered two distinct conceptions of the good citizen to the eighteenth-century public, alternatives which paralleled the division between the conservative High Church Angli-

1 J. C. D. Clark, *English Society, 1688–1832: Ideology, Social Structure and Political Practice during the Ancien Regime* (Cambridge University Press, 1985), 423.

cans and their more moderate, Low Church brethren. Disturbed by both the religious and political implications of the growing dissent from the established church, High Church Anglicans equated political virtue with religious conformity. Insisting on an indissoluble link between the religious and political constitutions of the English state, they claimed that the dissenters' rejection of the Anglican faith made them less than loyal to the English constitution in general and so properly disqualified them from representation and participation in public office. On the other hand, membership in the Church of England established individuals as supporters of the English constitution (and exposed them to much pious preaching regarding their political duties). It was both the necessary and sufficient condition of good citizenship.[2]

For reasons that are not fully clear, what was for other English citizens a period of transition in their conception of political virtue was for those with High Church commitments a period of consolidation. The same arguments for and against church establishment appear with tedious predictability until at least the late 1730s without much impact on those in power. (The publication in 1736 of William Warburton's *Alliance Between Church and State,* an unconventional defense of the establishment, marks some new thinking on this subject.) Parliament remained committed to the status quo: obligatory conformity to a state religion with relatively generous dispensations for conscientious protestant dissenters. As a matter of practical politics, those disadvantaged by this settlement were unable to dismantle those provisions in public law that guaranteed the Church of England its special political status. Disestablishment was hardly spoken of and the few efforts made to grant dissenters an equal role with Anglicans in public life failed dismally. Yet, the High Church and its parliamentary allies failed to secure any enduring legislation improving the Church's position or correspondingly weakening the dissenters'.[3]

Given this standoff between the Church's high-flying supporters and the Whig establishment, one might be tempted to dismiss the High Church politics of virtue as simply besides the point in Augustan political history, an annoying irrelevance that intrudes from time to time on the more crucial divisions between Court and Country, Whig and Tory. The fact that strong popular support persisted through much of the eighteenth century for High

2 I have deliberately framed this account of the good citizen in gender neutral terms. This is because High Church clerics would hardly approve of female dissenters while condemning their male consorts. Keep in mind however that women's opportunities as political actors were narrowly circumscribed, though not nonexistent, and that most discussion of the attributes of the good citizen took men alone to be fulfilling this role.

3 For an account of some of these efforts, see Tina Isaacs, "The Anglican Hierarchy and the Reformation of Manners, 1688–1738," *Journal of Ecclesiastical History* 33 (1982): 391–411.

Church and High Tory ideology makes this position difficult to sustain.[4] It is more plausible, I think, to treat the High Church conception of the good citizen as the relatively stable background against which all other debate about the dispositions of the virtuous citizen are played out. This is not to say that Low Church Anglicans or Country propagandists shared the High Church conviction that the good citizen must, whatever else, be a conforming Anglican. The nondenominational thrust of the reformation of manners movement explicitly repudiates this claim, while the Old Whig contingent of the Country party harbored distinctly anticlerical positions. Still, Low Church Anglicans stood with their conservative colleagues on the importance of the Test and Corporation Acts, although they were more willing to allow for occasional conformity, while the Country party united Old Whigs with High Tory elements strongly supportive of the High Church agenda. Given, then, that a significant portion of informed political society accepted the notion of religious conformity as an important element of a citizen's civic contribution (whether they took this position to High Church extremes or not), what were the other qualities necessary to the good citizen? It is in this debate that moral reformers (the subject of this chapter) and Country ideologists were embroiled and from this debate that the turn from public to private versions of political virtue issued.

For this reason, I focus in this chapter on the understanding of political virtue advanced by the latitudinarian or Low Church wing of the Anglican establishment. More tolerant than their high-flying brethren, these moderate Anglicans tended to measure the virtue of the citizen not by individual choice of church (although *some* choice was imperative) but by their personal morality. The qualities that made one a good individual in the eyes of God and the church were also those that made one a good citizen, an individual who contributed to the flourishing of the political community. This particular idea of the excellence of the citizen corresponds closely to the Anglican idea of the good state as a stable, hierarchically ordered community respectful of the codes of religious morality. Gamblers, drunkards, prostitutes and others whose behavior did not conform to the religious standards of personal morality (blasphemers and Sunday traders, for example) were not only irreligious or immoral individuals, they were bad

---

4 On this popular support, see Linda Colley, *In Defiance of Oligarchy: The Tory Party 1714–1760* (Cambridge University Press, 1982), 104–16. Nicholas Rogers provides a particularly illuminating local study, "Popular Jacobitism in Provincial Context: Eighteenth-Century Bristol and Norwich," in Eveline Cruickshanks and Jeremy Black, eds., *The Jacobite Challenge* (Edinburgh: John Donald Publishers, 1988). For the persistence of High Church/Tory ideas in political thought, see Clark, *English Society*, chapters 3 and 4 and J. A. W. Gunn, *Beyond Liberty and Property: The Process of Self-Recognition in Eighteenth-Century Political Thought* (Kingston and Montreal: McGill-Queen's University Press, 1983), chapter 4.

citizens as well. They impeded the flourishing of the good state as Christians understood it, threatening not only the judgment of God on a sinful nation, but the loss of English liberty through military defeat (vice effeminates) and the collapse of social order under a tide of vice-induced criminality. If we are to have a full picture of the transformation of political virtue in Augustan political argument and of the emergence of new understandings of this concept, we need some sense of where and why this Low Church account of political virtue went off-track as well, why it failed to establish itself as a plausible account of the good citizen accepted by the political nation at large.

I

The moderate Anglican understanding of political virtue is perhaps best traced in the literature of the Societies for Reformation of Manners (SRMs), the most visible and controversial arm of the religiously oriented moral reform movement that flourished in England in the decades after the Glorious Revolution.[5] Contemporary records offer two separate accounts of the SRMs' origins. Edward Stephens, an energetic propagandist for moral reform, but a bit of a crank, identified the first SRMs with two neighborhood associations (one headed by himself) formed in the 1690s to rid London's streets of vicious and debauched miscreants.[6] Whatever role Stephens played in forming the SRMs' precursors, he broke off relations with the Societies within the decade. An ardent Whig, he was disappointed with their nonpartisan approach to reformation.[7] The official histories of the SRMs stress their connection with lay religious societies aimed primarily at personal improvement and active in the 1670s and 1680s. These associations entered the reforming trade in the 1690s, encouraged by "four or five Gentleman of the Church of England" and desiring to "check those public and scandalous Sins which

5 On the history and ideology of the Societies, see in particular, Dudley Bahlman, *The Moral Revolution of 1688* (New Haven: Yale University Press, 1957); T. C. Curtis and W. A. Speck, "The Societies for Reformation of Manners: A Case Study in the Theory and Practice of Moral Reform," *Literature and History* 3 (1976): 45–64; Tina Isaacs, "Moral Crime, Moral Reform and the State in Early Eighteenth-Century England: A Study of Piety and Politics," unpublished Ph.D. dissertation, University of Rochester, 1980 as well as the works cited in the notes below.

6 [Edward Stephens], *A Plain Relation of the Late Action at Sea . . . with Reflections thereupon and upon the Present State of the Nation* (London, 1690); [Edward Stephens], *The Beginning and Progress of a Needful and Hopeful Reformation in England* (London, 1691); Edward Bristow, *Vice and Vigilance: Purity Movements in Britain since 1700* (Dublin: Gill and Macmillan, 1977), 16–17.

7 [Edward Stephens], *A Seasonable and Necessary Admonition to the Gentlemen of the First Society for Reformation of Manners* ([London?], [1700?]).

were become very insolent and crying in this City [London]."[8] Open to dissenters as well as Anglicans, these new societies sought to recall the nation from its vices in the most forceful way possible: public prosecution. Relying on the right of any English subject to prosecute criminal offenders, they distributed specially printed booklets of arrest warrants and urged their members "as their leasure should permit, to go out into the Streets and Markets, and public places on purpose, and to observe the people's behaviour there."[9] Those who violated the law and the SRMs' canon of respectability were to be reported and prosecuted. The Societies pursued drunkards, prostitutes, Sunday traders, gamblers and blasphemers with enthusiasm, prosecuting over 100,000 citizens during their forty-five year crusade.[10]

Despite the SRMs' explicit rejection of the traditional methods of church discipline, a substantial number of Anglican clergy welcomed the organizations' endeavors. These ecclesiastical well-wishers preached regularly to the SRMs, as did supportive dissenting clergy, encouraging flagging spirits and elaborating the spiritual significance of their work. Their sermons provide a classic example of how, in seeking to "sell" a broad public constituency on the desirability and appropriateness of a rather narrow conception of citizen virtue, advocates for such a virtue may in fact undercut, rather than strengthen, their own case, laying the groundwork for its later demise.

In general, a religiously inspired reformation of manners can pursue its goals in one of two ways. It may disdain the strong arm of the state, seeking

8 [Francis Grant, Lord Cullen], *A Brief Account of the Nature, Rise and Progress of the Societies, for Reformation of Manners, &c.* (Edinburgh, 1700), 21. See also the concurring accounts in [Thomas Bray], *A Short Account of the Several Kinds of Societies... for Carrying on the Reformation of Manners* (London, 1700) and Josiah Woodward, *An Account of the Progress of Reformation of Manners...* (London, 1704).

9 [Stephens], *Beginning and Progress,* 9.

10 The Societies detailed the number and kind of arrests and prosecutions they effected first in irregular "Black Lists" and then in annual "Accounts" appended to SRM sermons. The "Three and Twentieth Account" for 1 December 1716 to 1 December 1717 showed 1,927 prosecutions for lewd and disorderly practices (the common law offense under which prostitution was punished), 524 for trading on Sundays, 400 for profane swearing and cursing, 33 for keeping bawdy or disorderly houses and 25 for drunkenness (in Thomas Hayley, *A Sermon Preach'd to the Societies for Reformation of Manners...* [London, 1718]). For 1723–4, the figures were 1,951 for lewd and disorderly practices, 600 for Sunday trading, 108 for profane swearing, 29 for keeping bawdy or disorderly houses and 12 for drunkenness; the report also indicates that the SRMs assisted in the prosecution of 21 common gamesters and 2 gaming houses (in Edward Chandler, *A Sermon Preach'd to the Societies for Reformation of Manners...* [London, 1724]). The number of prosecutions dropped severely through the 1730s, the "Fortieth Account" for 1732–3 recording only 170 cases of lewd and disorderly practices and 240 Sabbath-breakers (in Robert Drew, *A Sermon Preach'd to the Societies for Reformation of Manners...* [London, 1735]). The "Four and Fortieth Account" gives the total number of prosecutions since the Societies' inception as 101,683 (in Samuel Smith, *A Sermon Preach'd to the Societies for Reformation of Manners...* [London, 1738]).

to effect its ends through less coercive means: education, preaching, private moral instruction and persuasion. Or it may enter the political realm, invoking the "terror of the magistrate's sword" and seeking a reformation of manners through prosecution and criminal punishment as the SRMs did. This second approach can be given two justifications. Supporters can offer a religious rationale for state action, in which the magistrate punishes the sins of drunkenness, profanity, fornication and gaming precisely because they are sins, prohibited by God and condemned by the church. Or they can appeal solely to material and temporal reasons for the legal enforcement of religious standards of personal morality, stressing the political benefits that states may expect from encouraging such behavior. By and large, Anglican clerics chose to frame their defense of the SRMs' activities in these latter terms, casting the reformers' attempts to enforce moral norms as above all a political task. In so doing they transformed personal morality from a private virtue, encouraged for pious reasons by a pious magistrate, to a political virtue, encouraged by the magistrate on the grounds of the public benefits it brings.

Framing the case for the prosecution of moral offenders in these political terms might seem, at first glance, a salutary adaptation of religious sentiment to the realities of eighteenth-century politics. It legitimates the use of secular authority to "enforce a largely religious code," while respecting contemporary conceptions of the scope of political authority.[11] Yet justifying the state's enforcement of religious norms of personal morality on civic rather than religious grounds had an unintended and unwelcome consequence. In adopting the political justifications they did, moral reformers directly engaged the debate about the good citizen that consumed so much of Augustan political argument. Although it would be quite difficult for anyone to challenge the ministers' claim for the sinfulness of, say, prostitution, all sorts of people could and did dispute the argument that whipping prostitutes and jailing drunkards substantially advanced the commonweal. The notion that the good state depended most crucially on personal good behavior proved too vulnerable to critical rebuttal to provide a persuasive ideal of political virtue to the Augustan citizenry.

To understand the difficulties the defenders of the SRMs got themselves into requires first understanding why they framed their arguments for moral reform the way they did. In sermons delivered on a quarterly basis to the Societies' faithful, Anglican and dissenting ministers insisted again and again that the public prosecution of moral offenders was both effective and legitimate. Such claims were not unfamiliar to the Augustan reformers' puritan

11 Isaacs, "Anglican Hierarchy," 410.

forebears, although puritans preferred a reformation grounded on an "appeal to reason . . . [and] to conscience" rather than on the coercive pressure of criminal courts.[12] But the *reasons* advanced by the SRMs to support their project reveals an understanding of moral reform not only different from earlier protestant rationales but more vulnerable to criticism as well.

The moral reformers' faith in the spiritual efficacy of temporal coercion followed easily from the widespread Augustan perception of sin as a species of lawlessness. If the problem with sinners is that they are lawless, then the cure lies less in a reconciliation with God, or a spiritual act of atonement, than in obedience. But obedience to law may properly be achieved by coercion as well as by persuasion. John Spademan, a dissenting minister and advocate of the SRMs' activities, thus urged the use of

the Magistrates Sword . . . that such, who fear not the Displeasure of God, or the Reproaches of Conscience, . . . may be check'd and awed by a menacing Law; which is the proper Instrument of repressing Evil doers.

John Waugh similarly believed that "they who will not be reformed and reclaimed from an evil Course, by Arguments fetched from another World, may be forced into better Manners by temporal Punishments." Understanding immorality as lawlessness, ministers could consider prosecution an effective substitute for religious persuasion.[13]

Ministers concerned with the social rather than the psychological causes of vice also cast problems of morality as problems of law and order, warning that a collapse in parental, ecclesiastical and even judicial discipline had created a dangerous vacuum of authority into which vice and infidelity rushed, threatening the stability and welfare of the entire community. Families, for example, suffered from the "too visible Neglect of Parents and Masters; who, many of them . . . make a constant Practice of spending whole

12 Margo Todd, *Christian Humanism and the Puritan Social Order* (Cambridge University Press, 1987), 202.

13 John Spademan, *A Sermon Preach'd November 14, 1698 and Now Publish'd at the Request of the Societies for Reformation of Manners* (London, 1699), 20; John Waugh, *A Sermon Preach'd to the Societies for Reformation of Manners. . .* (London, 1714), 8. Other SRM sermons that describe sin as lawlessness include Thomas Bray, *For God or for Satan: Being a Sermon Preach'd to the Societies for Reformation of Manners. . .* (London, 1709); St. George Ashe, *A Sermon Preach'd to the Societies for Reformation of Manners. . .* (London, 1717); Edmund Gibson, *A Sermon Preach'd to the Societies for Reformation of Manners. . .* (London, 1724); Smith, *Sermon.* See also *Proposals for a National Reformation of Manners. . . February 12, 1694/5* (London, 1695). Smith called sin "an Act of Hostility and Rebellion against God" (5). This understanding of sin is typical of Anglicanism. "If idolatry was the most comprehensive and evocative word in the puritan vocabulary of sin, disobedience held that place for Anglicans" (J. Sears McGee, *The Godly Man in Stuart England: Anglicans, Puritans, and the Two Tables, 1620–1670* [New Haven: Yale University Press, 1976], 100).

Nights in gratifying their Vices or Pleasures entirely neglecting Family Development and Order."[14] Magistrates had similarly abdicated their role as moral spurs and examples and the clergy had little influence over their wayward flocks.[15]

Given this diagnosis of the source of sin, moral reformers understandably cast secular prosecution as a process that would, as Francis Hare, an Anglican bishop, put it, "retrieve a just regard to Authority, human and divine."[16] Concerned citizens could not themselves reawaken respect for the church nor force fathers to better educate their children. But they could substitute the state's coercive power for the moral instruction no longer imparted by church, family or justice of the peace. Ministers, then, welcomed prosecution and punishment of sinful behavior as effectively replacing the traditional sources of moral socialization. A 1704 grand jury that encouraged the SRMs' efforts expressed the organizations' aims succinctly: "Vice," it asserted, "must give way to authority."[17]

By construing the process of moral reform as a reaffirmation of authority, Augustan reformers set themselves decisively at odds with the first genera-

---

14 John Denne, *The Duty of Doing All Things to the Glory of God. A Sermon Preach'd to the Societies for Reformation of Manners...* (London, 1730), 18–19. For other complaints about parents shirking their disciplinary duties, see Richard Dongworth, *The Necessity for Reformation: An Assizes Sermon* (London, 1708), 14; Thomas Newman, *Reformation or Mockery... A Sermon Preach'd to the Societies for Reformation of Manners at Salter's Hall...* (London, 1729), 18; Francis Hare, *A Sermon Preached to the Societies for Reformation of Manners...* (London, 1731), 32–5; Drew, *Sermon,* 2–3.

15 For concerns about the shortcomings of magistrates, see Hare, *Sermon,* 8–14; John Tutchin, *England's Happiness Consider'd, In Some Expedients...* (London, 1705), 10 and Thomas Penn, *A Sermon Preach'd Before the Societies for Reformation of Manners...* (London, 1708). Timothy Rogers, *A Sermon Preach'd to the Societies for Reformation of Manners...* (London, 1701); Penn, *Sermon*; Ashe, *Sermon,* 16; Arthur Bedford, *A Sermon Preach'd to the Societies for Reformation of Manners...* (London, 1734), 20; William Berriman, *Family-Religion Recommended* (London, 1735), 18; Drew, *Sermon,* 15–16 all complain about the neglect of the Sabbath. SRM supporters regretting the decline of ecclesiastical discipline include George Stanhope, *The Duty of Rebuking. A Sermon Preach'd at Bow-Church... Before... the Lord-Mayor and Aldermen... and the Societies for Reformation of Manners* (London, 1703) and Penn, *Sermon*. Some ministers however did not abandon the possibility of restoring church discipline. Edmund Gibson, later Bishop of London, issued a strong defense of the Church's rights to "the Administration of Discipline and Correction of Vice" in the introductory essay to his compilation of English church law. Such proponents of church discipline were usually suspicious of the SRMs' efforts. Thus Gibson's essay castigates the secular power for "taking the suppression of vice out of the hand of the spirituality (whose proper province it is...) and putting it into the hands of the Laity, who (to say no more) are generally too much taken up with Secular Cares and Diversions, to attend the Work" (*Codex Juris Ecclesiastici Anglicani* [London, 1713], xxxi). Gibson did however preach to the Societies a decade later (1723).

16 Hare, *Sermon,* 53.

17 Quoted in William Bragg Ewald, *Rogues, Royalty and Reporters: The Age of Queen Anne through its Newspapers* (Westport, CT: Greenwood Press, 1978), 125.

tion of English and continental protestants, substituting a political for a religious account of their good work. Understanding vice to be an absence of moral righteousness, earlier churchmen had considered its extirpation an exclusively religious goal – aimed both at securing the sinner's salvation and at protecting the "community of true believers from contamination." They believed the nation could remedy its moral ills only by cultivating a virtue that transformed individual and community, creating a truly Christian order where private and public activities unfolded in profound conformity to God's will.[18]

Comparing the SRMs' goals with Calvin's account of the ends of "church correction and excommunication" helps highlight the secular cast of Anglican thought. Calvin identifies three goals of church discipline: (1) that God not be insulted by actions dishonorable to His will and majesty; (2) that good church members not be corrupted by the example of the bad; and (3) that the sinner be ashamed and begin to repent.[19] Sermons preached to the SRMs also portrayed the public prosecution of moral offenses as upholding the honor of God and preventing the spread of immorality. But for the final term of Calvin's triad – the repentance of the sinner, inward change – Augustan clergy substituted a purely external goal. For them, the religious standards of personal morality deserved enforcement mainly because they contributed to restoring a social stability dangerously compromised by the nation's dissolute habits. Where puritans sought a spiritual regeneration of a depraved world that would create a community of saints, Anglicans wanted a reformation of unruly sinners that would uphold, indeed consist in, respect for public order and the hierarchy of spiritual and secular authority already established. "Orator" Henley captured this view in 1732, when he observed, "To preserve public order is the drift of Reformation."[20]

This shift of priorities from inward redemption to outward stability helps explain not only why Anglican ministers believed secular punishment could

18 Patrick Collinson, *The Elizabethan Puritan Movement* (London: Jonathan Cape, 1967), 40. For a general treatment of this transformative vision in Calvinist theology, see Ernst Troeltsch, *The Social Teaching of the Christian Churches*, 2 v. (New York: Harper and Row, 1960), II, 88ff. For this impulse in English puritanism, see among others, Todd, *Christian Humanism*, chapter 6; McGee, *Godly Man*, chapter 5; David Little, *Religion, Order, and Law: A Study in Pre-Revolutionary England* (New York: Harper and Row, 1969), chapters 3 and 4; John Wilson, *Pulpit in Parliament: Puritanism during the English Civil War, 1640–1648* (Princeton: Princeton University Press, 1969), 166–75. Wilson observes of the sermons preached before the Long Parliament 1640–8, "[their] explicit goal was an England conformed to the will of God, even united to Christ" (166).

19 John Calvin, *Institutes of the Christian Religion*, tr. John Allen (Grand Rapids, MI: Eerdmans Publishing Company, [1559] 1949), 504–8 (Book IV, chapter 12.2–5).

20 John Henley, *The Sermon that shou'd have been Preach'd before the Societies for Reformation of Manners . . .* (London, 1732), 17.

effectively promote personal morality but also why they found themselves characterizing the personal morality they wished to cultivate as a political as well as religious virtue. Although they desired reformation primarily for religious reasons, the benefits of moral reform could be described in exclusively temporal or secular terms as well. Having made this connection between personal morality and public good, reformers began to emphasize it at the expense of personal religious ideals. Where seventeenth-century puritans accepted the criminal prosecution of morals offenders as necessary to the elimination of sin in conformity with God's word, eighteenth-century Anglicans praised it for advancing the material goals and public welfare of the commonwealth. But in adapting the earlier case for the enforcement of personal morality to the more secular temper of the Augustan era, the SRMs came to characterize personal morality as a political virtue, substituting a political for a religious rationale for the reformation of manners. In so doing, the SRMs actually undermined their case for state involvement in reformation of manners, discrediting their particular version of what political virtue consisted in. We can trace this ironic outcome most clearly by looking more closely at the reformers' case for the legitimacy, as well as the efficacy, of secular punishment for moral sins.

II

Sixteenth-century protestant theologians usually defended the use of the state's coercive powers to cultivate virtue on what I would call theocentric grounds. They argued that God had ordained the temporal law and sword to serve an essentially moral function: the enforcement of His moral laws, as made known through the Ten Commandments. Thus Luther's disciple, Melanchthon, insisted in his *Loci Communes* (1555) that "worldly power serves above all to enforce the two commandments to maintain morality and peace. It is obliged, with all earnestness, zeal and determination, to punish adultery, incest and impurity contrary to nature, *even though these depravations do not concern the peace.*"[21] For these men, maintaining external moral discipline was as much the business of the civil magistrate as preserving peace and justice, and this responsibility independently justified the government's promotion of personal virtue.

Few eighteenth-century reformers absolutely repudiated this theocentric case for the magistrate's role in cultivating virtue. Not many authors however carried it beyond the level of pious exhortation. Rather, those who

21 Philip Melanchthon, *Selected Writings,* eds. E. E. Flack and Lowell Satre, tr. C. L. Hill (Minneapolis, MN: Augsburg Publishing House, 1962), 335; emphasis added.

made the most careful and consistent case for the legal enforcement of religious standards of personal morality offered an argument with a distinctly secular cast. Thus John Spademan defended the reformers' campaign by arguing, "If ungodly Persons did hurt only themselves, there might be some pretext for indulging, and conniving, at them; but the case is otherwise, they do a real harm to the Community, of which they are Members." Daniel Williams praised the SRMs for pursuing "the surest way to revive our Trade, prolong our Peace, and recover England's glory."[22] In sermon after sermon to the SRMs, ministers claim that the civil magistrate has a responsibility, indeed an obligation, to enforce religious standards of moral behavior – not only or merely on the basis of biblical accounts of God's will but as a consequence of the magistrate's primary civil duty: the maintenance of temporal peace and order.

This is not to say that the point of the reformers' work had suddenly ceased to be religious. In all likelihood, Spademan and Williams and the numerous other ministers who preached to the Societies embraced moral reform for primarily religious reasons; they wanted sin punished and destroyed, righteousness renewed, for the sake not only of a more godly commonwealth but of the sinners' souls. But to achieve this end they advanced arguments that provided political rather than religious reasons for supporting the reformation of manners undertaken by the SRMs; for this reason I characterize their arguments, not their final goals, as secular.[23]

SRM sermons identified two sorts of public dangers that might arise from the toleration of personal immorality. As Richard Smalbroke explained, the vicious "contribute to the Ruine of their Country" in two ways: "both by the natural Consequences of their Vices and by provoking God to send down his Judgements on a sinful Nation."[24] This concern with God's righteous wrath drew on the familiar Christian teaching that, although God balanced an individual's moral account in the afterlife, governments paid for the toleration of their citizens' sins within human history. Seventeenth-century cries for reform and repentance made much of the imminence of this cosmic

---

22 Spademan, *Sermon,* 36; Daniel Williams, *A Sermon Preach'd at Salter's-Hall to the Societies for Reformation of Manners* ... (London, 1698), 53.

23 It is worth noting as well the ideological cast to the reformers' arguments. Even as a religious ideal, their aims are heavily oriented towards the maintenance of law and order, due respect to authority and correction of the sins of the lower classes. Thus it is plausible, I think, to argue that while they conceived of their goals as religious, their interest in reformation had as well an unacknowledged political character. See Shelley Burtt, "The Virtue of Authority: Illiberalism and the Concern for Order in the Ideology of the Societies for Reformation of Manners, 1690–1740," unpublished paper, 1982.

24 Richard Smalbroke, *Reformation Necessary to prevent our Ruine. A Sermon Preach'd to the Societies for Reformation of Manners* (London, 1728), 6.

justice, warning of God's impending judgment on a covenanted nation.[25] But Smalbroke and his compatriots shared none of these millenarian expectations. Instead, they used the possibility of national judgment to appeal to the magistrate's temporal priorities, arguing that there is "not a Maxim more just in any Politicks [than that] Profanity and Debauchery are the worst Enemies to a State." The reason: "the Prosperity of States and Kingdoms depends entirely upon the Favour of... God... and that therefore a profound Contempt of Him ... Lewdness and other Vices, suffered without Restraint, draw down the divine Judgments upon them."[26] Ministers thus cast even the prospect of divine retribution as a secular concern, making it a matter of political expediency to punish citizens' lapses from virtue.

Most reformers however preferred to emphasize "the natural Consequences" of man's vices, arguing that immoral behavior brought enough temporal disadvantages in itself to justify its repression by the civil magistrate apart from religious or supernatural considerations. Ministers substantiated this charge with a litany of horrors, a list headed by the dire physical toll sinful living took on transgressors. By polluting the body with liquor and the fruits of lust, sinners increased their susceptibility to diseases, sapped their strength and suffered an early death. Worse, their physical degeneracy could be hereditary, "corrupt[ing] the Blood of the Nation." The indulgence of such passions also affected men emotionally, detracting from the hardiness and determination exhibited by more temperate souls, or as one critic had it, "Melt[ing] down the Courage of the Nation."[27]

Vicious living also affected the nation's productivity. Drunkenness and gaming were the major offenders in this category, encouraging not only idleness (a vice in itself) but financial ruin. The resulting impoverishment, creating an unwelcome drain on the public treasury, clearly made these vices a matter of public concern. As John Disney, Anglican vicar and moral reformer, warned, "The Poverty which these expensive Vices [Tippling,

25 Wilson, *Pulpit in Parliament,* 199–200; William Lamont, *Godly Rule: Politics and Religion, 1603–1660* (London: Macmillan, 1969), chapter 4.

26 *A Representation of the State of the Societies for Reformation of Manners, Humbly Offered to his Majesty* (London, 1715), 4. For similar fears, see Spademan, *Sermon* ("Wicked men are certainly Enemies to the public Good by provoking God to withdraw his protection"); Samuel Freeman, *A Sermon Preach'd at the Assizes, held at Northampton...* (London, 1690); Edward Calamy, *A Sermon Preach'd to the Societies for Reformation of Manners...* (London, 1699); Fowler, *Sermon;* William Colnett, *A Sermon Preach'd to the Societies for Reformation of Manners...* (London, 1711); Joseph Rawson, *Righteousness the Exaltation, and Sin the Reproach of a People. In a Sermon Preach'd at the Lent Assizes...* (London, 1714), 8; Thomas Coxe, *A Sermon Preach'd at the Assizes held at Bedford...* (Oxford, 1730).

27 Joseph Woodward, *A Short Disswasive from the Sin of Uncleanness* (London, 1701), n.p.; *An Essay on Conjugal Infidelity...* (London, [1727]), 12.

Drunkenness, Lewdness and Gaming] draw after them, is the Reason that Taxes seem to be so great a Burthen, that Trade ... languishes, your Markets want Money ... and your Prisons are crowded with Debtors."[28] Finally, all vices threatened to spill over into criminal enormities. Josiah Woodward solemnly accused promiscuity of providing the occasion or pretense for "Oppression, Theft, Robbery, Murder, etc." Drunkenness encouraged "profane Cursing and Swearing, Fighting, Robbery and Murder," as well as various sexual intrigues and offenses. Just as one virtue brought with it the practice of all others, each vice apparently encouraged its companions as well.[29]

John Disney's scholarly compendium, *A View of Antient Laws against Immorality and Profaneness* (1729), provides an especially good example of the newly secular cast of the reforming divines' argument. Disney, a one-time justice of the peace, devoted much of his efforts to the moral reform movement, although he was never explicitly associated with the SRMs. The first sentence of the book's introduction states plainly Disney's rationale for reformation.

If Impiety or Vice were to be considered only with regard to their Consequences in another World, it might be tolerable to leave it to Mens private Reflexion, and to the care of Divines ... but since they affect the *public* and *present,* as well as *personal* and *future* Interests of Mankind, 'tis fit the Civil Authority should exert itself, in a way of Coercion to suppress such practices.[30]

Again, Disney might personally desire a reformation of manners for religious reasons – for the glory of God, the salvation of sinners, the protection of the pious from offensive displays. He might also accept public prosecution and punishment of moral offenders as excellent ways to achieve these religious ends. But his writings explicitly set aside such religious rationales for state

28 John Disney, *An Address to Grand-Juries, Constables, and Church-Wardens* (London, 1710), 5. Philip Yorke, Earl of Hardwicke, and later Lord Chancellor, made a similar point in an address to a Grand Jury given most probably in the early 1730s: "Corruption of manners does not only tend to draw down just punishments upon persons guilty of such crimes, it enervates their minds and abates their industry. It introduces dissolution and sloth and consequently the ruin of trade, and at last is followed by poverty and beggary" (Philip Yorke, *The Life and Correspondence of Philip Yorke, Earl of Hardwicke, Lord High Chancellor of Great Britain,* 2 v. [Cambridge University Press, 1913], I,146). Other sermons reminded listeners of the burden the families of dissolute alcoholics or gamblers would make on parish funds (George Smyth, *A Sermon Preach'd at Salter's-Hall to the Societies for Reformation of Manners...* [London, 1727], 16–17).
29 Woodward, *Short Disswasive,* n.p.; Smalbroke, *Reformation Necessary,* 4. See also Moses Lowman, *A Sermon Preach'd to the Societies for Reformation of Manners at Salter's-Hall...* (London, 1720), 13 and Smith, *Sermon,* 16.
30 John Disney, *A View of Antient Laws against Immorality and Profaneness* (Cambridge, 1729), i.

action, focusing exclusively on secular, political reasons for enforcing morals legislation.

Most eighteenth-century jurists condemned profanity and Sabbath-breaking as offenses against God, a category that in itself explained their criminalization. Disney however offers primarily secular reasons to justify laws against such behavior. "There's a political reason too . . . to preserve the Honour of the Lord's Day; for Atheism would soon be the Consequence of a general Neglect of it, and Barbarism would not be far behind." And earlier, "The political Reason, why Magistrates are highly concerned to suppress Common Swearing, is, that it naturally leads to Perjury; which is destructive to the Safety, and all the Interests of Mankind."[31] Disney sets out the dangers of most other vices in the same way. Thus while drunkenness "is a Sin by the Law of God . . . the Arguments most proper here are of another kind; drawn from the vice itself, and the ill consequences of it [personal and political] in this life."[32] Disney's account of why immoral behavior deserves criminalization thus emphasizes its impact on the temporal welfare of society. Although the impulse behind his hefty folio volume, detailing the morals legislation enacted by past civilizations, is broadly religious, the arguments he advances to support his aims are not. They represent rather an effort to show that "the end of Government being the general Safety, Good Order, and Prosperity of the Subjects, there can be no just and careful Government . . . without care for the Suppression of Vice."[33]

SRM ministers and other proponents of moral reform thus staked their case for reformation of manners on the claim that the cultivation of personal morality was a "Matter of human Policy."[34] They contended that the promotion of popular morality served the explicitly temporal interest of English society and, for *this* reason, lay well within the legislative province of the civil authority. Two years prior to Disney's work, George Smyth's sermon to the SRMs similarly delimited the magistrate's authority in moral matters.

Vice and Immorality are faulty every way . . . offensive to God, Prejudicial to the Sinner's Personal Interests, and Injurious to Society . . . [But it is] upon this latter

---

31 Disney, *View of Antient Laws,* 234, 198. On the political danger of profanity, see also Gilbert Burnet, *Charitable Reproof. A Sermon Preached to the Societies for Reformation of Manners . . .* (London, 1700), 22; Matthew Heynes, *A Sermon for Reformation of Manners, Preach'd . . . at the Assizes . . .* (London, 1701), 13; Edward Cobden, *The Duty and Reward of Turning Others to Righteousness. A Sermon Preach'd to the Societies for Reformation of Manners . . .* (London, 1736), 17.

32 Disney, *View of Antient Laws,* 257.

33 *Ibid.,* iii.

34 George Stanhope, *The Duty of Juries. A Sermon Preach'd at the Lent-Assizes, holden at Maidstone, in Kent . . .* (London, 1701), 13.

Account principally, if not only, that they are punished by the civil Magistrate; and that you are justifiable in Detecting and Informing against them.[35]

Anglicans and dissenters of this period who supported the reformation of manners movement thus showed considerable reluctance to offer theo-centric justifications for the enforcement of morals legislation (despite the avowedly religious nature of their overall aims). The key to the Augustan reformation of manners movement was the claim that vice and immorality "may and ought to be restrained by the Magistrate's Coercive Power ... because they have an evil Aspect upon Civil Government."[36]

Why did the state's religious officials lean so heavily on secular rationales for the reformation of manners? Why did they not base their case for reform, as earlier protestants had, on the magistrate's responsibility to reform degenerate sinners – whatever the political effects of vice? Perhaps the most important reason was strategic. Because the sermons were after all hortatory exercises, the ministers can be understood as making those arguments they believed their listeners would find most persuasive. But why would this effort to characterize personal morality as a political virtue appeal to eighteenth-century moral reformers – or to their spiritual leaders? Three factors seem particularly helpful in explaining why Anglican supporters of the SRMs might feel especially comfortable in stressing the practical political benefits of a religiously inspired moral reform: the Thomistic heritage of Anglican political theory, seventeenth-century developments in Anglican moral theology and a new secularism in political philosophy itself.

III

Part of the reason Anglicans offered "merely civil" arguments for the magistrate's involvement in the reformation of manners lies with the understand-

---

35 Smyth, *Sermon,* 12.
36 Thomas Troughear, *The Magistrate's Duty to Honour God, Set Forth in a Sermon Preach'd at Southampton* (Oxford, 1733), 14. Other sermons to the Societies that rely on secular arguments to defend the SRMs' work include Heynes, *Sermon:* "The Immoralities of a Nation strike at that society which Government was design'd to cement ... it necessarily follows, that the Reasons of Government, even in its Original Design, require that open Vices and Immoralities, should be restrained" (6) and Smith, *Sermon:* although Christianity provides no "Precedent for enforcing Religion by the Civil Sword," the magistrate may still suppress sin given his "prior Engagements ... to advance the common Welfare for Vice, if suffer'd to spread ... will soon bring on a total Dissolution of any form of government" (15–16). See also *Representation,* 4; Hayley, *Sermon,* 26. Richard Smalbroke goes farther than most in suggesting a political rationale for suppressing sodomy: "But as the Good of Society is the particular care of the Magistrate, whatever has a direct tendency to lessen the Number of Subjects, and to weaken and dishonour the Government ... falls under his immediate Cognizance" (*Reformation Necessary,* 22).

ing of the state's responsibilities they had inherited from Aquinas through Richard Hooker, whose *Laws of Ecclesiastical Polity* (1593) provided the definitive formulation of Anglican political theology. Calvinist ministers considered the civil magistracy institutionally subordinate to the church, ordained by God to aid the ministry in the essentially religious task of establishing a truly righteous Christian commonwealth.[37] Hooker followed Aquinas who followed Aristotle in giving the state an independently valid end in the realm of nature: securing man's temporal flourishing. In this view, the magistrate's first responsibility is the maintenance of peace and civil justice; he serves the people's spiritual welfare by providing the peaceful conditions under which the church could go about its work. For Hooker, the Christian citizen lives in one society that governs him in two different modes: "which Society being termed a Commonweal as it liveth under ... Secular Law and Regiment; a Church as it liveth under the Spiritual Law of Christ."[38] Because England's supreme magistrate, the King, was also the head of its church, Anglicans could and did justify morals legislation as part of the Christian magistrate's religious responsibilities. But their Thomist heritage also enabled them to justify the reformation of manners on the grounds of "human policy," as Aquinas had done five centuries earlier.

Anglicans of the eighteenth century however went further than Aquinas in specifying the range of personal behavior that was not only ungodly but socially dangerous and thus properly criminalized. Aquinas had argued in the *Summa Theologica* that "because human law is enacted on behalf of the mass of men," the magistrate should not "prohibit every vice from which virtuous men abstain." Human law must focus on repressing only that type of vice or wrongdoing that actually threatens the conditions of social cooperation. To Aquinas this principle meant that the state should take aim only against "the graver vices from which the majority can abstain; and particularly those vices which are damaging to others, and which if they were not prohibited, would make it impossible for human society to endure:

---

37 Harro Höpfl, *The Christian Polity of John Calvin* (Cambridge University Press, 1982), 45–8, 189–93. See also Steven E. Ozment, *The Reformation in the Cities* (New Haven: Yale University Press, 1975), 135.

38 Richard Hooker, *Works* (Oxford: Clarendon Press, [1593] 1793), 293. Ernst Troeltsch describes the "Thomist Ethic of the State" to which Hooker subscribes thus: "The purpose of the State [in the Thomist Ethic] ... is the maintenance of order and the peace of the country; this implies that it is the duty of the government to create a setting for the peaceful exercise of vocation, the minimum at least of a legal morality, and the ideal of distributive and commutative justice," *Social Teaching*, 313. Robert Faulkner, *Richard Hooker and the Politics of a Christian England* (Berkeley: University of California Press, 1981), 104 stresses Hooker's conformity to this ethic. See especially Hooker, *Laws of Ecclesiastical Polity*, Book 7, chapter 2.5.

as murder, theft and suchlike."[39] To the moral reformers, this conclusion was too restrained. They argued that the populace's indulgence in such vices as drunkenness, lewdness, swearing, cursing and gaming threatened as well to "make it impossible for human society to endure." These vices thus required civil as well as religious condemnation.

Why did the moderate Anglicans who supported the SRMs repudiate Aquinas's cautious toleration of people's moral failings? One reason might be a comparatively recent development in Anglican moral theology. Reacting against the rigidity of puritanism, the latitudinarian Anglicans of the seventeenth century had begun to preach less the duty of virtue than its rewards. Foremost among the popularizers of this new view of moral virtue was Archbishop John Tillotson. The message he brought in his extremely popular sermons was that securing the good of one's soul coincided with finding one's happiness on earth; moral behavior was eminently in one's self-interest.[40] The sermons made to the SRMs reflect this approach to moral matters, transposing the temporal benefits to be gained from spiritual growth from the individual to the community level. The belief that, for each individual, virtue brings material rewards becomes the conviction that a community's enforcement of personal virtue will also bring that community tangible public benefits.

Both the Thomistic heritage of Anglican political theology and latitudinarian developments in moral philosophy helped determine the moral reformers' increasingly secular justification of their essentially religious politics of virtue. But perhaps most decisive in shaping the nature of their argument for state involvement in reformation of manners was the new account of the ends of magistracy gaining ground outside the church. Following the Revolution of 1688, popular accounts of the origin and end of civil government increasingly stressed temporal welfare as the predominant aim of the political community and cited the protection of individuals' prosperity and safety as the primary responsibility of the civil magistrate.[41] Rather than maintain

39 Aquinas, *Selected Political Writings,* ed. A. P. D'Entrèves (Oxford: Basil Blackwell, 1948), 135 (Ques. 96 Art. 2).
40 John Tillotson, Archbishop of Canterbury, *Works* (London, 1701). On latitudinarian theology in general and Tillotson in particular, see the accounts in G. R. Cragg, *From Puritanism to the Age of Reason* (Cambridge University Press, 1950), chapter 4; Norman Sykes, *Church and State in England in the Eighteenth Century* (Cambridge University Press, 1934), 343–432 and the more detailed treatments in H. R. McAdoo, *The Structure of Caroline Moral Theology* (London: Longmans, Green and Co., 1949) and C. F. Allison, *The Rise of Moralism: The Proclamation of the Gospel from Hooker to Baxter* (London: Society for Promoting Christian Knowledge, 1966).
41 See the works, both primary and secondary, cited in Richard Ashcraft and M. M. Goldsmith, "Locke, Revolution Principles, and the Formation of Whig Ideology," *The Historical Journal* 26 (1983): 773–800. Of course, to say that these themes were increasingly stressed is not to say that they predominated.

against this view a more theocentric account of the ends of civil society and the responsibilities of the civil magistrate (as responsive above all to God's will), Anglican ministers began to shape their case for moral reform to this secularized understanding of the scope of political action.

A 1720 sermon by Benjamin Ibbot, chaplain-in-ordinary to George I, suggests the extent to which some Anglicans at least embraced this new view of the civil magistrate's role. Ibbot's discussion of the proper province of state authority begins with a Lockean account of the ends of civil government. The only reason men "enter into Societies [is] for the mutual Security and Defence of their Person and Proprieties" Thus, "the proper Business of the Magistrate is to preserve the external Peace of the World, and the temporal Good of the Community." This account of the end of government means that immoral behavior should be publicly prosecuted only if it impinges upon the temporal concerns of the magistrate. Vices "fall under his Cognizance, as they are injurious to Mens Civil Interests, and destructive of the good Order and Government of the World; and not as they have an inherent Turpitude in them." A typical Augustan moralist, Ibbot is confident that all "Violations of the Divine Law are also prejudicial to Human Society." Still, he insists that the magistrate must abstract vices from their status as "Transgressions of the Laws of God" and consider them solely as disruptive political acts. On this basis alone he may punish them. "If the ill influence which these Vices have upon the Peace and Welfare of Human Society, could be separated from their Immorality . . . the Magistrate could have nothing to do with them."[42]

In accounting for the origin of government without reference to the will of God, Ibbot admittedly outstrips much of the Anglican clergy. Nor, preaching to London's Lord-Mayor on election day, is he specifically concerned to defend the SRMs' reforming efforts. But by firmly rejecting any civil involvement in religious affairs (in the course of an argument for religious toleration), he suggests the sort of political theory with which even religiously minded moral reformers had to grapple if they were to convince the broadest possible spectrum of public opinion that the prosecution and punishment of personal immorality was not only an effective but an appropriate use of state power.

Anglican ministers may have valued the reformation of manners for its religious goals and achievements. They may even have believed that it was as much the business of the civil magistrate as of the minister to make citizens more godly and less sinful. But both lay and religious audiences

---

42 Benjamin Ibbot, *The Nature and Extent of the Office of the Civil Magistrate* (London, 1720), 4–5, 6, 6–7.

were increasingly unlikely to understand the magistrate's role in these religious terms, as Ibbot's sermon illustrates. To the extent that moral reformers wanted a convincing justification for state involvement in the reformation of manners, they needed to find other grounds for public action. Thus the argument that reformation of manners met one of the least controversial goals of political action – furthering the temporal welfare of the state.

Ironically, in adapting the case for moral reform to suit the changing political sensibilities of the populace, this strictly political case for enforcing a virtue of personal morality became far more vulnerable to criticism than the more explicitly religious rationale for morals enforcement that Anglicans had abandoned as no longer persuasive to them or their contemporaries. Few if any students of the Bible would dispute the contention that vice and immorality are against the laws of God or that the sins the SRMs condemned (drunkenness, lewdness, profanity, gaming) counted as vice. The problem however for the moral reformers was that the role of the civil magistrate was no longer so uncontroversially characterized as upholding the laws of God. Supporters of the SRMs preferred to stress the political importance of personal morality in order to strengthen their case for aggressive enforcement of the nation's morals legislation. To the extent that reformers deployed this form of argument, they grounded their case for moral reform in a political goal that the devout and skeptical alike could agree on: the public welfare. But this switch from a religious to a secular justification of state action, intended to widen the popular appeal of the SRMs' efforts, had an unintended consequence. In establishing this link between personal morality and public good, moral reformers invited a more wide-ranging and aggressive attack on the church's position than if they had stuck with the traditional view that the magistrate as minister of God must enforce God's laws. In particular, their arguments sustained a variety of damaging objections from critics only too eager to show that a citizen's excellence consisted in something other than abstaining from the grosser vices of the age. By basing the rationale for the politics of virtue not on God's word, but on its contribution to temporal welfare, Anglicans exposed their case to an empirical scrutiny harsher than it could bear.

In the next few pages, I discuss a quartet of Augustan figures – Henry Sacheverell, Daniel Defoe, Jonathan Swift and Bernard Mandeville – whose criticisms of the Societies illustrate this difficulty. Although writing from different political perspectives, all challenged the assumption of Low Church Anglicans that the elimination of drunkenness, prostitution, gaming and the like was the best way to nurture the sort of virtues with which the modern polity would flourish.

IV

Sacheverell and Swift were both High Church Tories, the first a bitter-tongued polemicist with a special hatred for dissenters, the latter a brilliant, sardonic critic of his country's mores. Defoe placed his considerable political wit at the service of any who would have him. Despite decided Whig sympathies, he spent most of his journalistic career in the pay of the moderate Tory politician, Robert Harley.[43] Mandeville, a Dutch émigré and notorious social satirist, is the only one of these four authors to question directly the proposition that citizen virtue of any sort contributes importantly to the public welfare. The others consider certain behaviors to be politically virtuous and encourage the government to cultivate them. But, like Mandeville, their work confronts the SRMs on the reformers' chosen terrain, arguing that the SRMs neither understood the dispositions necessary to secure the common good nor followed the means best suited to cultivating them.

Perhaps the most notorious attack against the reforming societies came in Henry Sacheverell's 1709 assizes sermon, *The Communication of Sin*. Labeling moral reformers as "troublesome Wasps," he criticized the SRMs' efforts as "the unwarranted Effects of an Idle, Incroaching, Impertinent, and Medling Curiosity . . . the base Product of Ill-Nature, Spiritual Pride, Censoriousness and sanctified Spleen." Sacheverell's unstinting attack was largely prompted by the Societies' tolerance of dissenters among their ranks. Like most High Church clerics, Sacheverell considered the correction, not accommodation, of such schismatics to be the first step in the restoration of public virtue. However, he chose to frame his attack on the Societies in political rather than religious terms: reformers' activities "arrogantly intrench upon Other's Christian Liberty, and Innocence," and interfere with "our Neighbor's Proceedings, that don't belong to us." Such criticisms bluntly dismiss the moderate Anglican contention that the cultivation of personal morality makes an important contribution to national welfare; the Societies are meddling with behavior that has little effect on social or political order. By suggesting that the community must tolerate the moral shortcomings of its (Anglican) citizens, Sacheverell challenges the reformers' vision of personal morality as the keystone of political virtue. Those truly concerned about the morals of the citizen and the welfare of the community would prod dissenters back into the Anglican communion and give up the misguided effort to "carry on the

---

43 For the details of Defoe's political career, see James Sutherland, *Daniel Defoe: A Critical Study* (Cambridge: Harvard University Press, 1971) or Paula Backscheider, *Daniel Defoe: His Life* (Baltimore: The Johns Hopkins University Press, 1989). On Swift, see J. A. Downie, *Jonathan Swift, Political Writer* (London: Routledge and Kegan Paul, 1984) and J. P. Lock, *Swift's Tory Politics* (London: Duckworth, 1983). The best introduction to Sacheverell's life and politics is Geoffrey Holmes, *The Trial of Doctor Sacheverell* (London: Eyre Methuen, 1973).

Blessed Work of Reformation by Lying, Slandering, Whispering, Backbiting and Talebearing."[44]

Those outside the High Church also attacked the SRMs' effort to make personal morality the touchstone of citizen virtue. Defoe's 1713 squib, "The Groans of Great Britain," is a catalogue of Whig blunders written to support Harley's Tory government. In it, he suggests that the SRMs and their Whig allies have misconstrued the proper object of reformation. "They were Zealous against the poor Drury Lane Ladies of Pleasure; and the Smithfield Players and Poets were sensible of their Resentments . . . but Cheating, Bribery and Oppression found no zealous Reformers." To secure its safety and welfare, Great Britain needs a reformation not in "private Vices . . . [but] in the Public and Political Vices of a People . . . Avarice, blind Ambition and Luxury." Like Sacheverell, Defoe accuses the SRMs of misdirecting their efforts on behalf of public virtue: targeting not true political vices but behavior that is at worst irreligious, and at best, "Innocent Pleasures."[45]

Clerics supporting the SRMs had to admit that not even the justices of the peace (the officials charged with enforcing morals legislation) saw the profound political dangers of personal immorality. "'Tis shocking," complained one minister, "to hear such a one [a local magistrate] say, with an Air of Indifferency, 'tis but Swearing, but Drunkenness, but Sabbath-breaking, and ranging them under the Head of Necessary Liberties, which the common People must be allowed."[46] Yet, reformers invited just this response by suggesting that the reformation of manners be pursued precisely for its public benefits. If the Societies had continued to justify their cause as earlier reformers did – in terms of the magistrate's religious responsibility to exterminate vice, or his right to correct the private vices of individuals regardless of public impact – then the contention that immoral behaviors must be tolerated as "Necessary Liberties" would have lost much of its force as a convincing rejoinder.

Low Church Anglicans, in the eyes of their critics, had failed to target the true source of moral corruption in the kingdom. In what then should a proper reformation of manners consist? Those not sharing Sacheverell's high-flying prescription of imposing Anglican uniformity on all citizens focused on correcting the vices of the ruling classes. Although differences in temperament, religion and political allegiance usually put Defoe and Swift on opposite sides of any social issue, these two authors offer remarkably similar proposals for the moral reformation they both thought was badly needed.

44 Henry Sacheverell, *The Communication of Sin. A Sermon Preach'd at the Assizes held at Derby . . .* (London, 1709), 20–1, 15, 20, 21.
45 Daniel Defoe, *Les Soupirs de la Grand Britaigne: Or, the Groans of Great Britain . . .* (London, 1713), 14, 15.
46 Newman, *Reformation,* 28.

Jonathan Swift's *Project for the Advancement of Religion and Reformation of Manners* (1709) calls for the government to draw men to a personal
and public virtue through the persuasion of political and economic patronage. The Queen herself should begin this transformation by establishing
"Piety and Virtue ... [as] Qualifications necessary for Preferment," seeing
that her deputies and subordinates do likewise. By requiring good moral
character of all potential employees, the Queen and her court can make it in
"every Man's Interest and Honour to cultivate Religion and Virtue." Swift
also recommends restoring the authority of society's most public figures
(and thus their influence over the lower classes) by purging their ranks of
the "poor and corrupt." Until figures of authority discharge their responsibilities with dignity, the morals of the gentry and the masses remain in danger.
The Societies themselves he dismisses as "factious Clubs ... grown a Trade
to enrich little knavish Informers."[47]

Like Swift, Defoe locates the cause and cure of immorality in the upper
reaches of English society.

> Your Quest of Vice at Church and Court begin
> There lie the Seeds of high expiate Sin:
> 'Tis they can check the Vices of the Town,
> When e'er they please, but to suppress their own.[48]

But Defoe, more than Swift, fumes at the way in which the SRMs' campaign
targeted the less powerful members of society. Thus he complains that their
work enforces "Cobweb Laws, in which the small Flies are catch'd and the
great ones break through ... we do'nt fin'd [sic] the Rich Drunkard carri'd
before my Lord Mayor, nor a Swearing, Lewd Merchant punished."[49] He then

---

47 Jonathan Swift, *A Project for the Advancement of Religion and the Reformation of Manners*
   (London, 1709), 18, 16, 42. Swift's recent biographer, David Nokes, offers a sharply critical
   reading of this tract, calling the "scheme as narrow, naive, and Utopian as any that he sati-
   rizes ... Robespierre himself could not have formulated a more thoroughgoing apparatus for
   ensuring the tyranny of virtue" (*Jonathan Swift* [Oxford: Oxford University Press, 1985], 95,
   97). Irvin Ehrenpreis's classic biography, *Swift: The Man, His Works and the Age*, v. 2 (Cambridge: Harvard University Press, 1967), gives a similarly negative account, 289–94. These
   critics miss the fact that Swift, like Defoe, is offering a reforming plan designed to *moderate*
   the schemes of the SRMs. By relying on interest, rather than coercion, to secure virtue, he
   distances himself from such virtuecrats as Robespierre.
48 Daniel Defoe, *Reformation of Manners, A Satyr* (London, 1702), 61.
49 Daniel Defoe, *The Poor Man's Plea to all the Proclamations, Declarations, Acts of Parliament, etc ... for a Reformation of Manners* (London, [1698] 1703), 9. He returns to this
   theme four years later in *Reformation of Manners*:

   > Yet Ostia [England] boasts of her Regeneration
   > And tells us wondrous Tales of Reformation:
   > How against Vice she has been so severe,
   > That none but Men of Quality may swear (5).

goes on to argue that the class bias of the reformation of manners movement is not only unjust but, in terms of the ends served, misplaced. "To think then to effect a Reformation by Punishing the Poor, while the Rich seem to Enjoy a Charter for Wickedness, is like taking away the Effect, that the Cause may cease."[50]

Once again, the key to moral reform lies in "examples, not penalties."[51] Securing the reformation of leading citizens would remove the need to "push on the Laws" against their social inferiors. Because a remoralized gentry would seek out only sober and honest friends and employees, "Interest and Good Manners would Reform us of the poorer sort."[52] For both Defoe and Swift, true reformation comes from transforming the moral quality of the gentry's public life, reshaping the nation's attitudes towards the proper qualifications for political and economic service. The country's salvation lies not in the better execution of the nation's laws, but in better behavior from those who made them.

Bernard Mandeville offers a more radical critique of the Societies' efforts. It is not just that the Societies have misconstrued the proper object of a politics of virtue, but that a politics of virtue is a fundamentally misguided way to serve the interests of the community. Defoe, Swift and Sacheverell differed with the Societies over how best to nurture in citizens the moral excellences (either personal morality or religious conformity) that ground public welfare. Mandeville argues that from a strictly political perspective the modern state should be in the business of accommodating, not repressing, vice.

Mandeville's most famous work is *The Fable of the Bees,* first published in 1714 and brought to public attention in 1723 with the second edition. Although certain reformers took the *Fable*'s account of the "Publick Benefits" of "Private Vices" as a direct affront to their moral crusade, the book was not an explicit attack on the Societies. Rather, Mandeville turned his satiric genius against the reformers in a short publication of 1724, *A Modest Defence of Publick Stews,* dedicated to "the Gentlemen of the Societies." In this work, Mandeville suggested that the problem reformers were trying to combat by strict enforcement of existing laws would be far more appropriately handled by the establishment of state-run brothels. Setting up cheap, clean and accessible bordellos would "prevent most of the mischievous Effects of this Vice, [and] even lessen the Quantity of Whoring in general" by an appropriate supervision of this ubiquitous sin.[53]

50 Defoe, *Poor Man's Plea,* 16.
51 Defoe, *An Essay upon Projects* (London, 1697), 4.
52 Defoe, *Poor Man's Plea,* 23, 24.
53 Bernard Mandeville, *A Modest Defence of Publick Stews* (Los Angeles: Williams Andrews Clark Memorial Library, University of California, [1724] 1973), 11.

Here, Mandeville uses the moral reformers' own principle – that public
welfare, not moral character, should determine a behavior's legality – to
argue for the legalization of the trade in women. Properly regulated, public
brothels will prevent theft and other crimes related to prostitution, end the
spread of venereal diseases and assure the safety of bastard infants. They will
spare men the financial expenses of maintaining private mistresses and, by
satisfying men's natural urges, protect the wives and daughters of the upper
classes from seduction and debauchery.[54] Thus "few or none of [these evils
attributed to prostitution] are the necessary Effects of Whoring consider'd in
itself, but only proceed from the Abuse and ill Management of it."[55] From the
standpoint of public welfare, a judicious accommodation of the business of
prostitution makes as much if not more sense than a program of prosecution. Mandeville, then, meets and bests the Societies on their own ground.

Mandeville's rhetorical triumph neatly illustrates the dilemma that confronted the supporters of the SRMs. On the one hand, these individuals made
a genuine effort to adapt their arguments for a politics of virtue to contemporary sensibilities. On the other hand, by framing their case for the coercive
enforcement of personal morality in purely political terms, the Societies
initiated a debate which they would ultimately lose. Critics like those already discussed all too willingly challenged – or ridiculed – their claim that
adherence to religious standards of personal morality was the most important mark of the good citizen. Because Anglican moral reformers could not
convincingly defend this assertion, their case for the importance and legitimacy of a state enforcement of personal morality failed, and with it, their bid
for a public endorsement of their particular politics of public virtue.

One way to explain the failure of this religious politics of virtue is in terms
of social and political circumstances ill-suited to an enthusiastic embrace of
Low Church Anglican ideals. This view would attribute the reformers' difficulties primarily to an inhospitable social and political environment. A polity increasingly geared towards facilitating the success of large-scale commercial endeavors, governed by individuals increasingly attracted by liberal
characterizations of state authority, was no place to pursue the sort of moralistic politics of virtue favored by Low Church clerics. Moral reformers were
hopelessly out of step with their times, and for this reason their politics of
virtue went down to defeat.

But this argument misses an important intermediate step. The reformers'
agenda did not rest on some outdated or obsolescent view of political
authority that eighteenth-century citizens now rejected. One cannot say

54 *Ibid.*, 17–22, 25, 26, 50–1.
55 *Ibid.*, 6.

simply that times had passed them by. Rather, defenders of the SRMs made a genuine effort to engage the concerns of their coreligionists, to update their arguments for contemporary consumption. Thus, ministers defended the prosecution of moral offenders in terms of the temporal benefits such punishment promised, precisely because one of the more obvious justifications for coercive state intervention – the civil magistrate's religious responsibility for the welfare of the individual's soul – was no longer widely accepted in Augustan political argument. Because rehashing traditional theocentric rationales for reformation of manners would not have made political sense, moral reformers emphasized the secular advantages of their program.

This strategy might seem to hold considerable political promise. A politics of public virtue must make a convincing case for the administrative support or legislation it seeks; it must engage in political argument to persuade others of the correctness of its approach to cultivating and sustaining civic virtue. But it proved more difficult than moral reformers expected to translate the goals of a religiously motivated moral reform into a politically appealing language of public virtue. Their persuasives properly spoke to the concerns of the modern polity but in a way that ultimately made the case for state prosecution of moral offenders less rather than more compelling. Their fellow citizens simply did not accept their argument that the policing of personal morals was a central element of an effective politics of virtue.

One can see a similar dynamic at work in the republican or civic humanist politics of public virtue championed by writers associated with the Country party. Just as religious conceptions of political virtue lost their hold on the English political imagination by the middle of the eighteenth century, so too did the republican ideal of the good citizen as public-spirited patriot. Like moral reformers, advocates of a republican politics of public virtue adapted or updated a traditional understanding of political virtue to fit a new set of social and political circumstances. But the arguments they marshaled hardly strengthened the case for imposing a public virtue of the classical republican sort on the citizens of England. Instead, their efforts to grapple with the problem of public virtue transformed, and in transforming, helped privatize the traditional republican understanding of civic virtue.

4

◁══════════════════════════════════════▷

A republican politics of virtue: The selfish citizen in *Cato's Letters*

The pattern of political thought that we now call "classical republicanism" (or "civic humanism" or "civic republicanism")[1] has its roots in the work of ancient historians and statesmen who contemplated the fate of free republics, considering the conditions by which such self-governing political entities might sustain themselves through time. Its more immediate origins lie in the writings of a number of humanist scholars in Renaissance Italy who, departing from the earliest premises of humanism, asserted with Aristotle that the full development of men's moral excellences required not their withdrawal from the world but their political participation in a free community. The pressing question these "civic humanists" addressed was why such participation was fundamentally at risk in the republics of their day and how such a good might be safeguarded.[2] Drawing on lessons culled primarily

---

1 J. G. A. Pocock in a series of works culminating in *The Machiavellian Moment: Florentine Political Thought and the Atlantic Republican Tradition* (Princeton: Princeton University Press, 1975) identified an "Atlantic republican tradition" as sharing in and extending the civic humanism of the Florentine Renaissance. Pocock prefers to call the tradition as a whole civic humanist; Quentin Skinner, *The Foundations of Modern Political Thought, Volume I: The Renaissance* (Cambridge University Press, 1978) favors classical republicanism. For Pocock's reflections on the fungeability of the two terms, see "*The Machiavellian Moment* Revisited: A Study in History and Ideology," *Journal of Modern History* 53 (1981), 49 and *Virtue, Commerce, and History: Essays on Political Thought and History, Chiefly in the Eighteenth Century* (Cambridge University Press, 1985), 38–9. Others have opted for civic republicanism (J. H. Hexter, *On Historians* [Cambridge: Harvard University Press, 1979]; William Sullivan, *Reconstructing Public Philosophy* [Berkeley: University of California Press, 1986]) or even the civic tradition (John Robertson, "The Scottish Enlightenment at the Limits of the Civic Tradition," in Istvan Hont and Michael Ignatieff, eds., *Wealth and Virtue: The Shaping of Political Economy in the Scottish Enlightenment* [Cambridge University Press, 1985]).
2 The precise nature of civic humanism remains a matter of some dispute. The following description of the tenets of Renaissance civic humanism draws primarily on the work of Hans

from the historians of the Roman republic, they answered that republics crumbled once their people succumbed to corruption, an internal rot characterized by the onset of avarice, ambition and love of luxury. This moral decay exposed the nation to internal faction and external conquest – the two greatest threats to liberty. Their conclusion: the survival of the free city depended on the virtue of its citizens.

Early civic humanist tracts did not always delineate the precise characteristics that constituted "civic virtue" nor did they necessarily offer a unitary conception of the good citizen. (They differed for example on whether the rich citizen represented a contribution or threat to republican liberty.[3]) Most however affirmed the Ciceronian vision of the good citizen as fundamentally identical with the good man.[4] In this view, the virtues that contributed most importantly to the preservation of free government were also those that perfected the individual as a moral being: justice, courage, moderation, a practical wisdom and an abiding sense of duty to one's political community.

This optimistic identification of civic virtue with moral excellence did not survive the next generation of reflection about political liberty and the means to sustain it. Machiavelli's brilliant meditations on freedom and empire in the *Discourses on Livy* also recommended civic virtue to republics as an indispensable element of any community's liberty. But the dispositions Machiavelli called virtuous bore little resemblance to those that Renaissance humanists enthusiastically endorsed. Nor were they praised as allowing individuals to reach their full moral potential; the civic virtues in

Baron, who first identified and described this pattern of thought (*The Crisis of the Early Italian Renaissance,* rev. ed. [Princeton: Princeton University Press, 1966]), and on Quentin Skinner, *Foundations,* chapters 1–4, a careful amplification and correction of Baron's views. Both men stress the Roman sources of this tradition; J. G. A. Pocock in *Politics, Language and Time: Essays on Political Thought and History* (New York: Atheneum, 1973), chapter 3 and *Machiavellian Moment,* chapter 3 offers an alternative account that emphasizes civic humanism's Aristotelian roots.

The Renaissance authors whose work together constitutes the first flowering of civic humanism includes most prominently Coluccio Salutati (1331–1406), Leonardo Bruni (1370–1444), Poggio Bracciolini (1380–1459), Leon Battista Alberti (1404–72), Alamanno Rinuccini (1426–99). A useful English introduction to their work can be found in the translations of Benjamin Kohl and Ronald Witt, *The Earthly Republic: Italian Humanists on Government and Society* (Philadelphia: University of Pennsylvania Press, 1978) and Renée Watkins, *Humanism and Liberty: Writings on Freedom in Fifteenth-Century Florence* (Columbia: University of South Carolina Press, 1978).

3 Skinner, *Foundations,* 75.
4 Cicero, *De Officiis* 1.5.15, 2.5.18 and *Tusculan Disputations* 5.25.72 provide representative accounts of his understanding of virtue. D. C. Earl, *The Political Thought of Sallust* (Cambridge University Press, 1961), 47–52 helpfully distinguishes Ciceronian *virtus* from earlier Roman understandings of this quality; Skinner, *Foundations,* 88–101 discusses the Ciceronian ideal in the context of the Renaissance.

Machiavelli are valued for political reasons – the preservation of civic and personal liberty – alone.[5]

Given the changing content of civic virtue from Roman authors to Machiavelli and beyond, the identifying feature of classical republicanism as an ideology that persists over time is not its particular definition of civic virtue but the intimate connection it draws between virtue and political liberty. Alternative readings of the republican tradition place participation or self-realization through political participation at the center of republican thought. This is very much the theme of Aristotle's vision of the good polity and, with some qualifications, of the Renaissance's as well. But after Machiavelli, Aristotelian ideals simply do not figure very prominently in those works we now identify as part of the republican tradition until, perhaps, the writings of Hannah Arendt.[6] Certainly some republican or civic humanist works of the late Renaissance and early modern period praise the citizens' participation in a self-governing polity or their cultivation of civic virtue as intrinsic goods, as activities constitutive of and central to a good life. But others, Machiavelli for example, treat both civic virtue and political freedom instrumentally, valuing them particularly for their role in allowing citizens to achieve "whatever ends they may choose to set themselves."[7] In both cases, however, the central motive for pursuing a politics of virtue is the absolutely crucial role of civic virtue in preserving civic freedom. Liberty comes first.

I do not wish to deny a strong participatory element to much, if not most, republican theory. As Charles Taylor points out, it is indeed difficult to conceive of a free, self-governing polity preserving itself over time if it does not place a high value on citizen participation.[8] My point is that a theorist may legitimately separate both civic virtue and political liberty from active citizen participation without automatically forfeiting a place in the republican pantheon. The key question is whether the theorist preserves, with or without an emphasis on participation, the distinctive republican connection

---

5 Perhaps the only aspect of Machiavelli's account of *virtú* that scholars agree upon is that it is not equivalent to the *virtus* of the Ciceronian ideal. Quentin Skinner, *Machiavelli* (Oxford: Oxford University Press, 1981) provides a characteristically incisive comparison of Machiavellian and Ciceronian ideas of virtue (35–47) and a select bibliography of the debate (97). Felix Gilbert, *Machiavelli and Guicciardini* (Princeton: Princeton University Press, 1965) makes the important point that "the decisive aspects of Machiavelli's concept of *virtú* were taken from Latin historians, particularly Sallust" (328).

6 See in particular Hannah Arendt, "What is Freedom?" in *Between Past and Future: Eight Exercises in Political Thought* (New York: Penguin Books, 1961) and *The Human Condition* (Chicago: University of Chicago Press, 1958).

7 Quentin Skinner, "The Idea of Negative Liberty: Philosophical and Historical Perspectives," in Richard Rorty, J. B. Schneewind and Quentin Skinner, eds., *Philosophy in History: Essays on the Historiography of Philosophy* (Cambridge University Press, 1984), 205.

8 Charles Taylor, "Cross-Purposes: The Liberal-Communitarian Debate," in Nancy L. Rosenblum, ed., *Liberalism and the Moral Life* (Cambridge: Harvard University Press, 1989).

between liberty as the primary political good, corruption as the greatest threat to political liberty and civic virtue (most broadly defined as those dispositions of the individual citizen that combat corruption) as a crucial guarantor of continued freedom – a connection which is rarely if ever found in liberal thought.

Emphasizing liberty rather than participation as the central value of classical republicanism also allows a more constructive reading of the essential differences between liberalism and republicanism. The notion of two traditions of political thought deeply divided about the appropriate nature of political endeavor (self-realization through self-government versus the individual pursuit of the individual good life) can be replaced by an account of traditions differing primarily about the best way to achieve the same political end – a free (rather than despotic) society. This reading narrows the gap between the republican and liberal tradition by recognizing the common concerns that inform them both.[9]

Two of the most articulate expositors of republican themes in early eighteenth-century England are Henry St. John, Viscount Bolingbroke (1670–1750) and "Cato," the pseudonymous author of *Cato's Letters* (1720–3), the inspired creation of two accomplished political journalists, John Trenchard and Thomas Gordon. Although not republican (i.e., anti-monarchical) in the strict sense of the word, these writers continue to cast their reflections about the problems and prospects for constitutional monarchy in terms of the republican triumvirate of corruption, virtue and liberty. They stand at the end of a distinguished if short-lived British republican tradition, inaugurated with James Harrington and including John Milton, Marchamont Nedham, Algernon Sydney, Henry Neville, Walter Moyle, Andrew Fletcher, William Molesworth and John Toland.[10] This tradition

9 For an illuminating discussion of these issues that remains properly sensitive to the place of political participation in a free society, see Charles Taylor, "Cross-Purposes."

10 Z. S. Fink, *The Classical Republicans* (Chicago: Northwestern University Press, 1945) identified the seventeenth-century authors on this list, stressing their shared commitment to a republican form of government (and a Venetian model of it). Caroline Robbins, *The Eighteenth-Century Commonwealthman* (Cambridge: Harvard University Press, 1959) added to it various eighteenth-century authors who, she argued, retained a preference for a republican polity. Pocock in a series of works culminating in *The Machiavellian Moment* reinterpreted this Anglo-American tradition as primarily concerned with the preservation of civic virtue and autonomy (within a monarchical as well as republican context) and characterized the whole as fundamentally "Harringtonian" in outlook (see especially *Politics, Language and Time*, chapter 4). Pocock has further developed his argument in a number of publications including, most importantly, "*The Machiavellian Moment* Revisited"; "Cambridge Paradigms and Scotch Philosophers: A Study of the Relations Between the Civic Humanist and the Civil Jurisprudential Interpretation of Eighteenth-Century Social Thought," in Hont and Ignatieff, eds., *Wealth and Virtue* and *Virtue, Commerce, and History*. Noteworthy critical responses include Jesse Goodale, "Pocock's Neo-

bristles with idiosyncratic political programs and philosophical commitments, from Harrington's mechanized republic by ballot to Toland's mysti-
cal freemasonry. The thinkers within it are united however by the primacy
they accord to political liberty, the concern they manifest with corruption,
and the central role they assign, in securing liberty, to the operation of
civic virtue – however they define this quality.

Not all of these republican writers however define the qualities appropriate to the good citizen in the same way. In the next three chapters I look at
the quite different ways in which Cato, Bolingbroke and his Court Whig
opponents formulated the requirements of civic virtue and consider how
their various adaptations of traditional republican arguments contributed to
the transformation of virtue in this period.

I

John Trenchard was an accomplished veteran of political polemic when he
met Thomas Gordon, a young Scottish lawyer recently arrived in London
and eager to enter the world of political journalism. Impressed by a number
of his satirical attacks on the High Church party, Trenchard invited Gordon
to continue his case against "priestcraft" in a journal that they would edit
together: *The Independent Whig* (20 January 1720–4 January 1721).[11] The
collaboration thrived, and by the end of the year, the pair laid aside *The
Independent Whig* in favor of a new effort: *Cato's Letters,* published weekly
from 5 November 1720 to 27 July 1723 mostly in the *London Journal.*[12]

Harringtonians: A Reconsideration," *History of Political Thought* 1 (1980): 237–60; Isaac
Kramnick, "Republican Revisionism Revisited," *American Historical Review* 87 (1982):
629–64; Ian Shapiro, *Political Criticism* (Berkeley: University of California Press, 1990),
chapter 6.

11 For the little biographical data available on either author, see the *Dictionary of National
Biography* and Charles B. Realey, "The *London Journal* and Its Authors, 1720–23," *Humanistic Studies* 5 (3) in *Bulletin of University of Kansas* 36 (1935). John Trenchard (1660–
1723) was a country gentleman of comfortable means, the son of one of William III's
secretaries of state. Prior to his 1720 publications he was best known for his contributions
to the "standing army debates" of the late 1690s (see Lois Schwoerer, *"No Standing Armies!" The Anti-Army Ideology in Seventeenth-Century England* [Baltimore: The Johns
Hopkins University Press, 1974], chapter 8). Soon after Trenchard's death, Gordon (169?–
1750) married his collaborator's widow and left off opposition polemics for a government
sinecure (First Commissioner of Wine Licenses). He published successful translations of
Tacitus (1735) and Sallust (1744) accompanied by his own rather unremarkable "political
discourses" on these authors. At his death he left unfinished over 900 folio pages of a
History of England (J. M. Bulloch, *Thomas Gordon, the "Independent Whig"* [Aberdeen: At
the University Press], 30. Reprinted from *Aberdeen University Library Bulletin* 3 [1917]:
598–612, 733–49.)

12 The letters were published in the *London Journal* until that paper passed into government
hands in September 1722. They then appeared in the new *British Journal* from the 22nd of

The *Letters* begin with an attack on the government's handling of the infamous "South Sea Bubble." This financial scandal started with the authorized exchange of government debt for South Sea Company stock, an exchange intended to reduce the outstanding public debt. But the directors of the South Sea Company used this occasion to manipulate stock prices in such a way that thousands of investors were ruined. The affair, in which several government ministers were implicated, threatened to bring down the government. Walpole's skillful management of the crisis preserved the administration and made his political career, but left several guilty parties unpunished.[13]

Although furious at the "Harpies and Publick Robbers" whose schemes have "ruined thousands of innocent and well-meaning People," Cato does not agonize (as Bolingbroke will) over the growth of stockjobbers or monied men as a new class of citizens incapable of virtue.[14] His political world is not divided into the independent country gentry versus the dependent Whig banking interests, but into the power holders, always threatening tyranny, and the people, who if virtuous will thwart the power holders' corrupt plans. Cato simply considers the South Sea Bubble a typical example of the excesses to which government functionaries are liable. As such, the *Letters'* original cry for vengeance against these men soon evolves into a more reflective analysis of the sources and remedies of political evils in general.

Because those in power naturally look to their own rather than the public's benefit, a nation's freedom, supposed to be protected by its governors, is forever at risk. This image of liberty perpetually endangered by the lusts of rulers is endemic to republican literature. But Cato's explanation of the source of this problem differs from his classical republican and civic humanist predecessors. Roman historians who considered the unhappy fortunes of their republic tended to explain political villainy as the result of individual moral failings – a particular individual's lack of temperance, a certain person's weakness for luxury, one statesman's driving ambition.[15] Machiavelli

that month but never regained their previous level of readership (Realey, "The *London Journal* and Its Authors," 31). The letters were collected and reprinted at least six times between 1721 and 1754 (Bulloch, *Thomas Gordon,* 18).

13 On the political ramifications of the South Sea Bubble, see H. T. Dickinson, *Walpole and the Whig Supremacy* (London: The English Universities Press, 1973), chapter 4. The most thorough histories are John Carswell, *The South Sea Bubble* (Stanford: Stanford University Press, 1960) and P. G. M. Dickson, *The Financial Revolution in England* (London: Macmillan, 1967), chapters 5–8.

14 John Trenchard and Thomas Gordon, *Cato's Letters,* 4 v., 3d ed., facsimile reprint in 2 v. (New York: Russell and Russell, [1733] 1969), I, 15. Henceforth cited as *Letters.*

15 Thus Sallust's *Catiline Conspiracy* paints a brilliant portrait of a Roman noble, made desperate by his sensuality and avarice, choosing to bring down the republic rather than be

looked to social classes rather than individuals to explain the fragility of political liberty, warning, for example, against the "great desire to dominate" that characterizes a society's *uomini grandi.*[16] Cato locates the threat to political liberty neither in the vices of particular individuals nor in the impulses of the great. Rather he asserts that "this Evil has its Root in human Nature."[17] Thus he attributes the fragility of republican achievements to failings shared by all classes and conditions of men: "Whilst Men are Men, Ambition, Avarice, and Vanity, and other Passions, will govern their Actions; in spight of all Equity and Reason, they will be ever usurping, or attempting to usurp upon the Liberty and Fortunes of one another." Cato sees no point in hoping for a political regime that can deplete this "constant and certain Fund of Corruption and Malignity in human Nature."[18] Our selfish and passionate nature is the burden of corruption understood in the theological sense: "By the Sins of our first Parents, we are fallen into this unhappy and forlorn condition," laden from birth with a nature in which appetite triumphs over reason and self-love over benevolence.[19] A praiseworthy political system can hope only to regulate such iniquity, not remove it.

How precisely do people's passions endanger liberty? The answer, for Cato, depends in part on where one is in the social hierarchy. Those in power present the greatest threat to political liberty because "men will never think they have enough, whilst they can take more."[20] In fact, endowing men with political authority is almost by definition to encourage plots against liberty, violence against citizens' possessions and generally deplorable antisocial behavior. Few men "consider any publick Trust reposed in [them], with any other View, than as the Means to satiate [their] unruly and dangerous Desires!"[21]

The populace, reined in by the laws their masters too often transgress, present a different sort of danger to a community's freedom. Certainly, they are no friends of the magistrates' perpetual bid for unlimited power.[22] However this natural antipathy to tyrants hardly provides a sufficient protection

deprived of the consulship (5.1–8, 15.1–20.17). Livy's *History of Rome* similarly characterizes the despotism of the Decemvirs as the result of the pride and daring of one man, Appius Claudius, who inherited these traits from his family's character (III.33.7, 35.4–36.9). Although such vices are typical human failings, neither author suggests pride or avarice to be inescapable human passions, impelling all individuals to act, within or without the political world, with or without access to power.

16 Machiavelli, *The Prince and the Discourses* (New York: Modern Library, 1950), 122.
17 *Letters,* III, 78. See also II, 52; I, 239.
18 *Letters,* III, 13–14; II, 229.
19 *Letters,* III, 334.
20 *Letters,* III, 78.
21 *Letters,* II, 229–30.
22 *Letters,* IV, 81.

against their creation. Once again the problem lies with the passions – in particular the way in which people's passions corrupt their judgment. "Whoever would catch Mankind, has nothing to do, but to throw out a Bait to their Passions, and infallibly they are his Property."[23] Cato considers the South Sea Bubble a baleful illustration of the truth of this maxim. Rational citizens would scarcely have endangered both their own and their country's credit by such risky investment; but by "suffering one Passion [avarice] to get the better of all the rest," English citizens "are become wretched and poor, by a ravenous Appetite to grow great and rich." Nor should we expect bitter experience to temper people's "manifest and ill-grounded Credulity." Such is the "Folly and Feebleness of human Nature [that] . . . some little Art, and big Promises, would make us repeat it, and grow mad again."[24]

The disgraceful behavior of citizens in selecting their leaders is another example of the political dangers posed by the passions. "Rational and sober Instruction" mean nothing to "the Crowd, who are always taken with shallow Pomp and Sound, and with Men of little Restraints." Thus self-interested politicians ply them with liquor and inflammatory rhetoric and soon win not only their affection but their vote. "A foolish Speech, supported with Vehemence and Brandy, will conquer the best Sense, and the best Cause in the World."[25] None of these demagogues would succeed "were the Passions properly balanced"; but the fact that men "are governed not by Judgment but by Sensation" constantly exposes them to such deception and betrayal.[26]

Although their motives may differ, the populace and magistrate are thus equally to blame for the desperate situation in which free polities find themselves.

In surveying the State of the World, one is often at a great Loss, whether to ascribe the political Misery of Mankind to their own Folly and Credulity, or to the Knavery and Impudence of their pretended Managers. Both these Causes, in all Appearance, concur to produce the same Evil; and if there were no Bubbles, there would be no Sharpers.[27]

The great may plunder the commonwealth to satisfy their own ambitions, but the people, Cato warns, all too frequently abet this crime from ignorance, avarice or credulity. For all, the downfall is their irrational, passionate nature.

Given this pessimistic psychology, Cato necessarily agonizes over the prospects for political liberty in any society. The "restless and selfish Spirit of

23 *Letters,* I, 27.
24 *Letters,* I, 25; I, 27.
25 *Letters,* IV, 248.
26 *Letters,* I, 25; IV, 247.
27 *Letters,* I, 82.

Man"[28] makes it imperative to set governors over the people to preserve the peace and respect for others' rights that necessarily underlie civil freedom. But this same spirit renders those governors an inevitable threat to the liberty they are charged with protecting. Cato explains this dilemma, never far from the thought of most republicans, in this way: "Whereas Power can ... subsist where Liberty is not, Liberty cannot subsist without Power; so that she has, as it were, the Enemy always at her Gates."[29] How then to preserve political liberty? How to disarm this enemy, leaving the nation's governors strong enough to lend the necessary terror to the laws that preserve liberty and yet docile enough not to take the laws into their own hands?

Like most republicans, Cato's strategy for protecting liberty from the power necessary to sustain it involves first placing "Checks upon those who would otherwise put Chains upon them [societies]." Above all, a polity wishing to retain its freedom must substitute a mixed constitution for the "simple Forms of Government."[30] The salutary effect of this constitutional arrangement derives first of all from the distribution of authority among a wide range of individuals and social classes. It is not that sharing power all of a sudden renders individuals more concerned for public liberty. Rather they find their schemes for greater power sabotaged by others jealous of their authority. Thus Cato says of magistrates under a mixed constitution, "Their Emulation, Envy, Fear or Interest, always made them Spies and Checks upon one another."[31] More importantly, the mixed constitution gives a formal political voice to those most committed to restraining political abuses: the people. As the objects of political power and the potential victims of the despot's arbitrary will, the people are more likely to protest infringements on public liberty than any other social group. Thus Cato assumes that popular representatives in parliament "will always act for their Country's Interest; their own being so interwoven with the People's Happiness, that they must stand and fall together."[32] To ensure that the people's chosen representatives do not themselves fall victim to the temptations of power Cato recommends a large chamber and frequent elections: "These Deputies must be either so numerous, that there can be no Means of corrupting the Majority; or so often changed, that there shall be no Time to do it so as to answer any End by doing it."[33] Of these two alternatives, the rotation in office is more

28 *Letters,* II, 50.
29 *Letters,* I, 261.
30 *Letters,* II, 230; III, 13.
31 *Letters,* II, 231.
32 *Letters,* I, 181.
33 *Letters,* II, 237.

important. Only by making one's representatives from time to time subject to political power can one preclude the necessarily vicious effects of the exercise of it.[34]

These constitutional arrangements represent typical republican expedients for restraining the inevitable excesses of men in power. They derive their value from their negative function; they prevent man's passions from working directly at odds with the public good. But neither Cato nor his predecessors consider such preventive measures sufficient to protect the precious jewel of liberty. Preserving political freedom requires as well the cultivation of civic virtue – the development of dispositions in citizens and statesmen that lead them positively to further the public good of liberty, stability and national prosperity.

II

Despite their universal agreement on the importance of civic virtue to the preservation and flourishing of any free political community, republican texts do not share a common account of the nature or content of this quality. Some authors call for a virtue in which right reason triumphs over selfish passions. Others see civic virtue as itself a sort of passion, a "love of country" that impels the citizen to forsake the private for public ends. A few theorists see virtuous citizens defending their country, and their country's liberty, from motives of personal advantage–to win glory and reputation, for example. These quite different accounts of civic virtue nevertheless share an important theme. They all characterize the good citizen as one whose interest or passion is publicly focused, either directly (from a sense of duty or love) or mediately (as a necessary means to win the fame he craves).[35]

Cato's account of the virtues that will safeguard political liberty jettisons these standard formulations. Because he understands individuals as consumed by selfish passions, the stoic ideal of a virtue grounded in reason appears to Cato as "too Heroick . . . for the living Generation." Nor does Cato countenance the idea of a public-spirited passion, of citizens endowed with "Views purely publick and disinterested." He bluntly reminds his readers that "the best Things that Men do, as well as the worst are selfish."[36] To call then for a virtue based on the rational suppression of our passions or in the noble expression of a truly "public spirit" is, for Cato, to ground liberty's survival in a psychological impossibility.

34 *Letters,* II, 240.
35 I elaborate on this tripartite distinction in Shelley Burtt, "The Good Citizen's Psyche: On the Psychology of Civic Virtue," *Polity* 23 (1990): 23–38.
36 *Letters,* II, 13; II, 54; II, 77.

But Cato's skeptical assessment of the standard republican notions of civic virtue does not prompt a rejection of this ideal altogether. Rather it leads him to argue that any successful account of civic virtue must incorporate the corrosive view of human nature expressed throughout the *Letters*. The patriot, in Cato's view, is simply a person for whom "to serve his country is his private Pleasure;... he does good to [Mankind] by gratifying himself."[37] In this paradoxical portrait of the good citizen, Cato argues that the aspect of human nature that most endangers liberty – self-interest – can and must be brought to protect it.

One might reasonably inquire at this point about how different Cato's account of the good citizen is from his contemporaries'. To conceive of individuals as fundamentally egoistic, beset by selfish passions they rarely if ever bring under control, is hardly a new view of human nature, however much Cato seeks to distinguish it from some earlier, more noble ideals. The pessimistic psychology that Cato espouses can be found not only in the work of seventeenth-century moral skeptics but in Calvinist theology as well. It is also a commonplace of the late seventeenth-century "Discourse of Trade" literature in England, which stressed the self-interested nature of most commercial endeavor.[38] Nor was it a particularly original departure in political thought to argue that fundamentally selfish individuals might advance the public welfare. Economists had pursued precisely this argument for a generation at least while Bernard Mandeville had advanced an especially extreme version of this claim in *The Fable of the Bees,* first published in 1714.

What is different and, I think, unique about *Cato's Letters* is the idea that the pursuit of one's private interests can properly and effectively ground civically virtuous actions. Two examples can perhaps suggest the vast gap between Cato's selfish citizen and the approach to civic virtue taken by most republican thinkers in early modern England.

Trenchard and Gordon cite Algernon Sydney's *Discourses of Government* with warm enthusiasm. The book, first published in 1698, fifteen years after Sydney had gone to the scaffold, is praised for its insight into the workings of free government and its uncompromising stance against the evils of tyranny. Yet *Cato's Letters* abandons the ideal of public-spirited patriotism so strongly

---

37 *Letters,* II, 52.
38 Joyce Oldham Appleby, *Economic Thought and Ideology in Eighteenth-Century England* (Princeton: Princeton University Press, 1978), 115, 247–8; see also J. A. W. Gunn, *Politics and the Public Interest in the Seventeenth Century* (London: Routledge, Kegan and Paul, 1969), especially chapters 4–6 on the emergence of egoistic psychologies in seventeenth-century English political theory.

affirmed in the *Discourses*. Cato considers this ideal unrealistic in contemporary politics, but Sydney argues that

> Time changes nothing... The same order that made men valiant and industrious in the services of their country during the first ages would have the same effect if it were now in being. Men would have the same love to the public as the Spartans and Romans had if there were the same reason for it.[39]

The egoistic psychology that had for several generations formed the backdrop for much continental moral philosophy and protestant theology notably fails to persuade Sydney; in his view, human beings are still psychologically capable of a traditional publicly oriented form of civic virtue. All that is wanting is a government worthy of them.

Charles Davenant, writing in the later years of William III's reign, also endorses a publicly oriented account of citizen virtue. His widely read political essays criticize those who "mingle with the interests of the publick [their] own inclinations." Individuals must "reduce themselves to the terms of justice, and right reason[,]... every man... suppressing his own vain thought of himself." Davenant remains confident that English citizens can pursue the good of the public before their own interests, suggesting that they practice an intellectual exercise familiar from religious devotions: "As to think lowly of ourselves, is the first step that leads us to revere the Deity... so he who has considered of what little value his single self is compared to the whole commonwealth, will be soon brought to prefer its interest much beyond his own."[40] Davenant, like Sydney, offers a surprisingly optimistic account of the psychological resources of the modern citizen at a time when both theology and moral philosophy were ceding increasing scope and power to the selfish tendencies of human nature.

Cato's Letters, then, does not introduce a new view of human nature to English political argument. Instead it seeks to graft a rather widely accepted account of human psychology onto a tradition of political reflection that had, by and large, refused to make room for it. Among English authors writing within the republican tradition only Harrington shares Cato's belief in the insurmountable selfishness of the republican citizen. But the two authors cope with the fact of egoistic citizens in quite different ways. For Harrington, securing a republican polity for citizens congenitally incapable of public spiritedness requires a constitutional solution. Political institutions must be structured so as to produce a virtuous (just) outcome from the

39 Algernon Sydney, *The Works* (London, 1772), 184.
40 Charles Davenant, *The Political and Commerical Works*, 4 v. (London, 1771), IV, 275, 366, 364.

actions of nonvirtuous, self-regarding individuals. Harrington relies in particular on a judicious division of political labor in which a nation's elite deliberates but does not vote on political choices and the nation's populace votes but does not deliberate. Cato, by contrast, calls egoistic citizens themselves to civic virtue, arguing that for statesman and citizen alike a devoted pursuit of their own self-interest can produce behavior that is a genuine expression of civic virtue.

I offer below a more detailed account of how Cato expects this process to work. My point here is that such an argument constitutes not only a decisive rejection of Harrington's solution to the problem of an egoistic citizenry but a significant departure from the traditional republican or civic humanist understanding of civic virtue as grounded in the setting aside or transcending of private interests and desires. One can see Cato's argument as paving the way for later accounts in which the pursuit of self-interest rightly understood substitutes for the civic virtue cherished by republicans. Cato, however, has not reached this point; he remains committed to producing classically virtuous citizens (even if by unorthodox means). In the *Letters,* civic virtue is privatized, its roots given a self-interested, personally focused foundation; but it is not dispensed with altogether.

One possible objection to this account of Cato's argument as marking a break with a traditional politics of public virtue concerns its contemporary reception. If *Cato's Letters* were actually transforming the republican understanding of civic virtue in this way, why was this fact not more extensively noted and commented upon? One possibility is that to readers increasingly convinced of the accuracy of an egoistic account of human psychology, Cato's arguments appear appropriate, unremarkable. Cato continued to call for the same sort of civically virtuous actions as earlier writers in the republican tradition had; he simply explained their genesis in a different, more realistic way. We should also remember that few, if any, of Cato's eighteenth-century readers were deliberately comparing the *Letters'* account of civic virtue with earlier accounts to be found in something called the "classical republican" or "civic humanist" tradition.

But, these points made, one must admit that Cato's distinctive approach to the grounding of civic virtue was not generally embraced at this time. In fact, just a few years after the *Letters* ceased publication, Bolingbroke began to offer in the pages of *The Craftsman* an aggressively public-oriented, if somewhat unconventional, account of the virtue to be displayed by the good English citizen. And his writings were, if anything, more eagerly consumed than Cato's. The *Letters* suffered in part from being sandwiched chronologically between Davenant's widely read essays and Bolingbroke's masterful propaganda, both of which extolled a traditional, publicly oriented civic virtue. Whether for this or another reason, Cato's reworking of the grounds of civic virtue represents a road not traveled in republican political argument.

However, the failure of Cato's contemporaries to remark on or embrace the new account of civic virtue found in the *Letters* does not mean that this new account does not appear there. In the *Letters*, Cato redescribes civic virtue so as to suit it to a polity that increasingly expected individuals to put their own interests in front of the public's (as a psychological inevitability). In so doing, he kept alive, in a particularly distinctive and compelling way, the republican option in modern polities – whether his contemporaries recognized it as such or not.

III

Cato's account of the dispositions that will, in the context of the Augustan monarchy, further the republican ideals of political liberty, self-government and national prosperity comes in two parts. The virtues of the people and of their magistrates differ significantly. In both cases, however, it is personal interest rather than public-mindedness that produces the behavior that Cato and other republicans regard as civically virtuous.

The civic virtue of the magistrate consists, for Cato, in two related achievements: the honest discharge of duty and the cultivation of popular affections. Obviously, good magistrates must exercise their power "for the Sake of the People" – and for the people alone.[41] But good magistrates must do more than punctiliously conform to constitutional constraints on their behavior. They must enter into sympathy with the citizenry, make the citizens' desires their own and strive above all in the fulfillment of their duties to win the citizens' affection. "Those Ministers who cannot make the People their Friends, it is to be shrewdly suspected, do not deserve their Friendship; it is certain, that much Honesty, and small Management, rarely miss to gain it."[42] Cato thus considers the friendship of the people the best guarantor of a magistrate's trustworthy performance of his duty.

Cato goes on to argue, although not very successfully, that it is possible to ground the magistrate's civic virtues independently of a self-denying public spirit. Cato pursues this subject in an essay plaintively titled, "Every Man's True Interest found in the General Interest – how little this is considered!" He offers no new revelations under this heading, only variations on the

41 *Letters,* II, 248.
42 *Letters,* I, 87.

familiar theme that "every Man's private Advantage is so much wrapt up in the publick Felicity, that by every Step which he takes to depreciate his Country's Happiness, he undermines and destroys his own." Does a ruler desire riches? "A free and happy People, will bring more Money into his Coffers, than Racks and Armies can extort from enslaved Countries." Does he desire a peaceful and lengthy reign? "Princes, who have trusted wholly to the People, have seldom been deceived or deserted." Cato argues here that statesmen should "preserve the Affections of the people," not because doing so is virtuous – in his view, such moralistic appeals have no impact on people's actions – but because their personal appetite for power, security and riches will be best met by furthering the public interest in limited government, personal freedom and national prosperity.[43]

On the other hand, as Cato reluctantly admits, enlightening selfish individuals as to their own "best interests" does not always produce the desired behavior. In fact, in the short run, the dictates of self-interest work against cooperation with the public, as people tend "to prefer themselves and their own Family before [the Whole]... whatever becomes of Conscience, Honour, and Generosity." The problem is exacerbated by the corrupting effect of political power: "the Possession of Power soon alters and viciates [sic] their [men's] Hearts," causing those in government to trade "all their virtuous and beneficent Qualities [for]... a new Spirit, of Arrogance, Injustice and Oppression."[44]

In these circumstances, appeals to reason must be replaced by threats. "We do not expect philosophical Virtue from them [Mankind]; but only that they follow Virtue as their Interest, and find it penal and dangerous to depart from it." In the case of magistrates, this means instituting laws that "make Honesty and Equity their Interest."[45] Threatening magistrates with costly punishments and swift retribution for any betrayal of political trust provides the necessary incentive to bring the magistrate's selfish passions round to the service of public good – most of the time.

But, convinced that "Men will be Rogues where they dare," Cato rarely affirms the practical possibility of magisterial virtue, even when encouraged by the coercive force of the law. Instead, Cato warns the masses to treat those endowed with political authority warily.

All these Discoveries and Complaints of the Crookedness and Corruption of human Nature... are made to shew, that as Selfishness is the strongest Bias of Men, every Man ought to be upon his Guard against another, that he become not [his] Prey.[46]

43 *Letters*, III, 193–4; III, 195; I, 180; I, 181.
44 *Letters*, III, 200; II, 239, 98.
45 *Letters*, II, 56; II, 258.
46 *Letters*, II, 53.

The public manifestation of this vigilant attitude constitutes the virtue of the citizen, a virtue that Cato sees as within the reach of most men, because it is so very much in their interest.

Virtuous citizens, as Cato describes them, are angry, jealous and eager to hound from office government officials who overstep the bounds of their authority. Far from identifying sympathetically with the wishes and aims of those in power, these exemplary citizens will quickly seek to humble those whose riches or influence threaten to endanger the commonwealth. Although such vengeful behavior in an individual is neither prudent nor pious, "Jealousy and Revenge, in a whole People ... are laudable and politick Virtues; without which they will never thrive, never be esteemed."[47] Good citizens thus willingly and critically judge the performance of their rulers, calling them angrily to account whenever their actions endanger national liberty.[48]

One might object that any truly republican account of civic virtue must expect citizens not only to participate in public (as Cato's do) but to deliberate impartially on the public good. This, for example, is what Harrington's scheme for a bicameral legislature is trying to achieve and what Cato's account of civic virtue as a more or less reactive fury appears to leave out. In one sense, the objection is correct: to the extent that citizens of a free, self-governing polity are usually engaged in public decision making, their virtue necessarily includes independent and fair-minded deliberation on the public good. But Cato is transposing the republican themes of liberty, corruption and virtue from the familiar setting of a democratic city-state or tiny commonwealth to a populous constitutional monarchy with a highly restricted franchise. In this setting, the legislature is open only to political elites; the virtue of the ordinary citizen is thus properly directed not to public deliberation itself, but to controlling those who are engaged in it.

Cato's call to action in the aftermath of the South Sea Bubble provides a concrete example of the sort of civic virtue he wants English citizens to display. Over a third of Cato's letters in the first six months of publication address the question of bringing South Sea schemers to justice. Two points register with particular vehemence. First is the fact that citizens' personal interests and misfortunes provide not stumbling blocks to civic virtue but its starting point. "Our present Misfortunes will rouse up our Spirits, and as it were awaken us out of a deep Lethargy," Cato predicts. Good citizens should "make a Virtue of their present Anger" and insist that the state "take full Vengeance of [sic] all those whom we can discover to be guilty."[49] The

47 *Letters*, I, 6–7.
48 *Letters*, I, 260.
49 *Letters*, I, 122; I, 9; I, 142.

impulse to civically virtuous action comes for Cato not from disinterested love of country, a selfless public spirit, but from righteous anger at personal interest betrayed. Citizens should enter the political arena, Cato urges, to claim what is rightfully theirs and punish those who have tried to abscond with it. In case citizens should hesitate to act with sufficient ruthlessness, Cato enforces his point with a reference to Roman history. "To this Spirit of Jealousy and Revenge, was formerly the Roman Commonwealth beholden for the long Preservation of its Liberty."[50]

The fact that Cato is writing his letters at all suggests that he is not fully prepared to trust a spontaneous "Spirit of Jealousy and Revenge" to provide the impetus for purging the body politic of "the noxious Juices and morbisick Matter that oppresses us."[51] Rather, citizens whose interests have been trampled on must be directed and encouraged in their task of vengeance, whipped on to action by virulent denunciations of villains and fervent appeals to popular interest and conscience. Thus the second distinctive feature of Cato's account is the role he assigns to the politically engaged journalist or partisan like himself. Cato does not precisely lecture the public on its self-interest or the connection of self-interest to the public good. He assumes that the dire circumstances in which they find themselves, following their craze for stockjobbing, is lesson enough. However he is not quite willing to credit the populace with the ability to sustain their anger or direct it correctly. Thus Cato's virulent rhetoric provides a primer in public-spiritedness, suggesting proper channels for their vengeance, the means by which to topple the would-be architects of their subjection.

Cato's effort to ground this popular virtue of vigilance and vengeance in the selfish desires of the masses proves a good deal more successful than his attempt to root the virtue of the magistrate in the personal interests of those in power. Cato makes his case particularly persuasive by arguing for a closer connection between private and public interest in the life of the ordinary citizen than in that of the public figure. The reason for this difference lies in the varying political circumstances of "great Men" and the masses. Individuals who possess great wealth or high office will often find their personal interests at odds with their public responsibilities.[52] But respectable citizens who do not aspire to a seat in parliament experience no such conflict:

No Ambition prompts them ... No aspiring or unsociable Passions incite them; they have no Rivals for Place, no Competitor to pull down; they have no darling Child, Pimp, or Relation to Raise; they have no Occasion for Dissimulation or Intrigue.[53]

50 *Letters,* I, 7.
51 *Letters,* I, 142.
52 *Letters,* III, 200.
53 *Letters,* I, 178.

Protected in this way from the corrupting corridors of power, the people's only desires are for goods entirely consonant with the public welfare: "The Security of their Persons and Property is their highest Aim." Cato has this coincidence of private and public good in mind when he asserts, "The People's Interest is the Publick Interest; it signifies the same Thing."[54]

It follows from this fact that the prospects for persuading citizens to act virtuously through an appeal to their own interests are very good. Left to their own devices, citizens will jealously defend their property and persons against any unjust usurpation by the government, vigorously resisting any effort by parliament or Crown to restrict their civil liberties. They will do so not out of an abstracted sense of duty or public spirit, but because they personally value their freedoms. They will be acting politically to defend their own stake in the polity but their behavior, because it preserves the ends of government from perversion by corrupt magistrates, will be a classic example of civic virtue in action. Thus ordinary citizens can serve the public simply by following their self-interest: "The Whole People, by consulting their own Interest, consult the Publick, and act for the Publick by acting for themselves."[55]

Cato's acceptance of Lockean premises plays a crucial role in allowing him to link the pursuit of private interest so successfully to the achievement of public good. Following Locke, Cato argues that the business of government is to satisfy the governed in the possession of their property, persons and liberty.[56] Once these individual satisfactions are made the touchstone of good government, it makes a great deal of sense to say, with Cato, "The Whole People, by consulting their own Interest, consult the Publick, and act for the Publick by acting for themselves." If, on the other hand, the business of government is understood as the pursuit of goods that do not reduce in this way to the satisfaction of individuals' expectations, making this connection is much harder. The challenge naturally becomes getting individuals to set aside personal interests in preference for public goods of a completely different order. And the answer, just as naturally, can appear to lie in a character trait, a virtue, that disposes individuals to do precisely that.

Those familiar with the tradition of republican thought know that by describing the demands on the virtuous citizen in this second way, republican theorists continually confront the challenge of corruption. To slip from public-mindedness to private-interestedness is both a natural human weakness and the epitome of political corruption. Cato's reconceptualization of

54 *Letters,* I, 178; I, 106.
55 *Letters,* II, 41.
56 *Letters,* II, 35.

the grounds of civic virtue allows him also to recast the problem of citizen corruption.

IV

Country ideologists usually pointed to the financial and political innovations following upon the Glorious Revolution as the corrupting force in modern politics, the cancer that transformed virtuous citizens into greedy, self-aggrandizing political hacks. But Cato, despite the fact that he writes in the wake of the South Sea Bubble's financial disaster, does not attack recent developments in public credit or ministerial government for the corruption of citizen virtue. Rather he blames the errors of judgment to which the unruly masses in all ages are liable. Like most republicans, Cato worries that the populace will not always assess its interests correctly.

When strong Liquor, or Money, or false Terrors intervene, and Government is turned into Faction; the Judgment of the people is vitiated, and worse than none. They then prefer the worst Men to the best . . . and the most popular Man is he who bribes highest, or imposes upon them best.[57]

But he breaks with republican tradition in arguing that the people's departure from "the open and plain Paths of Virtue"[58] is self-correcting. Their corruption is not a sickness of the soul, but a momentary misperception of interest under strong temptation. Luxury, avarice and personal dependence can never permanently distort their political judgment. As soon as citizens' immediate interests are harmed by such degeneration, the natural desire for a free government will reassert itself.

Cato's confidence that a corrupt people can redeem itself rests in his conviction that despite its faults no citizenry will tolerate for long true dereliction of duty among its governors. This claim rests in turn on two related propositions: first, that "temporal Felicity is the whole End of Government"[59] and second, that people rarely if ever mistake the signs of good and bad government because they rarely err in assessing their own personal happiness. Thus Cato says, "Every Ploughman knows a good Government from a bad one, from the Effects of it; he knows whether the Fruits of his Labour be his own, and whether he enjoy them in Peace and Security."[60] This ability to judge of public measures from their effects on personal experience protects people from ever supporting a truly iniquitous government.

57 *Letters,* II, 130.
58 *Letters,* I, 178.
59 *Letters,* I, 87.
60 *Letters,* II, 35; see also I, 155.

But what of Cato's own admission that the citizenry can be misled or corrupted by unscrupulous politicians? The *Letters* insist that such deception can never persist past the point where it substantively harms the citizen's primary interests. "People will for some Time be dallied with and amused with false Reasonings, Misrepresentations and Promises," but when taxes soar, war drags on and the government succumbs to incompetent sycophants, "all Parties will at last confer Notes" and turn against the "wicked Men" whom they once supported.[61] Thus Cato argues that freeholders may be willing enough to sell their votes to the highest bidder in times of plenty, but they are rarely deceived when it comes to their own pocketbooks, their own personal interest and advantage.

By explaining how a more or less democratic political culture can preserve liberty despite the pressures of corruption, Cato restates and resolves a recurring dilemma forcefully articulated in Machiavelli's *Discourses*. Machiavelli worried that once the people's passions were successfully aroused in the service of erroneous ends or of loyalties pledged to corrupt individuals, they would not recover their judgment until it was too late, their liberty gone for good. Once compromised, Machiavelli doubted that virtue could be renewed; a people rarely recovered from the corruption of its public sentiments.[62] For Cato, an initial failure in popular judgment marks not the beginning of the end, but a way station in a process that will recall the nation to virtue. As government goes from bad to worse, the spectre of tyranny necessarily galvanizes a population, he argues. Newly angered by the deception practiced upon them and finally frightened for their freedom, the people will turn on those who seduced them and purge the polity of the enemies of liberty.[63]

The key to this more optimistic account of the persistence of civic virtue is Cato's recognition that self-interested individuals maintain a constant potential for public action. Citizens whose primary commitments are not political but economic, focused not on office or political participation but on their crop acreage and account books, understand their self-interest in a way that limits the impact of their political mistakes or "corruption." By reconceiving civic virtue as grounded in private interest, Cato explains how states might break the cycle of corruption that earlier republicans considered inevitable.

In making the case for the self-interested roots of virtuous public action, *Cato's Letters* represents an innovative but little appreciated effort to recast traditional republican fears and values in a mold more suited to the realities

61 *Letters,* III, 267.
62 Machiavelli, *Discourses,* Book I, chapters 17, 18, 47, 53.
63 *Letters,* I, 37.

of eighteenth-century politics and culture. In place of the standard conception of civic virtue as public spiritedness, Cato makes a case for a political virtue grounded in the citizens' pursuit of their own satisfaction. This account can and should be described as transforming a republican politics of civic virtue. It substitutes, within a discourse concerned above all with the relationship between virtue, liberty and corruption, a privately oriented for a publicly oriented conception of the good citizen. Thus Cato envisions a polity of individuals who act in the political arena for the public good (thus exhibiting civic virtue), but who do so out of concern for their own freedom and prosperity.

It remains appropriate to characterize individuals behaving in this way as civically, rather than socially or morally, virtuous. They are vigilant critics of their representatives' decisions and of ministerial policies; they are quick to demand the resignation of those politicians who abuse their trust; they insist that government serve the wants of the people not the powerful – all dispositions that sustain a civic way of life (as far as a constitutional monarchy can be described as supporting one at all). But they do all these things for their own, rather than their country's good.

On the whole, Cato succeeds remarkably well in drawing republican thought in this direction. But Cato's bifurcated political world with its sharp contrast between virtuous citizens and power-hungry statesmen strangely fails to encompass in its territory the devoted friend of liberty, Cato himself. Neither a statesman accustomed to political power, nor an ordinary citizen vulnerable to the appeals of dishonest politicians, Cato's persona appears to disprove the egoistic psychology on which he bases his claims. Surely, in ceaselessly unveiling the machinations of selfish men, in warning the populace of the means used to deceive it, Cato represents the selfless patriot, toiling independently of personal gain for the nation's welfare.

Cato's political psychology in fact makes room for "wise and honest Men" who might support rather than hinder the cause of liberty. Characterizing good government as "the Art of applying to the Passions," Cato holds out the possibility that some honest politicians will seek to manipulate the citizens' "reigning Appetites, appearing Interests, and predominant Foibles" to good ends rather than bad.[64] Although Cato believes it impossible for even well-intentioned governors to wean individuals from prejudice to reason, those concerned for the public good might manage "to make use of [man's] Weaknesses to render him happy, as wicked Men do to make him miserable."[65]

64 *Letters,* II, 48; III, 331.
65 *Letters,* III, 335.

Cato's political prescriptions thus explicitly make room for political elites interested in public service rather than personal aggrandizement.

But what, according to Cato, could motivate these friends of humanity? Cato's egoistic psychology rules out an appeal to disinterested benevolence or public spirit to explain such behavior. We are all creatures of our passions or, at best, our interests. Yet even a cursory reading of Cato's essays suggests an engagement with the ideal of liberty far more passionate than a careful calculation of self-interest would presumably produce. The fervor in Cato's writings simply does not mesh with his notion that people interpret their interests and find their happiness in purely self-regarding ways.

The problem Cato's doctrines encounter here recalls the difficulties he had in accounting for the magistrate's civic virtue. There Cato reluctantly concluded that the individual's passions were such that a rational appeal to self-interest alone could not effectively persuade power holders to act virtuously: institutional constraints were necessary to produce appropriately public-regarding behavior. But in reaching this pessimistic conclusion, Cato overlooked the possibility that the selfish passions of magistrate and citizen might be shaped or educated to find satisfaction in civically virtuous activity. Throughout the *Letters,* Cato warns of unscrupulous appeals to people's appetites and desires that confuse their judgment, complaining that "men scarcely ever have proper Objects for their Passions."[66] But positing such negative manipulation of the passions suggests as well the possibility of a more positive shaping of the objects of desire, an education of the sentiments that might bring "great Men" to derive satisfaction from public reputation and service. This is the route towards civic virtue traveled by Machiavelli and, after Cato, by Rousseau.

The same point holds for the patrons of liberty who take it upon themselves to defend the public good. As Cato himself argues, the individual's psyche is terribly impressionable; it is not impossible that the passions, through education, temperament or culture, could come to find their happiness in the service of a public rather than a private ideal. We should not expect to find a polity wholly peopled by such public-spirited souls – nor, as Cato's speculations on popular virtue reveal, do we need to. But Cato's own account of the virtues of the citizen would be enhanced were he to recognize a third political type between the ambitious, corruptible power holders and the populace devoted to the ends of personal comfort and well-being: patriots, who finding their personal satisfaction in the explicit advancement of public ends, help goad the populace to their self-interested defense of liberty and national prosperity.

66 *Letters,* I, 42.

Cato's Letters thus provides a suggestive vision of how the Augustan polity might, without transforming itself into a classical republic, still nurture in its citizens an effective form of civic virtue. England's constitutional monarchy is, of course, too large and participation in it too limited for liberty to be preserved through an Athenian-style democracy in which all citizens rule and are ruled in turn. And people – not just the people of England – are too weak and selfish to make the public-spirited civic virtue celebrated in the Roman tradition anything more than a compelling historical myth. But modern individuals in love mostly with their own comfort can still be encouraged and expected to defend their polity against the most egregious attacks against it. Such individuals do need to understand themselves as citizens, do need to conceive of themselves as joined in a community structured by law, possessing certain rights which they are entitled to demand that their government respect. But this sense of a political self is all the public orientation one needs to ground the performance of civic virtue. Once it is in place, the nation awaits only a friend of liberty to urge its self-interested citizens to take appropriate vengeance on those who have proved themselves enemies of the public good.

5

◁══▷

Bolingbroke's politics of virtue

From 1726 to 1736, Henry St. John, Viscount Bolingbroke occupied center stage in the English political drama we have come to call "Court versus Country." On one side was ranged the Court Whig oligarchy, increasingly confident of its hold on power and led by the brilliant politician, England's first prime minister, Robert Walpole. On the other was the Country opposition, an unstable coalition of Jacobites, Country Tories and dissident Whigs claiming to speak for the country at large against the presumed political excesses of the Court or government.[1] A gifted, wealthy and ambitious young Tory statesman, Bolingbroke became a member of parliament in 1700, secretary of war in 1704 and secretary of state in 1710. His political maneuvering around the death of Queen Anne raised sufficient suspicion of his Jacobitism for him to flee to France on the accession of George I; he briefly served as private secretary to the pretender James Stuart (1715–16). He returned to England a decade later after winning a pardon and the return of his substantial estates – but not, at Walpole's insistence, his seat in the House of Lords. For the next ten years, until he again gave up the political struggle and returned to France, Bolingbroke worked with the Country opposition to unseat Robert Walpole or at least derail his increasingly effective centralization of power.[2]

1 On the division between Court and Country, see chapter 2.
2 The details of Bolingbroke's life and career are well set out in H. T. Dickinson, *Bolingbroke* (London: Constable, 1970) and, in Bolingbroke's own words, in *Letter to Sir William Wind-ham* (London, 1753). For his moral and political philosophy, see Isaac Kramnick, *Boling-broke and His Circle: The Politics of Nostalgia in the Age of Walpole* (Cambridge: Harvard University Press, 1968). Other intellectual biographies include Jeffrey Hart, *Viscount Bolingbroke: Tory Humanist* (London: Routledge and Kegan Paul, 1965); Sydney Wayne Jackman, *Man of Mercury: An Appreciation of the Mind of Henry St. John, Viscount Bolingbroke* (London: Pall Mall Publishers, 1965); Simon Varey, *Henry St. John, Viscount Bolingbroke* (Boston: Twayne Publishers, 1984).

Unable to use his considerable rhetorical gifts in parliament, Bolingbroke breathed life into the Country case against Walpole through the pages of his phenomenally successful weekly, *The Craftsman*, launched in the autumn of 1726.[3] Bolingbroke's plan of attack was simple: use language that we now identify as within the tradition of classical republicanism or civic humanism to persuade contemporaries that the policies and practices of Walpole's ministry were both corrupt and corrupting. By this claim, Bolingbroke meant to accuse Walpole and his colleagues of more than simple venality or unethical behavior, although he made these charges as well. Rather, he sought to cast contemporary politics as one more act in the republican drama of the rise and fall of free governments. The same corruption that had brought down Rome and subjected Italian cities to the rule of princes was threatening England under the Hanovers, or more appositely, England under Walpole. Thus Whig government was both corrupt (plotting against its citizens' liberties, scheming to extend executive power) and corrupting (pursuing policies that transformed the character of citizen and polity in such a way that the practice of public virtue would soon become impossible). No time could be spared to recall the nation to a politics of virtue – a step that required first of all ridding the government of Walpole and his cronies.

As a matter of practical politics, Bolingbroke's denunciations of Walpole had little effect. The Country opposition only once posed a serious threat to Walpole's preeminence (during the 1733 excise crisis), and the difficulty in this case was of Walpole's own making.[4] However, the infrequent political achievements of this opposition should not obscure the substantial impact of its political propaganda on the nation's political ideas and ideals. In particular, Bolingbroke's decision to cast the drama of contemporary politics as

3 *The Craftsman*, founded by Bolingbroke and William Pulteney and edited by Nicholas Amhurst, had the highest circulation of any newspaper of the period. Varey, *Bolingbroke* places it at 13,000 in 1731 and at "little less than 10,000 at any time between 1729 and 1732" (32). These figures revise upwards the estimates in Simon Varey, ed., *Bolingbroke: Contributions to The Craftsman* (Oxford: Clarendon Press, 1982), xiv. A contemporary work critical of Bolingbroke assumed 40 readers per paper (*Liberty and the Craftsman: A Project for Improving the Country Journal* [London: 1730]).

4 Walpole's effort in 1733 to extend the taxes on consumer goods and expand the bureaucracy necessary to administer them gave the opposition its most promising opening for political agitation in the decade. For the political difficulties the proposal caused, see J. H. Plumb, *Sir Robert Walpole: The King's Minister* (Boston: Houghton Mifflin Company, 1961), 260–70 and Paul Langford, *The Excise Crisis: Society and Politics in the Age of Walpole* (Oxford: Clarendon Press, 1975). For more general political histories of the Country opposition, its activities and ideology, see Archibald Foord, *His Majesty's Opposition, 1714–1830* (Oxford: Clarendon Press, 1964), chapters 4 and 5; H. T. Dickinson, *Walpole and the Whig Supremacy* (London: The English Universities Press, 1975), esp. chapter 5; Paul Langford, *A Polite and Commercial People: England, 1727–1785* (Oxford: Clarendon Press, 1989), chapter 1.

a battle for the soul of English citizens played an important role in the process I have called the transformation of virtue.

I argued in the introduction that the transformation of virtue in eighteenth-century English political argument proceeded along roughly the following lines. There was first a change in external circumstances (culture, politics, economic realities) that in some way called into question the possibility or desirability of a traditional politics of public virtue. Advocates of such politics then adapted their arguments in order to meet these new circumstances, a response that, paradoxically, resulted in the emergence of a more privately oriented understanding of civic virtue rather than the reenergizing of a politics of public virtue.

This process played itself out in a number of different ways. Low Church Anglicans found themselves struggling to adapt the case for moral reform to a more secularized understanding of the role of the civil magistrate. Cato rejected traditional republican accounts of civic virtue as inconsistent with an egoistic understanding of human psychology. And Bolingbroke began to tinker with the arguments of the republican tradition in order better to serve his partisan goals.

To understand how Bolingbroke's articulation of a new, but still publicly oriented, conception of republican civic virtue contributes to the development of a more privately oriented alternative, we must consider the response Bolingbroke's writings elicited from his contemporaries. Faced with an argument carefully tailored to portray Whig rule as irredeemably corrupt, Bolingbroke's opponents hurriedly developed an alternate politics of virtue, a politics built around an argument that liberty and the good state might be preserved without the sort of public virtue Bolingbroke insists on. To Bolingbroke's charge of a balanced constitution betrayed, civic virtue undermined, Court Whigs responded that liberty consisted in more than preserving the fiction of a balanced constitution; it was to be measured by concrete political achievements that improved the life of the individual citizen. A government that adhered to the rule of law, allowed for the increase of wealth and the expansion of trade, secured property and person against attack was free, whatever the balance of power between Court and parliament. And the civic virtue required to sustain liberty conceived of in this way was not love of the constitution but temperance, frugality, diligence, honesty – personal qualities that well-intentioned citizens might cultivate themselves. Bolingbroke does not then articulate a privately oriented conception of civic virtue himself. But his determined effort, in the service of partisan aims, to produce a politics of public virtue that would condemn Walpole as corrupt provides the impetus for the reconceptualization – and privatization – of virtue undertaken by his opponents, the Court Whigs.[5]

I

Central to Bolingbroke's partisan project of denouncing the Whig regime is his claim that a balanced constitution provides the only adequate safeguard for political liberty. Bolingbroke argues, in good republican fashion, that a nation's freedom will always be threatened by the ambitions of those in power.[6] The mixed constitution is the obvious, and again traditionally republican, solution to such a perpetual danger. It parcels out power between King, Lords and Commons, ensuring that "if any one part of the three which compose our government, should at any time usurp more power than the law gives ... the other two parts may, by uniting their strength, reduce this power into its proper bounds, or correct the abuse of it."[7] Bolingbroke goes on to claim, however, that for such reciprocal supervision to work each of the parts must remain strictly independent from the others' influence. In particular, no member of parliament should receive any emoluments from the ministry, no offices, honors or grants that carry with them an implicit expectation of a quid pro quo in crucial votes. Only such independence keeps the constitution in proper balance and only such a balanced constitution can assure liberty.

Bolingbroke narrows the conditions of liberty in this way (linking continued political freedom to the maintenance of a balanced constitution) in order to portray Whig politics in the worst possible light. One can easily imagine an interpretation of Walpole's activities in which the obvious political and moral shortcomings of the Whig regime do not automatically translate into tyrannical schemes and the death of the virtuous citizen. But the whole aim of Bolingbroke's political writings is to place the Whigs on the political defensive. To do so, he deploys the emotionally charged language of what we now call classical republicanism or civic humanism, casting Court Whigs as the agents of corruption and their Country opponents as the epitome of public virtue.[8]

5 This paragraph briefly summarizes the argument to be found in chapter 6.
6 Bolingbroke, Henry St. John, Viscount, *Historical Writings,* ed. Isaac Kramnick (Chicago: University of Chicago Press, 1972), 157–8.
7 *Ibid.,* 197.
8 Certain aspects of the following argument will be familiar from Quentin Skinner, "The Principles and Practice of Opposition: The Case of Bolingbroke versus Walpole," in Neil Mac-Kendrick, ed., *Historical Perspectives: Studies in English Thought and Society* (London: Europa Publications, 1974). I share Skinner's view of the reasons Bolingbroke chose to make the sorts of political arguments he did. But this chapter focuses, as Skinner's does not, on the

But to make this portrait in black and white convincing, Bolingbroke must give the familiar categories of republican thought – liberty, virtue and corruption – new content. Without reworking, they will not yield the uncompromising condemnation of Walpole that Bolingbroke wants. Thus Bolingbroke reduces the notion of political liberty to the maintenance of formal constitutional structures: an independent parliament and balanced constitution. To deviate from this ideal, either through error or innovation is to enslave – whatever the actual political experiences of English citizens.

By arguing that political liberty is impossible without the balanced constitution, Bolingbroke makes this fictional construct not only the measure of political freedom, but the arbiter of civic virtue. Just as no society can be free that allows its governors to compromise the "mutual independency" of King and Commons, so no citizen can be virtuous who fails to defend this political ideal. Civic virtue becomes nothing more nor less than the disposition to support a balanced constitution (a disposition which, Bolingbroke goes on to argue, the Whigs definitively lack), and the presence of corruption is indicated not by attacks on public liberty broadly conceived, but simply by a vote or other form of support for the Whig ministry.

By defining virtue and corruption in this way, Bolingbroke strengthens in the short run the polemical impact of his work. But he also creates the conditions under which others can more easily question the need for a politics of public virtue in the first place. Bolingbroke's politically motivated recasting of republican ideals, intended to bolster the fortune of the Country opposition, invites a Court Whig response that disposes with publicly oriented conceptions of civic virtue altogether.

The next chapter considers the consequences of orienting the politics of public virtue around an almost claustrophobic focus on the constitution and constitutional integrity as the benchmarks of good government. Here, in a sequential examination of his major political writings – *Remarks on the History of England* (1730–1), *A Dissertation upon Parties* (1733–4), *A Letter on the Spirit of Patriotism* (1736) and *The Idea of a Patriot King* (1738) – I consider Bolingbroke's case for a public virtue conceived as love of the balanced constitution.

Bolingbroke is perhaps best known for his paeans to an elite virtue of civic responsibility, offered in his later writings on patriotism and the patriot king. But his earlier essays for the *Craftsman* focus on a popular political virtue which Bolingbroke defines variously as "a disposition to oppose all instances of mal-administration," a "public spirit of watchfulness over all national inter-

particular use Bolingbroke makes of the ideas of civic virtue and corruption and how this use differs from that of the tradition on which he draws.

ests ... a perpetual jealousy of the governors by the governed."⁹ In these passages, Bolingbroke seems to embrace a fairly typical republican account of the civic virtue appropriate to the populace at large, one that emphasizes, as did Cato's, the passionate and defensive nature of the people's virtue, their vigilant scrutiny of the exercise of magisterial power, their readiness to take decisive action whenever the ruler oversteps the allotted bounds. The difference lies in the object of the virtuous citizen's attention.

In place of the traditional republican invocation of "love of one's country" as the crucial characteristic of civic virtue, Bolingbroke calls on citizens "to value ourselves in the first place on our zeal for the constitution."¹⁰ Good citizens do not defend an expansive if somewhat indeterminate public good nor act in defense of a general notion of liberty. Rather they make "the conformity, or repugnancy of things to this [their] constitution, the rule by which [they] accept them as favorable or reject them as dangerous to liberty."¹¹ Packed parliaments, corrupt elections, encroachments on the ancient privileges of the commons are the stuff of the virtuous citizens' dissatisfaction and the target of their wrath. Bolingbroke ferrets out evidence of such "zeal for the constitution" as early as the fifteenth century when, he argues, "the watchful spirit of liberty was soon alarmed" by the "influence which the crown had obtained in the elections of members of parliament." The patriotic gentlemen of that time acted quickly to preserve the balance of the constitution, making "such regulations about elections ... as seemed at that time sufficient to prevent this influence for the future."¹² With liberty resting on nothing more nor less than the maintenance of a mixed constitution, properly balanced, the people's virtue becomes nothing more nor less than love for the good constitution, as Bolingbroke has defined it.

This conception of civic virtue is both different from and less convincing than the position staked out by Bolingbroke's republican predecessors. Republican thinkers expect constitutions to do double duty. First, constitutional arrangements themselves provide certain goods, such as political participation, to a virtuous citizenry. Second, by structuring governmental institutions so as to prevent egregious abuses of power, constitutions protect and maintain the public (nondomestic) space in which various nonpolitical goods are pursued. Given this understanding of the ends of the constitution, virtuous citizens need not be committed to constitutional stasis.

9 Bolingbroke, Henry St. John, Viscount, *The Works of Lord Bolingbroke,* 4 v. (London: Henry Bohn, 1844. Reprinted New York: A.M. Kelley, 1967), II, 387; *Historical Writings,* 162, 163.
10 Bolingbroke, *Works,* II, 116.
11 *Ibid.,* II, 112.
12 Bolingbroke, *Historical Writings,* 195–6.

Rather they are expected to judge constitutional innovation by its effects on the sorts of goods a constitution is supposed to provide and protect.

In his *Letters*, Cato follows this more traditional republican conception, urging citizens to measure political liberty not by an abstract formula for constitutional balance but in terms of their own happiness and that of their countrymen. Are they free from fear and oppression, from the arbitrary actions of those in power? Does government foster opportunities by which they might increase their wealth? Does it respect established rights of political participation and representation? The answers to these questions provide more concrete indications of when liberty is in danger and thus of when citizen action is needed than Bolingbroke's constitutional gauge. Absent evidence that citizen interests are substantively harmed, constitutional innovations may be tolerated and even encouraged without compromising a citizenry's virtue.

Bolingbroke, however, needed an account of civic virtue, resonant with the republican tradition, that would still allow him to brand Walpole's ministry as dangerously corrupt. The extent to which Whig government actually threatened those substantive goods that citizens expect from government was a matter of genuine debate. Perhaps it did; perhaps it didn't. But there was little question that the ministry's policies contravened the balanced constitution as Bolingbroke defined it. Thus defining virtue as loyalty to the constitution allowed Bolingbroke to brand Walpole and his colleagues as *prima facie* corrupt, without probing too deeply into the actual effects of the ministry's policies on the citizens' life and livelihood.

Bolingbroke also used this narrow definition of virtue to attack Walpole, not just for being corrupt himself, but for corrupting the nation's citizenry. A citizenry still in possession of its spirit of liberty would recognize Walpole's cultivation of a Court party in parliament as contrary to the principles of a balanced constitution and thus, by extension, dangerous to public freedom. That the nation has failed to do so, that in fact Whigs continue to be elected to parliament, is evidence, Bolingbroke argues, of a disturbing decline in public spirit precipitated by the Whigs' own principles and practices.

Such a conclusion follows neatly from Bolingbroke's account of virtue as loyalty to the balanced constitution. Yet if one were to measure civic virtue by other, broader standards, the electorate's toleration of Walpole might indicate not a lack of virtue but a lack of occasion to exercise this quality. Walpole's supporter William Arnall makes this point in a 1727 article:

You [the opposition] complain that the Nation is seized with a political Lethargy. People of your easy Circumstances ... may be in Danger of such a Distemper; but we [the people], who labour hard for a comfortable Living, are in no great Hazard of

such a Disease . . . No less than real Oppression, harsh Usage, or unsufferable Insolence can make an Impression upon us . . . Never fear a political Lethargy, as you call
it, or Stupidity in us; for however far Luxury may have prevail'd amongst the great
and wealthy, yet the Mass remains uncorrupt and untainted.[13]

Bolingbroke though has little incentive or desire to portray fellow citizens
as still in possession of a robust "spirit of liberty" that they do not yet see the
necessity of using. If the English citizen were still capable of defending the
constitution against truly disequilibriating innovations, if freeholders still
preserved the will to champion public freedom when genuinely threatened,
the nation would have far less to fear from Walpole than Bolingbroke
claims – and far less need of "patriots" like Bolingbroke himself.

For Bolingbroke, then, the disposition that makes Englishmen good citizens is not a general attachment to the public good but a more restricted
passion for the constitution and the constitution alone. This description of
civic virtue remains publicly oriented – the good citizen protests government malfeasance not to advance personal interests but to preserve and
protect the balanced constitution, an ideal to which he is unselfishly devoted. It is, however, an account of public virtue transformed to meet
specific partisan needs.

It remains possible to read Bolingbroke's advocacy of public virtue as
something other than pure political posturing. Persuasive arguments have
been made in particular for seeing it as a critique of or nostalgic reaction to a
new social order that seemed to be undercutting the conditions that nurtured virtuous citizens as Bolingbroke understood them.[14] My point, however, is that to portray the new social order as so fraught with danger and
prone to corruption, Bolingbroke had first to rework the republican notions
of liberty, virtue and corruption that supposedly provided the basis for such
a critique.

Bolingbroke thus offers an account of what it means to be civically virtuous that emphasizes precisely those qualities that Walpole and his colleagues
might be said to lack. They have little reverence or use for the constitutional
balance Bolingbroke esteems so highly and little interest in cultivating
among citizens a "spirit of liberty" that might express itself in defending this
balance. I have already argued that this recasting of republican themes is
intended to advance the opposition's political agenda and, in print at least, it
does so quite effectively. But it is not a vision of the virtuous citizen to which

13 [William Arnall], *The Free Briton: Or, the Opinion of the People. Number II* (London, 1727),
   27–8.
14 J. G. A. Pocock, *The Machiavellian Moment: Florentine Political Thought and the Atlantic
   Republican Tradition* (Princeton: Princeton University Press, 1975), 478–86 and Kramnick, *Bolingbroke's Circle*, respectively.

Bolingbroke is willing to commit himself wholeheartedly. Beginning in the *Remarks on the History of England* and culminating in *The Idea of a Patriot King,* Bolingbroke struggles with the dominant classical republican vision of the polity as the locus of conflict not consensus.[15] Uncomfortable with such a confrontational view of political community, he substitutes a notion of "political friendship" between prince and people that devalues the popular expression of civic virtue and transforms the republican understanding of the good citizen's nature.

Bolingbroke believes with most republicans that those in positions of political authority develop a love for power that places political liberty in perpetual danger.[16] He affirms as well the notion of a virtuous people as ever vigilant defenders of their political privileges against just such untrustworthy magistrates.[17] But Bolingbroke does not accept the standard republican assessment of free society as perpetually conflict-ridden, preserving peace and political liberty only through some sort of wary truce between a grasping ruler and a suspicious and demanding people. Rather, he takes seriously, in a way his contemporaries and predecessors do not, the possibility that a ruling magistrate might naturally embrace and perpetuate a regime of virtue. The good prince, Bolingbroke argues, can and will govern in such a way as to transcend the usual adversarial nature of government.

Queen Elizabeth's reign exemplifies, for Bolingbroke, the possibilities available when a virtuous monarch assumes the rule of a virtuous people. Rather than struggling to dominate a powerful and jealous Commons through her prerogative, Elizabeth "threw herself so entirely on the affections of her subjects that she seemed to decline all other terms of the crown."[18] In Bolingbroke's view, this willingness to seek the affection of the populace can transform the political community from an arena in which the competing interests of ruler and ruled are painfully adjudicated to a locus of harmonious cooperation. When a people find their prince thus devoted to their welfare, their "spirit of jealousy and watchfulness" gives way to a devotion to that monarch who has so generously guaranteed their freedom.

Bolingbroke calls this ideal relationship "political or state friendship," an

---

15 The shared vision I have in mind here begins with the Roman historians, especially Livy, continues with Machiavelli and emerges in the writings of English civic humanists like Algernon Sydney and Cato. It might be conceived as the "realist" or "pragmatic" side of the civic humanist tradition in contrast to the more idealized understanding of the state presented in Cicero and articulated in the works of some of the earliest Florentine humanists. Aristotle too tends towards this "realist" camp (*Politics,* Book 3), although I do not see him as central to the classical republican-civic humanist tradition (see chapter 4).
16 Bolingbroke, *Historical Writings,* 158.
17 *Ibid.,* 157.
18 *Ibid.,* 243.

"intimate and affectionate union" grounded by "good government on one part and ... gratitude and expectation on the other."[19] At its most successful, these complementary virtues call forth a relationship not just of friendship but of filial obedience. Thus Bolingbroke writes in *The Idea of a Patriot King,* the "true image of a free people ... is that of a patriarchal family ... united by one common interest and animated by one common spirit."[20]

With this image of the patriarchal family, Bolingbroke rejects not only the inevitability of conflict assumed in much of the classical republican-civic humanist writings, but also the centrality of popular virtue. The good state for Bolingbroke transcends the need for the demanding and fractious citizen, for the citizen "animated by a generous resolution of defending [his] liberties at any risk." Instead the reformed patriot need only bow to the orders and governance of the good prince and find his liberty in his affection for his monarch.[21]

Portraying popular virtue as a quality that obligingly dissipates under the rule of the good monarch is politically expedient in at least one way, shifting the blame for political acrimony from the opposition to the Court. There would be no need for the people to express their spirit of liberty (through opposition politicking) were the king the type of virtuous monarch whose rule brought a reign of political harmony. But the partisan purposes of this vision of political community should not be overemphasized. Whether the appeal lies in a "reactive" conservatism or a Tory humanism,[22] Bolingbroke seems to be powerfully drawn to the image of a cohesive, hierarchical community for reasons not related to immediate political ends.

This idealized understanding of political community underlines Bolingbroke's problematic treatment of popular civic virtue. Just as Bolingbroke narrows the scope of publicly oriented civic virtue, his "spirit of liberty," by defining its object exclusively as the constitution, so he restricts its role in politics by portraying it as irrelevant to the ideal polity. Civic virtue be-

---

19 *Ibid.,* 278–9.
20 Bolingbroke, *Works,* II, 401.
21 Bolingbroke, *Historical Writings,* 157. One could argue that, because popular virtue would presumably reassert itself at the onset of tyranny, Bolingbroke accords it at least an implicit role in the good state. Or perhaps popular virtue plays a role because the threat of its exercise keeps the good prince honest. Bolingbroke explicitly denies the latter point; his understanding of the good prince is that he acts from duty not interest or necessity (see the argument at the end of the chapter). And while it may be true that when the prince stops exercising his virtue, the spirit of liberty may reassert itself, this argument does not speak to my main point: that in the best state, ruled by a virtuous monarch, popular virtue, as Bolingbroke himself defines it, is given no role.
22 For the first label see Kramnick, *Bolingbroke's Circle,* 265 and 79–81 for an elaboration. For the second view see Hart, *Bolingbroke.*

comes above all something that Walpole's regime lacks and his account of the disposition is shaped so as to secure this conclusion.

II

Corruption is the grand theme of the *Dissertation upon Parties,* a collection of nineteen essays published in *The Craftsman* between October 1733 and December 1734 and issued in book form soon thereafter.[23] In this work, Bolingbroke charges that the Whig regime is destroying the conditions necessary for the practice of civic virtue, condemning Augustan England to the same debilitating corruption that in the past sapped the vitality of other great nations. Here Bolingbroke seeks to cast his country as suffering the same sort of political crisis described most compellingly in the works of Machiavelli and the Roman historian Sallust. But for such an account to be persuasive, Bolingbroke must systematically revise the understanding of the nature and processes of corruption as put forward by earlier authors in this tradition.

As with most republicans, Bolingbroke uses the term "corruption" in a variety of ways, only one of which I am particularly concerned with here. Bolingbroke first uses it to refer to those practices by which money is made to grease the wheels of politics. Buying the loyalty of a member of parliament by offering him a sinecure, purchasing a borough's votes through pre-election largesse, underwriting a pamphlet war through treasury funds are all examples of the political venality which for Bolingbroke deserves the name corruption.[24]

Bolingbroke also deploys the term in an institutional sense to denote any deviation from the balanced constitution. This is the "corruption" against which the civic virtue of loyalty to the constitution must especially be mobilized. The characteristic manifestation of such institutional corruption is the cultivation of a Court party in parliament, a project which violates the fundamental tenet of the balanced constitution: the "mutual independency" of Court and parliament.

In debating the actual extent of corruption in Walpole's England, scholars usually use the word in one of these two senses. They argue for example that

23 The work divides itself logically into two parts. The first eleven essays were published in a space of fourteen weeks, with the final one suggesting a conclusion. Ten months later (November 1734), Bolingbroke took up the cudgels again, adding eight additional essays with more pointed references to contemporary politics. Collected editions appeared quickly thereafter (Varey, *Bolingbroke,* 61, 63). The later essays, which focus more closely on the issue of corruption, form the basis of my discussion.

24 The extent of corruption of this sort under Walpole is discussed in a number of histories, including Dickinson, *Walpole and the Whig Supremacy,* chapters 5 and 8; J. B. Owen, *The Eighteenth Century, 1714–1815* (New York: W. W. Norton and Company, 1974), chapter 5.

Walpole's efforts to establish a Court party, while at times pursued by unsavory means, are more fairly characterized as a legitimate constitutional innovation than as a corrupt departure from tradition.[25] Bolingbroke wants the charge of corruption to evoke more, however, than underhanded financial dealings or inappropriate efforts at political influence. Whig rule, he charges, is breeding a generation of citizens too spineless to defend the nation's liberties, too concerned with advancing their own ambitions and estates to resist the Court's nefarious scheme to establish for itself a "bulky majority" in parliament. His querulous cry echoes in *The Idea of a Patriot King:*

Will the minds of men, which this ministry has narrowed to personal regards alone ... be so easily or so soon enlarged? Will their sentiments, which are debased from the love of liberty ... to a rapacious eagerness after wealth that may sate their avarice ... be so easily or so soon elevated?[26]

Bolingbroke here accuses Walpole of fomenting corruption in the classical republican sense, of cultivating political conditions that nourish ambition and avarice rather than civic virtue. The result, Bolingbroke charges, is a spiritual decay that renders a nation's citizenry unable or unwilling to defend its freedom.

But consider for a moment how Machiavelli and Sallust portray the progress of corruption. Both authors blame the individual's essentially desiring nature for a nation's loss of liberty. Good laws and strict discipline (usually of the military variety) can for a time nurture the love for personal glory or public liberty that constitutes public virtue. But once this culture succumbs (to peace in Sallust's scheme or to inevitable decay in Machiavelli's), corruption must set in. Citizens no longer straitjacketed by military discipline or sternly executed laws will quickly seek out ends more consistent with their animal than their rational nature. Ambition and avarice will overtake their souls, and they will turn to an unrestrained accumulation of power, money, popularity, comfort; any sense of moral limits on these various endeavors will completely drop away.

The political consequences of such a development, for Machiavelli and Sallust, are immediate and devastating. First comes the perversion of political leadership: a corrupt people begin to elect their rulers on the basis of wealth or popularity, not political merit. Faction quickly follows, as those competing for office value only the possession of power not public service.

---

25 See for example H. N. Fieldhouse, "Bolingbroke and the Idea of Non-Party Government," *History* 23 (1938), 50–3; Kramnick, *Bolingbroke's Circle,* 152; Dickinson, *Bolingbroke,* 205; Pocock, *Machiavellian Moment,* 482.
26 Bolingbroke, *Works,* II, 374.

Finally, and most dangerously, the citizens' corruption shatters the fragile equilibrium of social life. With neither populace nor nobility willing or able to set limits to the pursuit of their desires, the stage is set for murderous sedition, lengthy civil war or the emergence of a dictator – in any case, the overthrow of the citizens' freedom.[27]

Bolingbroke may wish to insist that the preconditions for political tyranny as set out in the classical republican tradition have generally been established in eighteenth-century England; citizens increasingly prefer money and power over a selfless advancement of policies favorable to liberty, for example. But it is hard to imagine England under George II collapsing into the sort of chaos both Sallust and Machiavelli document as the wages of this sin. In particular, the radical repudiation of civic values so terrifyingly portrayed in Sallust's portrait of Catiline simply does not obtain in the more ordered world of Augustan England.

How then does Bolingbroke make his case for the spiritual corruption of England's citizenry? As with his treatment of civic virtue, Bolingbroke simply offers a new definition of the corrupt citizen. Thus, the *Dissertation* cites no evidence that citizens have actually lost their love of liberty or shifted their object of desire from public good to private advancement – proof of corruption as Sallust and Machiavelli understand this term. Rather, the primary evidence for the unsettling civic degeneration of the English people is the fact that the electorate continues to return Court officials to parliamentary seats, thus betraying the constitutional balance Bolingbroke so reveres.

Whenever the people of Britain become so degenerate and base, as to be induced by corruption ... to choose persons to represent them in parliament, whom they have found by experience to be ... dependents on a court, and the creatures of a minister ... then may the enemies of our constitution boast that they have got the better of it.[28]

---

27 For Sallust's account of corruption see both *The Conspiracy of Catiline* and *The Jugurthine War* as well as the discussion in D. C. Earl, *The Political Thought of Sallust* (Cambridge University Press, 1961). Alfredo Bonadeo, "Corruption, Conflict and Power in the Works and Times of Niccolo Machiavelli," *University of California Publications in Modern Philology* 108 (Berkeley: University of California Press, 1973), 6–35, offers one of the few systematic analyses of Machiavelli's understanding of corruption, but does not stress its links to Sallust as much as I do here. Not all English civic humanists accepted this classical republican account of political corruption. James Harrington argued that "corruption" denoted only the unfitness of a people for a certain form of government caused by a shift in the underlying balance of property (*The Political Works*, ed. J. G. A. Pocock [Cambridge University Press, 1977], 202) and this characterization convinced at least some later writers. Walter Moyle, for example, makes a similar point in *An Essay upon the Constitution of the Roman Government* in *Two English Republican Tracts*, ed. Caroline Robbins (Cambridge University Press, 1969), 231.

28 Bolingbroke, *Works*, II, 151.

Here Bolingbroke identifies popular corruption, the loss of civic virtue, with support of parliamentary candidates attached to the Court Whig interest. It is important to note that Bolingbroke is not complaining about popular endorsement of actual malfeasance, of real abuses of the political system, of laws ignored, of small (or great) landowners oppressed, of trade ruined, or of justice undone. For Bolingbroke, simply to support a Court Whig is itself proof of moral debilitation for it implies an acceptance of the unconstitutional and thus institutionally corrupt Court party. In essence, he measures the populace's moral state by its performance at the polls.

Characterizing corruption in this way usefully expands the opposition's polemical repertoire; any vote for a Walpole associate can now be attacked as not only mistaken but corrupt. But to label all support of Court Whigs as corrupt, as evidence of the decline of civic virtue, accords neither with common sense nor with the standard republican conception of corruption. Absent proof that the policies of the Court party are substantively affecting the nation's liberty, the reelection of Walpole's allies does not itself demonstrate the moral corruption of the citizenry, their abandonment of civic ideals for more immediate personal gain.

The difficulties with Bolingbroke's account of corruption persists when he turns to an explanation of how the English people have fallen into this deplorable state. Here, too, Bolingbroke draws on a familiar republican theme (pinpointing avarice as responsible for the Augustans' loss of virtue) but recasts it to suit his polemical purposes.

Bolingbroke places the blame for the nation's loss of virtue on an almost fantastic cause: the deficit financing of the English state. As he explains it, the Whigs in power, by spending beyond their immediate means, have created a traffic in public debt that in turn feeds a speculative trade in state securities, a practice derogatorily known as stockjobbing. This new form of commercial endeavor, Bolingbroke argues, fatally attacks the spirit of liberty, substituting for the nation's traditional love of liberty a "spirit of rapine and venality, fraud and corruption."[29]

But why does the extension of government debt and creation of a stock market so completely transform England's civic culture? Bolingbroke's basic argument is that the fortunes to be made and lost through trading in the public debt have upset the traditional social structure to such a degree that good citizens can no longer resist the temptation to collude in public corruption. He describes this problem as having two dimensions.

By allowing a few men to amass vast riches, the financial markets contribute to a "general poverty." And "general poverty ... lay[s] numbers of men

29 *Ibid.*, II, 166.

open to the attacks of corruption" simply because they are in need of the money Walpole promises to supply. Bolingbroke then goes on to stress the deleterious effects of stockjobbing even on those "who do not feel the publick want." Because the "new money" accumulated by Whig financiers can dwarf the fortunes of landed gentlemen, Bolingbroke argues that "he, who thought himself rich before, may begin to think himself poor."[30] And to think oneself poor is to open oneself to corruption, at least in those circumstances where money has become the touchstone of political and social power.

The problem is compounded, Bolingbroke warns, by the lowly origins of the newly wealthy.

He, who would have been ashamed to participate in fraud, or to yield to corruption, may begin to think the faults venial, when he sees men, who were far below him, rise above him by fraud and by corruption.[31]

Here Bolingbroke blames the social mobility created by the market in public debt and commercial securities for completely demoralizing England's landed gentry. Unable to bear the political success of "men, whom [they] hath been used to esteem . . . far inferior to [themselves] in all respects," they begin to collaborate with Walpole's corrupt regime, prostituting themselves in order to maintain a comparable power and influence with Walpole's "monied men."

Through such arguments, Bolingbroke seeks to convince his readers that the wealth derived from a new form of public finance is as intrinsically destructive of a public spirit as the corrupting conditions described in Machiavelli's *Discourses* and the Roman histories. His argument is that the public debt so radically transforms the culture of the British commonwealth as to infect previously virtuous citizens with the deadly virus of avarice and ambition in the same way that the decay of a polity's established *ordini* or the fall of Carthage (Machiavelli's and Sallust's argument respectively) threatened the political fabric of earlier republics.

As an account of the dangers to which the Augustan polity was actually subject, Bolingbroke's argument approaches the absurd.[32] Consider for ex-

---

30 *Ibid.*, II, 165.
31 *Ibid.*
32 Pocock argues that to men steeped in the idiom of Machiavelli and Harrington, the emergence of public debt as an influential social force was inevitably disturbing. Rootless, fickle, influenced by passion not reason, Credit represented the modern version of *fortuna* against which virtuous men must struggle (*Machiavellian Moment,* 453). This argument may well capture what early Augustan writers found unsettling about the new commercial polity. Certainly, Bolingbroke's account of the damaging nature of stockjobbing is considerably more heavy-handed.

ample the centerpiece of his case for the corruption of the parliamentary majority – the claim that the established gentry find the financial and political success of stockjobbers so insupportable that they corrupt themselves and expose the nation's liberty simply to maintain their social and political status. This account is not only an exceedingly awkward way of explaining parliamentary majorities for Walpole's policies but a peculiar tribute to those whom Bolingbroke takes to be the backbone of English society. Could the popular spirit of liberty so enthusiastically described in the *Remarks* be dealt such a serious blow by a new means of financing government expenditure? Would the gentry really trade away its liberties for some slight comparative advantage in political status? It seems more likely that backbenchers allied themselves with Walpole because they saw no good reason to attack the minister's policies or performance. Their political virtue remains intact but dormant, because unnecessary.

One cannot and should not dismiss the fact that the emergence of a new system of public credit was a significant political and economic innovation, recognized as such by Augustan writers and feared by some for its potential impact on civic commitments. Since the fortunes of virtue did indeed flag during this period, one can be tempted to link these two developments directly, adopting the Country party's own account of how civic virtue came to be endangered as historical truth. Yet this account, as perfected in Bolingbroke's *Dissertation upon Parties,* does not provide convincing evidence that the rise of the stock market was responsible for the decline in public virtue. The story Bolingbroke constructs, in which a resentful gentry corrupts itself to maintain social equality with a collection of financial parvenus, makes for good reading in the coffeehouses, but it does not in itself explain the turn away from public virtue evident in the political argument of the time.

It is far more helpful to take Bolingbroke's argument as the catalyst for a protracted political debate in which a number of alternatives to the sort of civic virtue supported by Bolingbroke are deliberately put forward for public consideration. The arguments of the *Remarks* and the *Dissertation upon Parties* should be read as brilliant efforts to adapt the republican language of Country polemic to the particular political occasion at hand: the unseating of Walpole and his Whig associates. By painting a political world in which civic virtue equaled loyalty to the constitution and corruption followed upon the introduction of deficit finance, Bolingbroke seeks to cast Whig policies as desperately in need of the Country's corrective politics of public virtue. The practical effect of Bolingbroke's arguments, however, is to encourage Court Whigs to develop an account of political liberty and civic virtue that deliberately renders the Country politics of public virtue superfluous.

Against Bolingbroke's argument for the impossibility of civic virtue under Walpole, the Court Whigs affirm its possibility, imagining a citizen who advances the good of the nation, protects political liberty through the practice of familiar moral virtues: frugality, industry, honesty. In thus replying to Bolingbroke, the Court Whigs effect the transformation of civic virtue we are tracking in this period. But they do not do so in shared despair at the corruption of a polity led astray by new forms of public finance. By no means converts to Bolingbroke's vision, they are simply reaching, in the rough and tumble of political debate, for arguments to counter Bolingbroke's cleverly targeted polemical journalism.

III

The final act in Bolingbroke's drama of national corruption and renewal concerns the virtue of patriotism, an elite virtue that Bolingbroke considers the only hope for a nation "whose ruin is so far advanced."[33] Strictly speaking, Bolingbroke's writings on patriotism lie beyond the scope of this essay. Composed in the late 1730s, they were not formally published for another decade and their proposals thus exerted little influence on the political debate traced here. Still, Bolingbroke's prescription for the English nation as contained in his two essays on patriotism (*A Letter on the Spirit of Patriotism* [1736] and *The Idea of a Patriot King* [1738]) represent such a distinctive response to the breakdown in the politics of public virtue that they deserve examination. Having himself created a picture of the modern polity in which the citizens' spirit of liberty, their "disposition to oppose all instances of maladministration" has sadly degenerated, Bolingbroke resurrects the notion of a selfless love for one's country as the quality needed to restore civic virtue to a corrupted populace and to redeem the nation from destruction.[34]

The spirit of patriotism differs from the more plebeian spirit of liberty in three ways. It is first of all a virtue grounded in duty, not in passion or interest, and it is therefore a quality available only to those few endowed with sufficient "ethereal spirit" to follow a life responsive solely to the dictates of moral responsibility.[35] Bolingbroke limits the practice of patriotism first to a natural aristocracy (those few men "who engross almost the whole reason of the species; who are born to instruct, to guide and to preserve") and then, in *The Idea of a Patriot King*, solely to the person of the prince.[36] Finally, unlike the weakened, popular spirit of liberty, the virtue

33 Bolingbroke, *Works,* II, 395.
34 *Ibid.,* II, 387.
35 *Ibid.,* II, 352.
36 *Ibid.*

of patriotism acts effectively against corruption; indeed the characteristic function of this quality is to free the state and its citizens from corruption's clutches.

The patriot begins his reformation by "bring[ing] men from strong habits of corruption, to prefer honour to profit, and liberty to luxury." Once the patriot effects this moral transformation (at least among members of parliament), he consolidates his gains in legal action, "shut[ting] up, with all the bars and bolts of the law, the primary entries through which these torrents of corruption have been let in on us." Although the *Spirit of Patriotism* does not entertain specifics, the *Dissertation upon Parties* leaves little question of the holes to be plugged. The patriot will not only "wrest the power of the government . . . out of the hands that have employed it weakly and wickedly" but abolish the means by which government promotes its corrupt designs: the civil list, bloated treasury rolls and the public debt.[37]

The Idea of a Patriot King, written two years later, advertises similar goals. But here the reforming agent is not parliament, which has proved itself beyond redemption, but a virtuous monarch. The patriot king is the only individual who unites the will to reform the state with the authority to do so. Whereas the natural aristocracy has first to reeducate morally an entire parliament before implementing procedures to end corruption, the patriot king, because of his unique position in the constitution, requires only his own good will to halt the populace's moral rot. Not only can he abolish such corrupt expedients as the civil list with a single word, he also presents by such actions a powerful moral example that inexorably prompts popular emulation. Most importantly, the patriot king's patronage can reverse the dangerous political culture that, in making money the coin of political favor, creates the social conditions for a loss of popular virtue. "By rendering public virtue and real capacity the sole means of acquiring any degree of power or profit in the state, he will set the passions of [the citizens'] hearts on the side of liberty and good government . . . reinfusing into the minds of men the spirit of this constitution."[38] The patriot king's decision to abandon political corruption as an "expedient of government" (or the patriotic parliament's legal exclusion of such policies) provides an effective antidote to the moral corruption besetting Augustan culture. Such remedies will restore "the orders and forms of the constitution . . . to their primitive integrity," a reformation which will in turn renew the citizenry's love of liberty and good government.[39]

Perhaps the most distinctive aspect of Bolingbroke's account of the virtue

37 *Ibid.,* II, 365, 364, 364.
38 *Ibid.,* II, 396.
39 *Ibid.*

of patriotism is the optimistic psychology that lies behind it, the faith that a select group of persons will and can be virtuous simply because reason tells them it is right to be so. In staking out this position, Bolingbroke distances himself from the most influential moral and political philosophies of his day which tended to accept the durability of the citizen's selfish impulses, making their manipulation rather than transcendence the ground of man's moral and political life.[40] Bolingbroke does include considerations of interest in his prescription for virtue. From the *Remarks on the History of England* to *The Idea of a Patriot King,* Bolingbroke argues that "interest and duty remain indivisibly united, however they may be separated in opinion."[41] But while Bolingbroke cites the personal advantages that the patriot derives from the performance of virtue, Bolingbroke chooses to clinch his case for the performance of civic virtue by stressing its morally obligatory nature.

It may be easily proved from a consideration of the circumstances in which we stand as individuals, that the general good of society is the particular interest of every member. Our Creator designed therefore that we should promote this general good. It is by consequence our duty to do so.[42]

He makes a similar plea in the *Spirit of Patriotism:*

The service of our country is not chimerical, but a real duty. He who admits the proofs of any other moral duty, drawn from the constitution of human nature or from the moral fitness and unfitness of things, must admit them in favor of this duty, or be reduced to the most absurd inconsistency.[43]

Bolingbroke's point: civic virtue need not and should not be grounded in arguments of self-interest, in appeals to personal passions. Rather, rational contemplation of the world reveals God's intention for human action ("Reason collects the will of God from the constitution of things")[44] and truly virtuous behavior, political or otherwise, is that in which human will is brought into conformity with God's.

But is reason alone sufficient to determine human will in this way? Eighteenth-century moral psychology and theology generally answer in the

---

40 Consider for example Hume's celebrated passage, published in *Essays, Moral and Political* in 1741: "Political writers have established it as a maxim, that, in contriving any system of government... every man ought to be supposed a *knave,* and to have no other end, in all his actions, than private interest. By this interest we must govern him, and, by means of it, make him, notwithstanding his insatiable avarice and ambition [the classical republican marks of corruption], co-operate to public good" ("On the Independency of Parliament," in David Hume, *Essays Moral, Political and Literary,* ed. Eugene F. Miller [Indianapolis, IN: LibertyClassics, 1987], 42).

41 Bolingbroke, *Historical Writings,* 280. See also *Works,* II, 359–60.

42 Bolingbroke, *Historical Writings,* 279.

43 Bolingbroke, *Works,* II, 358–9.

44 *Ibid.,* II, 354.

negative. Bolingbroke's affirmative answer requires two qualifications. First, virtue born of a rational consent to duty occurs only in the rarefied few; only those endowed with a surfeit of intelligence and talent are eligible to become "patriots." Second, even these select individuals must be carefully instructed if they are not to misuse their ability. The statesman must be taught from childhood that his position and talents are given for the service of the community and not for "the gratification of his ambition and his other passions."[45] Only in these circumstances, Bolingbroke argues, can we expect reason to operate forcefully enough to bring the elite citizen to virtue.

This argument that the primary source of patriotic virtue is a selfless dedication to the public good puts Bolingbroke at odds not only with much Augustan moral and political philosophy but with the classical republican tradition as well. Cicero aside, the Romans who celebrate the achievements of their republic ground the citizens' virtue not in submission to natural law but in praiseworthy passions: love of liberty, love of glory and fame.[46] But Bolingbroke, in a slashing attack on Machiavelli's views, roundly rejects the propriety of basing virtue in such passions.[47] Not only is this appeal to self-interest unworthy of a potential patriot ("superior talents and superior rank . . . are noble prerogatives," not to be enlisted by degrading applications to selfish advantage).[48] It is downright dangerous, staking the nation's prospects on too fickle a foundation. A civic virtue grounded in enlightened self-interest transforms itself too easily into a passion for private advantage "which [men] endeavor to palliate and to reconcile as well as they can to that of the public."[49] Only individuals disciplined by a sense of moral or religious duty can be relied upon to resist the temptation to turn public service to the service of their own ambition and transcend the petty views of "particular, separate interest" for the "general and common interest of society."[50] In contrast then to both his contemporaries and to the civic humanist-classical republican tradition, Bolingbroke questions both the necessity and reliability of an appeal to the baser aspects of human nature in order to assure the performance of virtue. Statesmen act virtuously not because they seek fame or glory but because their reason reveals to them the duty of pursuing vigorously and selflessly public happiness.

45 *Ibid.*
46 See in particular the writings of Sallust, Livy and Tacitus and the account of them offered in Earl, *Political Thought of Sallust* and *The Moral and Political Tradition of Rome* (Ithaca: Cornell University Press, 1967).
47 Bolingbroke, *Works*, II, 390. The passage in Machiavelli that so arouses Bolingbroke's ire is in the *Discourses*, Book I, chapter 10.
48 *Ibid.,* II, 359.
49 *Ibid.,* II, 357.
50 Bolingbroke, *Historical Writings*, 280.

Partisan considerations may play some role in Bolingbroke's portrait of the good statesman as unsullied by self-interested passions. These essays not only set out a program of political reform but also seek to persuade ambitious young politicians and a restive Crown Prince to oppose and overturn the policies of the ministry in office. Both the *Spirit of Patriotism* and the *Patriot King* bolster the case for such action with an unfavorable comparison between a wicked ministry "animated from the first by ambition and avarice, the love of power and money" and praiseworthy patriots who undertake "opposition ... as a duty," from a selfless concern for the good of the country as a whole.[51] To portray both sides as motivated by interest or passions (however different the object) would prove less effective as both a persuasive to and justification for opposition activity.

But political purposes do not appear paramount in this call for a virtue grounded in reason and duty. Bolingbroke, after all, chose not to publish the essays when written, but circulated them privately. In them, he seems to extol the virtue of patriotism primarily from a genuinely felt sympathy for this ideal – and a corresponding distrust of the ability of interest to ground a satisfactory political virtue. Even Bolingbroke's early works demonstrate a fascination for what Bolingbroke takes to be the selfless devotion of the Roman citizen to his polity.[52] The *Spirit of Patriotism* and the *Patriot King* seek to recall this sentiment to contemporary England, affirming against the skeptical psychology of the day Cicero's faith in a reason that can perceive the plan of the universe and can determine man's will to its fulfillment.

Considered in sequence, then, Bolingbroke's chief writings – *Remarks on the History of England* (1730–1), *A Dissertation upon Parties* (1733–4), *A Letter on the Spirit of Patriotism* (1736) and *The Idea of a Patriot King* (1738) – provide an extended meditation on the nature and possibility of public virtue in the modern world. The *Remarks* and *Dissertation* describe a popular civic virtue dangerously undermined by Walpole's pursuit of political advantage; the essays on patriotism consider whether some more elite version of public virtue might still save the nation from corruption.

In the next chapter, I set out the way in which Bolingbroke's critique of Whig politics prompted Walpole's defenders to articulate a new, privately oriented conception of civic virtue more appropriate, so they claimed, to the political and cultural circumstances of the Augustan polity. But what of Bolingbroke's own proposals? In calling for a civic virtue grounded in the self-sacrificing public service of a political elite, does he offer a politics of

51 Bolingbroke, *Works*, II, 358.
52 Bolingbroke, *Historical Writings*, 157.

public virtue available to and appropriate for English citizens of the mid-eighteenth century? The answer to this question is both yes and no.

In the first place, Bolingbroke's belief in the possibility of patriotism – his assumption that individual citizens can serve the general good independently of any immediate personal gain – is not necessarily misplaced. Any theory of civic virtue probably needs to make room for such friends of liberty, although it need not repudiate egoistic psychology to do so. Many of Bolingbroke's philosophical contemporaries, Cato included, had begun to investigate how public-regarding behavior might be elicited without reliance on purely benevolent dispositions or the operations of a disinterested reason. But even these theories must account for public crusaders like Cato himself or fail to persuade fully. Although the motives that lead individual men and women into generally self-denying public service are more complex and less noble than Bolingbroke would have it, the possibility remains high that some citizens will speak for liberty and virtue out of concern for certain interests conceived of as common rather than personal. This possibility holds good throughout the spectrum of political regimes and economic structures. The virtue of patriotism is in fact the one form of civic excellence that Bolingbroke concedes survives the radical political and economic innovations of his day. The practice of patriotism is thus not limited to aristocratic republics or agrarian societies; a constitutional monarchy, a commercial economy can nurture such virtue as well.

If it remains possible to make an elite patriotism the centerpiece of a modern politics of public virtue, the more pressing question is whether one would want to. In answering this question, it is important to remember that Bolingbroke's case for the necessity of an elite civic virtue rests on a semantic problem of his own making: his redefinition of classical republican terms so as to narrow and concentrate their meanings in a highly artificial way. Once civic virtue is defined as love of the constitution and corruption as support of the Whigs (who undermine the constitution), then, and only then, can Country politicians argue for virtue's disappearance from the modern polity. As a politics of public virtue, then, Bolingbroke's advocacy of patriotism is not so much objectionable – the relatively disinterested contributions of friends of liberty can and should be welcomed in any polity – as besides the point. It offers a solution to a problem that does not actually exist.

But to affirm the possibility of civic virtue in the eighteenth-century polity is not to settle the question of what sort of civic virtue it will be. Here we return to the question at the center of this chapter and the study as a whole: what happened to the politics of public virtue in early eighteenth-century English political argument and why? As I have already indicated, there is not one but several answers to this question. For Cato, human nature is simply not capable of the heroic virtues lauded by classical republicans. Yet rather than abandon the republican ideal of the citizen active in defense of liberty, his *Letters* puzzle out the conditions under which self-interested individuals might remain vigorous defenders of the public good without embracing a public form of civic virtue.

Bolingbroke, too, contributes to the process I have called the transformation of virtue, though not as directly. In seeking to advance the cause of the Country opposition by attacking both the political process and the English citizenry as corrupt, Bolingbroke drove defenders of Walpole's regime to rework the conventional assumptions of what made a good citizen. By the time the essays on patriotism appeared, these theorists had already elaborated a vision of virtuous citizenship that required no recourse to an elite ethic of civic service, or for that matter, to a public virtue of any kind. Instead, the Court Whigs suggested, the civic virtue most needed in England at this time was privately oriented. Individuals could best ready themselves to defend liberty and deliberate on the public good by keeping their own house in order, cultivating the personal excellences of honesty, frugality, industry and moderation. Bolingbroke's own manipulation of the republican tradition had, ironically, encouraged others to conceive of civic virtue in a way that rendered his own solution to political corruption – the revival of patriotism – both irrelevant and obsolete.

6

⊲══════════════════════════════════════▷

The Court Whig conception of
civic virtue

Whatever the accuracy of the portrait, the bleak picture painted by Boling-broke of a citizenry and constitution corrupted by a power-hungry ministry crystallized some of the more potent themes of opposition polemic in the early eighteenth century. Since its formation in the previous century, the Country opposition had complained that the distribution of places, pensions and electoral bribes threatened to establish a parliament perfectly submissive to the Crown's pleasure at the expense of liberty, good government and public virtue. Walpole's aggressive use of patronage to consolidate his position, his unprecedented centralization of power in the office of the Treasury and the carefully marshaled influence exercised in his behalf in the nation's elections only lent new force to these opposition accusations.[1] Any Whig victory in the pitched propaganda battle waged throughout this period would thus depend on Walpole's mounting a vigorous and convincing response to such charges.

To defend his policies against the *Craftsman*'s weekly barrage of criticism, Walpole relied on a diverse group of pro-ministerial writers that included a number of bishops, a lord (Hervey), a sibling (Horace Walpole), an Irishman (Matthew Concanen), dissenters (James Pitt) and one-half of the "illustrious Cato" (Thomas Gordon, who accepted a profitable government post soon after Trenchard's death).[2] From their pens flowed a steady stream of pro-ministerial propaganda and anti-opposition polemic which raged far beyond the single issue of parliamentary corruption. When the *Craftsman* called for

1 For the realities of political patronage and influence in eighteenth-century Britain, see the works cited in chapter 5, n. 24.
2 "An Account of the Reputed Writers in the News-Papers," *Gentleman's Magazine* 3 (1733), 91 and Laurence Hanson, *Government and the Press, 1695–1763* (London: Humphrey Milford, 1936), 117. Gordon was appointed a commissioner of wine licenses sometime in the 1720s, in return for which, most probably, he made himself useful as an editor for the government press (Hanson, *Government and the Press,* 114).

war against Spain, they made the case for Walpole's policy of accommodation and peace. They also defended the administration's handling of the public debt and the "standing army," while reminding readers of the flourishing state of domestic and international trade. When substantive themes palled, they attacked the personalities, motives and conduct of the "patriots" of the opposition, initiating a tiresome exchange of denunciations in which the Court Whigs rarely got the better of their opponents.[3]

Despite the decidedly tawdry aspects of such public polemics, the discipline of joining in journalistic debate nurtured two of the sharpest minds in the Court Whig coterie – James Pitt and William Arnall. Arnall was a brief and bright star on the political scene, breaking into print at age seventeen, dead at age twenty-six.[4] His lively talent, first displayed in the pro-ministerial pamphlet *Clodius and Cicero* (1727), not only won him a spot on the *British Journal* (where he wrote under the name Roger Manley) but soon secured him his own paper, the *Free Briton* (for which he adopted the pseudonym Francis Walsingham). A favorite of Walpole and King George, he commanded a handsome fee for his propaganda efforts.[5] Much less is known about James Pitt. A dissenter, he came to London and the ministerial service from a schoolmaster's post in Norwich, assuming the editorship of the *London Journal* in the fall of 1729 and working diligently for the Court interest through 1736. As with Gordon, Walpole most probably secured his loyalty and income with a post, this one in the customs office.[6] The works of these two authors represent perhaps the most thorough response to the Country charge of corruption in Court Whig literature. Their writings thus offer an ideal prism through which to examine the transformation of virtue that Bolingbroke's attack on Walpole helped to bring about.[7]

3 See for example [William Yonge], *Sedition and Defamation Display'd: In a Letter to the Author of the Craftsman* (London, 1731) and the fierce exchanges that followed.
4 The *Dictionary of National Biography* gives his dates as 1715?–1741? but this would have him publishing *Clodius and Cicero* at the tender age of twelve. If he did indeed die at age 26, a 1710?–1736 dating, also suggested by the *DNB*, seems more likely.
5 For these facts, see [James Ralph], *The Case of Authors by Profession or Trade, Stated* (London, 1758), 38 and Hanson, *Government and the Press*, 113. On Arnall's political thought in general, see Thomas Horne, "Politics in a Corrupt Society: William Arnall's Defense of Robert Walpole," *Journal of the History of Ideas* 41 (1980): 601–14.
6 "Account of the Reputed Writers," 91.
7 There are few modern accounts of Court Whig ideology in general or of its conception of virtue. Duncan Forbes, *Hume's Philosophical Politics* (Cambridge University Press, 1975), chapter 5 and H. T. Dickinson, *Liberty and Property: Political Ideology in Eighteenth-Century Britain* (New York: Holmes and Meier Publishers, 1977), chapter 4 define Court Whiggism quite broadly and focus on its understanding of liberty. Reed Browning, *Political and Constitutional Ideas of the Court Whigs* (Baton Rouge: Louisiana State University Press, 1982) examines a number of individuals allied with Walpole, but does not include either Pitt or Arnall.

One can imagine at least two ways in which Court Whigs might defend Walpole's policies. They might admit to Walpole's corruption but excuse it on the grounds that the good state might flourish without the virtue of statesman or citizen. Thus J. G. A. Pocock argues that "the ideology of the Court ... did not regard virtue as politically paradigmatic" and sought instead to provide another more practical foundation for good government.[8] Or, they might challenge the opposition's charges at their source, rejecting the accusation of corruption and championing Walpole's policies as beneficent and public-spirited. Such a tactic would not require Court Whigs to defend as either possible or present the sort of civic virtue lauded by Bolingbroke. But neither would they have to abandon the idea of civic virtue altogether. Rather, Court Whigs might seek to redefine the term so as to make it a practical possibility among citizens that Bolingbroke would damn as corrupt.

In this chapter I want to make the case that Pitt and Arnall, in defending Walpole against the onslaught of Country propaganda, elaborate some version of the second possibility. Although their writings answer the opposition's charges of corruption in different ways, neither writer defends Walpole's politics by abandoning a politics of virtue altogether. What they do dispute is Bolingbroke's idea that the good citizen is one who defends the balanced constitution against all comers, who resists all forms of executive influence in parliament, who eschews involvement in the "corrupting" worlds of finance and Whig politics. Against this ideal they offer their own more privately oriented conception of civic virtue, of citizens who advance the public good not through a publicly oriented spirit of liberty but through a select set of moral virtues (temperance, honesty, industry, frugality) exercised in the private sphere.

I

Like all Arnall's writings, his first pamphlet, *Clodius and Cicero* (1727), was particularly concerned to justify Walpole's use of favors, pensions and elec-

---

8 J. G. A. Pocock, *The Machiavellian Moment: Florentine Political Thought and the Atlantic Republican Tradition* (Princeton: Princeton University Press, 1975), 487. The complete passage reads: "The ideology of the Court ... did not regard virtue as politically paradigmatic, it did not regard government as founded upon principles of virtue which needed to be regularly reasserted; it readily accepted that men were factious and interested beings and, instead of regarding these characteristics as fatal if unchecked to virtue and government, proposed to have them policed by a strong central executive, which did not itself need to be disciplined by the principles of virtue, but might without suffering harm appeal to the passions and interests of men." That is, the Court replaced a politics of virtue with one that looked to the manipulation of citizens' passions and interests. In *Virtue, Commerce, and History: Essays on Political Thought and History, Chiefly in the Eighteenth Century* (Cambridge University Press, 1985), Pocock argues that the preferred Court substitutes for public virtue are the "social, cultural and commercial values" we associate with Addison (235).

toral bribes to cultivate a loyal party of supporters in parliament. The Country opposition condemned such practices as both corrupt (principles, not pounds sterling, should dictate public policy) and corrupting (depriving those in receipt of ministerial favors and pensions of the autonomy that made them good deliberators on the public welfare). Arnall's response to these charges registers two themes with particular vehemence.

First, any influence-peddling that occurs is not the engine of civic corruption, but a necessary response to a citizenry no longer interested in acting for the public good without personal reward. To this extent, Arnall concedes the Country charge that English citizens are politically corrupt, unable or unwilling to place the public interest ahead of private advantage. "The noble Virtues are long since lost, that engag'd those Patriot Volunteers, whose Names do Honour to Humanity." He vigorously disputes however the correlative charge that Walpole's ministry must be held responsible for this development or criticized for adapting to it. "Can the Ministry then be complain'd of, who purchase Friends for the Publick, when so Few will appear in the cause without valuable Considerations?"[9] The Whigs buy votes only from those citizens already willing to offer them for sale.

The administration should not be taken to task for tolerating, indeed accommodating, the vices of the Augustan citizenry. Borrowing a page from Machiavelli, Arnall warns, "Such frequently is the Situation of Things, and such the Malignity of Men, that Measures strictly Virtuous would bring present Confusion and Ruin." Practical experience shows the futility of embarking on large-scale reform: "What have avail'd all our sumptuary Laws; what all those against Gaming and Duelling; what those against Bribery?" Arnall asks. "Only to demonstrate how much more Force there is in Luxury, and Vanity and Avarice, than there is in Laws with all their Penalties."[10] Thus, in tailoring his policies to the venality of English citizens, Walpole is wisely enduring a social evil that he lacks the power to cure. "Governors must indulge the Humours and submit to the Necessity of the Times, or Government will soon be at an End."[11]

But such an analysis, although perhaps exonerating Walpole, provides a meager rallying point for friends of the administration, justifying the ministry as it does by condemning the people it is appointed to govern. More promis-

---

9 *British Journal,* no. 19, 25 May 1728. Newspaper dates are given Old Style to match dates given on the masthead. Note that the *British Journal,* which had been published since 1722, renames and renumbers itself *The British Journal; or the Censor, by Roger Manley of Lincoln's Inn, Esq., no. 1* on 20 January 1728.
10 William Arnall, *Clodius and Cicero* (London, 1727), 28.
11 *British Journal,* no. 19, 25 May 1728. See also *British Journal,* no. 74, 31 May 1729: "When Corruption has universally prevail'd no Man can administer the Publick without it; and to attempt an immediate Suppression of this Evil will infallibly ruin the Minister, peradventure his Country also."

ing is the second prong of Arnall's defense of Walpole. Here he vindicates the administration's practices and contests the charge of corruption by pointing to the freedom and prosperity currently enjoyed by the nation's citizens. Why, he asks, does the opposition insist on harrying the government

> when Liberty is well protected; when the Laws only are the Rule of Right and Wrong; when a Minister can have no Interest repugnant to the Public Interest; when no Demands are made upon the Subject but what the Law makes; at such a Conjuncture as this...to distress [the Ministry] and weaken their Hands...'tis Faction barefac'd.[12]

Arnall here turns the republican linkage of virtue and liberty against opposition rhetoric. Corruption is to be feared and condemned, so the republican line goes, because of its effect on public liberty: tyranny, poverty, instability, injustice. But if corruption is indeed made manifest by its fruits, how ridiculous to raise the alarm against it in a prosperous, well-functioning constitutional monarchy such as Great Britain. Liberty is so clearly enjoyed by English citizens, how could their governors be corrupt or their policies corrupting?

The themes of *Clodius and Cicero* are expanded and applied more specifically to the problem of electoral bribery in an anonymous article published in the *British Journal*, no. 265, 21 October 1727. Arnall did not assume the paper's editorship until three months after this date, but the work's candid discussion of ministerial corruption and light style make an attribution to Arnall possible. In any case, the "Conversation between Mr. Hopewell and Mr. Sullen," one of the very few dialogues published in the pro-ministerial press, deploys the two themes characteristic of Arnall's argument: both blaming the people for a corruption to which the government must respond and using evidence of prosperity and liberty to deny that the government's actions are appropriately characterized as corrupt in the first place.

Hopewell begins his defense of the Court's practices by echoing two points made forcefully in *Clodius and Cicero*: first, that corruption is not a problem particular to Walpole's ministry and second, that its presence is no barrier to good government. "Why all this Clamour rais'd at present? Are the English the first or only Offenders of this Kind?" he says of the opposition's charge of corruption. The claim that the Whigs are responsible for this evil is completely unfounded; corruption "has been the Complaint of all Times and under the best Governments, and has been redress'd by none." In a sense, the pervasiveness of corruption proves its innocuousness. "Why from one bad Symptom do we pronounce the Ruin of the Constitution?"[13]

12 Arnall, *Clodius and Cicero*, 31–2.
13 *British Journal*, no. 265, 21 October 1727.

Sullen responds to such assurances skeptically: whatever the historical presence of corruption in England, the fact remains that the Whigs are buying their candidates seats in parliament. By compromising in this way the autonomy of members of parliament, the administration's conduct on the hustings *is* corrupting. Hopewell agrees that the loss of autonomy is an appropriate criterion of corruption, but he denies that the Whigs' electoral practices threaten such an outcome. Most Whig members of parliament possess sufficient "natural Interest" to win their seats without the ministry's help, Hopewell argues. The money they take from the government goes only to offset the massive expenditures made by opposition candidates; it does not buy the candidates' loyalty or votes. Nor should the administration be criticized for recommending "old and fast Friends to such Corporations where [it has] Credit and Influence."[14] Such actions simply discharge a debt of gratitude while prudently assuring that the ministry's supporters remain in parliament. No one's autonomy is compromised in either of these cases because those receiving the money would support the government in any case. The same sort of argument can be made in defense of the Whig practice of trading favors for votes. Offering money or place to "a Man who does really in his private Judgment prefer me to my Antagonist" is not improper because it does not implicate the administration in the essence of corruption: the seduction of honest souls or the compromising of individual autonomy.[15]

In these passages, the "Conversation" defends Walpole on the grounds that the electorate is genuinely attached to Whig interests. But Arnall's other defense of administration behavior is also broached in the "Conversation." Here he baldly concedes the corruption of the English citizenry. "Such is the Turn of Mankind," Arnall warns in the *British Journal's* leading article for 31 May 1729 (no. 74) that "he frequently sells his Judgment to his Appetite." What is a minister to do when faced with such "amazing Discontentedness," this restless dissatisfaction with their current stock of goods that renders voters vulnerable to corrupt temptations? Reform, the renewal of virtue, Arnall treats as impossible: no government can alter the tendencies of human nature. However, a wise statesman can "defeat [corruption], not by Declamation, but by over-bidding, and out-buying it. Corruption, like Violence, must be oppos'd by itself." With these arguments, Arnall cleverly pries apart the republican linkage of virtue as the only safeguard to liberty and corruption as liberty's greatest threat. In fact, he suggests, behavior that among a virtuous people would be properly labeled corrupt – purchasing

14 *Ibid.*
15 *Ibid.*

power with money or favors – turns out, in a compromised polity, to sustain rather than undermine liberty.[16] In this case, the force of identifying such actions as "corrupt" is substantially muted.

Will nothing then count as truly corrupt behavior, in the sense of actually endangering political liberty and citizen autonomy? Yes, genuine corruption could threaten any polity, England's included, but its presence or absence should be a matter for empirical judgment, not Country sloganeering. Judge the state of your liberties, Arnall pleads, not by the fantasies conjured up in the *Craftsman* but by your everyday experiences. If "real Oppression, harsh Usage or unsufferable Insolence" are absent, if "the Laws of the Land ... are not infring'd, or dispens'd with," then the administration cannot be and should not be called corrupt.[17] The opposition prompts citizens to judge the ministry's policies by their conformity to certain abstract principles of good government. Far more sensible, Arnall retorts, to praise or condemn them on the basis of the good or evil they actually achieve.[18]

Reed Browning has criticized Court Whig arguments structured along these lines as "crude utilitarianism."[19] But justifying a government's acts by the real goods to be reaped from them has much to be said for it, especially in a climate of vituperative partisan rhetoric. Arnall's writings seek to debunk opposition complaints of corruption, incipient tyranny and nefarious politicking, by focusing popular attention on the actual consequences of the condemned behavior. "When idle, unnecessary and hurtful Bounties are bestow'd ... Men may well complain; but otherwise I cannot see how Reason will justify the Clamour," Arnall states.[20] His confidence that a utilitarian or empirical standard of virtue and corruption will reveal the opposition's charges of wrongdoing as so much political posturing may be mistaken. But

16 Thus Arnall states in the same issue of the *British Journal:* "Nor is it a Crime, but a meritorious Action, to buy [Men] off from their favourite Follies, and gain them, tho' by Purchase, to Truth and good Sense" (no. 74, 31 May 1729). See also *British Journal,* no. 19, 25 May 1728: "The severest Virtue cannot complain if the Arms of Vice are turned against itself; nor can a People complain if they sell their Vote to their own Advantage."

17 [William Arnall], *The Free Briton: Or, The Opinion of the People. Number II* (London, 1727), 27, 31.

18 See a similar argument of Arnall's in the *Free Briton,* no. 140, 3 August 1732. James Pitt makes comparable appeals to empirical standards as a basis for refuting charges of corruption in the *London Journal:* "Tis impossible, I say, that this Noise of a Country Interest should spring from the People, for I would seriously ask them, what are their Grievances? Don't they flow in Wealth? [and] Trade? ... and are not their liberties so extensive that every Man says what he will, and does what he will?" See also the exhortations in the *London Journal,* no. 608, 20 March 1731; no. 767, 9 March 1734; no. 800, 26 October 1734.

19 Browning, *Political and Constitutional Ideas,* 236. See also Horne, "Politics in a Corrupt Society," 610–11.

20 *British Journal,* no. 19, 25 May 1728.

his use of such a standard as a sensible basis on which to judge a government's worthiness is not.[21]

Arnall's arguments may at first seem to mark him as a traveler along the first route I mapped out above: someone who defends Walpole's policies by conceding both the presence of corruption and the dispensability of civic virtue, going on from there to make the best of politics in a corrupt world. In fact, Arnall both defends the virtue of Walpole's policies and sketches the means by which the populace, now quite corrupt, might find its virtue renewed. In making the case for the uprightness of Walpole's actions, Arnall once again asks citizens to judge the ministry's policies not by their questionable appearance but by their intended effect. In a polity where the "common People are naturally prone to corruption . . . those who wish well to Mankind" must use any means available to "secure their Affections for the Public Interest."[22] The expedient of purchasing government supporters cannot be labeled corrupt when it preserves freedom and stability against Jacobites, nonjurors and the generally disaffected. In fact, Hopewell proudly asserts, "To this Practice [of electoral bribery], we owe the present Enjoyment of our Liberties and Preservation of our Constitution."[23] Because the Whigs use their financial resources and patronage network to advance the cause of freedom and prosperity – an assertion Arnall is willing to submit to the test of popular opinion – their behavior should be deemed virtuous, not corrupt.

Despite the fact that for Arnall the virtue of the current ministry hangs on the alleged corruption of the people, he also refuses to write the morals of the populace off altogether. English citizens can be brought from the corrupt dependence they now exhibit to the vigor of civic virtue by a simple reform of their personal lives. For Arnall, the great inlet to corruption in the contemporary polity is luxury, which he, with most of his contemporaries, defines as living beyond one's means. This vice breeds corruption simply by making people necessitous enough to welcome bribes. The cure for such corruption, however, lies as close as a balanced bank account; one must only determine to be temperate, frugal and honest. If the populace would "return from luxurious, irregular Ways of Living, to the more easy and natural Means

21 Browning's most powerful objection to the utilitarian defense of the Court Whig regime – in which the Whigs are said to deserve "support because they brought happiness to the people" – is that such an argument provides no critical purchase against an absolutist regime that makes its citizens happy as well (*Political and Constitutional Ideas*, 236). But this is to miss the fact that Court Whigs furnish their "utilitarian" standard with a specific political content that includes popular involvement in government, the protection of liberty and property, and the achievement of constitutional government as defined by tradition, law and the Revolution of 1688. No absolutist government could meet these criteria for approval, and no nation deprived of these goods would, in their view, be happy.

22 *British Journal*, no. 19, 25 May 1728.

23 *British Journal*, no. 265, 21 October 1727.

of national Industry," they could easily avoid the "various Misfortunes attending Slavery and Debauchery." And once citizens manifested such virtues, England's governors could themselves return to more conventionally praiseworthy behavior. "If they [the People] would be honest, just and disinterested, they will never create a Necessity for good Ministers, or a Temptation for bad ones to buy them."[24]

Civically virtuous behavior then remains within the reach of English citizens – but it will not be the sort of public virtue recommended so warmly by Bolingbroke and his allies. For the Country opposition, the primary cause of corruption is the Whig regime's new "Constitution of the Revenue" and the unprecedented possibilities it provides for purchasing the allegiance of the citizenry. They argue that in these circumstances, civic virtue is best expressed as "zeal for the constitution."[25] Of course, the last thing Arnall wants is citizens made virtuous by the defense of a balanced constitution. The whole point of his journalistic endeavors is to defend as reasonable, just and virtuous policies that subvert the good constitution as Bolingbroke defines it. But Arnall does not, on this account, give up on a notion of civic virtue altogether. Instead he argues that the best protection against citizens being corrupted by government money is a well-lined pocketbook, protected by a frugal lifestyle, temperate tastes and industrious impulses. The character traits linked to such behavior are properly denominated civic (as well as moral) virtues because they are the attributes of the citizen most necessary (in Arnall's view at least) to the preservation of a free, self-governing polity.

Arnall, then, never concedes the irrelevance of civic virtue to the good polity or its impossibility in the modern state.[26] Instead, he uses empirical standards of good government, pointing to well-functioning courts of law, rising trade figures and comfortable personal lives, to argue that none of Walpole's political stratagems should count as corrupt or corrupting. In fact, by sustaining liberty in the face of a greedy and untrustworthy electorate, Walpole's policies are as virtuous, if not more so, than the "reforms" the Country opposition is always trying to introduce. This argument represents Arnall's main offensive against the opposition. In it he concedes the corruption of the populace and argues that the policies to which the Country opposition objects are made necessary by this corruption. But in considering how the nation might combat the evils of luxury, Arnall articulates a

24 *British Journal,* no. 74, 31 May 1729. See also *British Journal,* no. 19, 25 May 1728.
25 Henry St. John, Viscount Bolingbroke, *The Works of Lord Bolingbroke,* 4 v. (London: Henry Bohn, 1844. Reprinted New York: A. M. Kelley, 1967), II, 116.
26 For an alternate account of Arnall as someone who "had given up on the political importance of virtue," see Horne, "Politics in a Corrupt Society," 614 and *passim.*

more positive program. Does the opposition want more virtue in political life? Let all citizens look first to their personal habits; cultivating the virtues of personal moderation will create the civic personality best suited to sustaining a free and flourishing polity and most able to fight off the temptations of corruption. In this account we find the beginning of a politics of civic virtue privately rather than publicly oriented, an approach to the good citizen given fuller expression in the work of James Pitt.

II

James Pitt, recruited to the ministry's cause a year or two after Arnall, devotes much of his editorial efforts to answering the charges leveled by Bolingbroke in his best polemical works, *Remarks on the History of England* and *A Dissertation upon Parties.* In these essays, first published serially in the *Craftsman,* Bolingbroke pursued the opposition argument that, in strengthening the Court's influence over members of parliament, Walpole and his ministers were actually corrupting England's constitution, by compromising the balance between King, Lords and Commons. The task of rebuttal, assigned to Pitt, was not an easy one. As a matter of fact, Walpole *was* lining up parliamentary supporters through the distribution of favors, places and patronage before and after elections. In addition, Bolingbroke's main thesis – that a parliament inordinately dependent on the Crown spelled political disaster – struck a sympathetic chord with the Norwich schoolmaster.[27]

The problem Pitt faced, then, was to explain why Walpole's cultivation of patronage and place should not be taken as compromising the cherished independence of parliament. His generally successful strategy is to meet and best Bolingbroke on his own ground. Agreeing that Walpole seeks to establish "dependencies" in parliament, Pitt challenges first the claim that "dependencies" are necessarily corrupt and second the assertion that a properly balanced constitution would be rid of them completely. A properly balanced constitution in fact requires the interpenetration of executive and legislative that Bolingbroke identifies as corrupt.[28] Pitt then goes on to attack Bolingbroke's suggestion that laws be passed to prevent any further erosion of parliamentary independence. Laws designed to end the practices by which Whigs built their power will not make citizens more virtuous nor liberty more secure. What corrupt individuals need is an education in virtue, and

27 *London Journal,* no. 673, 20 May 1732.
28 This argument is most famously made by David Hume in his essay, "On the Independency of Parliament," first published in 1741 (David Hume, *Essays, Moral, Political and Literary,* ed. Eugene F. Miller, rev. ed. [Indianapolis, IN: LibertyClassics, 1987], Part I, chapter 6).

the virtues in which they should be educated are, as Arnall argued, the personal ones of temperance, frugality and industry.

It is possible to read recent histories of the political thought of this period as suggesting that Court Whigs were just as convinced of the corruption of Walpole's practices as Bolingbroke. Accepting the picture of history Bolingbroke presented to his contemporaries, yet nevertheless favoring the established Whig regime, they had no choice but to admit that their politics were corrupt and corrupting and to defend the viability and attractiveness of such politics without reference to civic virtue. Pitt's arguments however, like Arnall's, demonstrate that Court Whigs did possess the theoretical resources to respond effectively to Country criticism while still granting civic virtue a prominent role in the contemporary polity. The civic virtue they end up defending is not the publicly oriented one favored by Bolingbroke. But it remains a civic virtue: a set of dispositions that lead citizens to further, through their actions, the public good of a free polity.

Pitt begins his response to Bolingbroke by challenging the idea that placemen in parliament are dependent and, because dependent, necessarily corrupt.[29] We should distinguish, he says, between truly corrupt individuals, who act against their consciences in return for a Court favor and loyal supporters of the government who are justly recompensed for their efforts. "All the Places, Honours, and Preferments which True Whigs enjoy, are not Bribes to induce them to act against their Judgments but Rewards for their Services."[30] To condemn such men as corrupt purely on the basis of a formal political relationship (allegiance to a ministry) strikes Pitt as absurd and offensive. Individuals should be judged virtuous or corrupt on the basis of the policies they promote, not on the company they keep. An association with the ministry does not make one corrupt; voting for a measure that actually undermines citizen liberties does.

Pitt further defends Walpole's cultivation of a Court party by arguing that the exercise of Crown influence actually preserves the constitutional balance Bolingbroke praises so highly. To ask the king to renounce or reduce his right of appointing members of parliament to executive service would, Pitt contends, remove the last barrier that stands between England's constitutional monarchy and a "regal commonwealth." The distribution of patronage and place simply preserves the Court's already fragile independence.

To ground this case for the constitutional validity of places and pensions, Pitt invokes the Harringtonian thesis that power follows property. While Bolingbroke argues that the cultivation of a parliamentary party has given

29 *London Journal,* no. 805, 30 November 1734.
30 *London Journal,* no. 770, 30 March 1734.

the Crown even more power than it enjoyed in the heyday of prerogative, Pitt paints a sorry portrait of a king deprived of almost all his social and political resources.[31] In this newly humbled position, the Court is forced to cling to one or two expedients – such as the disposal of places – to maintain its position in a balanced constitution. The "real power of disposing places is as absolutely necessary to preserve His Majesty's real constitutional Independence, as the Power of giving Money" is to the Commons.[32] In fact, a careful look at the distribution of power and property in the kingdom reveals that the House of Commons, not the Crown, is the primary threat to constitutional balance. By seeking to make the nation's representatives ever more independent of the Crown, the Country interest is doing greater damage to an ideal of constitutional balance than Walpole ever could.[33] With this argument, Pitt counters Bolingbroke's critique of Court influence on its own terms. Far from conceding that Walpole's influence in parliament represents a corruption of the constitution and then arguing that this corruption must somehow be accommodated or embraced, Pitt vigorously denies the impropriety of such behavior and charges the *Craftsman*'s proposals with constitutional corruption.

Having defended in principle Court efforts to secure a loyal parliamentary following, Pitt turns to the question of what can be done to prevent the exercise of influence and patronage from going too far. Arnall had argued that the ministry's dispensing of favors could never count as corrupt or corrupting in itself. Either the largesse distributed rewarded individuals already well disposed to the administration or it bought off representatives and electors corrupted enough in the first place to sell their vote to the higher bidder. Pitt however accepts that under certain circumstances gifts of money or office might prove too great a temptation for men's consciences.[34] To this extent, he admits Bolingbroke is right to be concerned about ministerial influence. But he goes on to argue that the Country interest has completely misconceived both the extent of this threat and what the nation should do about it. In the first place, the wealth and property already enjoyed by the Commons make it unlikely that many persons will succumb to corrupt temptation, actually abandoning their political principles for govern-

31 "The material foundation of kingly government being removed (which consists in real strength arising from Lands, and the Dependencies created by Tenures) the monarchy now stands on a more precarious and popular Foundation" (*London Journal*, no. 768, 16 March 1734).
32 *London Journal*, no. 796, 28 September 1734.
33 For other versions of this argument see *London Journal*, no. 631, 28 August 1731; no. 765, 23 February 1734; *Daily Gazetteer*, no. 48, 23 August 1735. See also Benjamin Hoadly's speech reported in the *London Journal*, no. 621, 19 June 1731.
34 *London Journal*, no. 673, 20 May 1732.

ment favors. Secondly, the best way to guard against such infrequent eventualities is not the place bill so rabidly sought by the Country interest (banning both civil servants and military officers from sitting in parliament) but the cultivation of what Pitt calls private virtue. Only the personal virtues of temperance and industry, thrift and honesty can effectively safeguard the nation and its liberties from Crown influence.

In making this argument, Pitt begins by challenging Bolingbroke's claim that the Whigs' financial revolution has created a generation of statesmen ripe for corruption. In the *Dissertation upon Parties,* Bolingbroke advances the argument that the rise of new "monied men" to positions of power and influence places an unbearable strain on the political virtue of the established gentry. Unable to tolerate the preeminence of such parvenus, they abandon their Country principles and strike corrupt bargains with a power-hungry Court simply to regain some of their former status.[35] Pitt rightly dismisses this scenario as completely implausible. It is, he says, "absolutely unreasonable to insinuate that the Gentlemen of England who have large Estates, Families and Interest in the Kingdom, will give up the Liberties of their Country, for the Sake of little Precarious Places."[36] Members of parliament are simply too well off under current conditions of liberty to risk their "own Estates and Interest in the Country" for some momentary favors of an ill-designing ministry.[37] They cooperate with Walpole's ministry because they approve of its policies. In suggesting otherwise, Bolingbroke has completely misrepresented the material and psychological resources of England's leading families.[38]

Are English citizens then immune to corruption? Pitt's writings argue not for this unlikely possibility but for a better understanding of the source of corruption and the strategy for containing it. The true threat to the gentry's morals and the nation's liberties is not the advent of monied men in the corridors of power but that old republican nemesis, luxury. Like Arnall, Pitt explains that "the cause of Corruption (if 'tis more general than it used to be) is Luxury and Vanity, introduced by the general Wealth diffused through the Kingdom within these 40 or 50 Years."[39] Here Pitt offers a genealogy of moral corruption that reaffirms, against Bolingbroke's innovations, the conventional civic humanist or classical republican understanding of its roots. It is not a new class of people or a new form of wealth that threatens the

---

35 See Bolingbroke, *Works,* II, 165–6, as well as the discussion in chapter 5.
36 *London Journal,* no. 673, 20 May 1732.
37 *London Journal,* no. 799, 19 October 1734.
38 See also *London Journal,* no. 801, 2 November 1734; no. 805, 30 November 1734; no. 814, 8 February 1735 and William Arnall's contribution to the *Free Briton,* no. 119, 9 March 1732.
39 *London Journal,* no. 832, 14 June 1735.

morals of the nation, but the age-old problem of money and desire. Men whose extravagant style of life has left them bankrupt, indebted or simply thirsty for ever more pleasures will be easy prey for a Crown eager to buy converts. These men alone will be "so weak or so wicked as for the Sake of a temporary precarious Possession, to part with a more certain, valuable and lasting good."[40]

But if luxury and the necessity it brings are the true sources of corruption, the place bills championed by the Country party as the best preventive to corruption are of little real help in warding it off. These place bills, proposed in almost every parliamentary session, were intended to prevent undue ministerial influence in parliament by banning individuals who held government and military offices from sitting there.[41] But, says Pitt, a place bill would eliminate only a few of the pressures that invite corrupt collusion between members of parliament and the Court. All governments must appoint someone to fill executive offices and these officeholders must be supplied with funds – occasions that can always be turned into opportunities for corruption.[42] By limiting the pool of members of parliament from which the Court might draw its helpers, the *Craftsman* simply shifts the power of appointment and thus influence to parliament, an expedient which, in strengthening parliament against the Crown, Pitt has shown to be unconstitutional.

In addition, corruption is not simply a function of places and pensions that parliament may allow or withhold, but of dependence. And the feeling or experience of dependence cannot be legislated away.

Every Man who has more Understanding, Sagacity or Money than his Neighbor, has it in his power to influence; and this Power of influencing will eternally remain, unless a way is found out to exclude all Man's Capacities, Passions, Appetites, Desires ... and also to level their Fortunes.[43]

Thus Pitt argues that no law in itself could completely protect the nation's representatives from unseemly political pressure. The exercise of influence can occur on too many levels and in too many ways to be contained by legislative fiat alone.

In fact, Pitt argues, laws which pretend to protect us from our own corrupt dispositions go beyond the bounds of legitimate state regulation.

The End and Design of Government is not to keep us from hurting ourselves but to keep others from hurting us ... [Government] can do nothing but secure us against

40 *London Journal,* no. 801, 2 November 1734.
41 For the legislative history of place bills, see chapter 2, note 22.
42 *London Journal,* no. 820, 22 March 1735.
43 *Daily Gazetteer,* no. 222, 13 March 1736.

the violence of wicked Men; but it cannot secure [us] against the Arts of other Men, nor against ourselves.[44]

Corruption, Pitt insists, is a moral problem; it rests not in specific material opportunities to trade votes for favors (which when identified, parliament might legislate against) but in the disposition to accept such trades. If there are "any Men in the kingdom so profligate to sell their Freedom: who can help it?" That individual will find a way to do so whatever legislation exists.[45] Given the fact that "Men may be corrupt in so many ways and so secretly, that 'tis impossible Human Laws shall ever reach them," law is neither an appropriate nor adequate medium through which to prevent citizens from selling their votes.[46] Pitt thus argues for an understanding of the nature and sources of corruption that renders the Country's favorite legislative cure – the place bill – profoundly suspect.

The only effective way to prevent the exercise of the corrupt influence that both Pitt and the opposition fear is a concerted effort to promote personal virtue. "Let the People of England then ... get their Livings by Industry, and never exceed the limits of their private Fortunes, and all complaints of venality and Corruption will fall to the Ground."[47] Industrious individuals living within their incomes will simply not fall prey to the schemes of designing politicians. Like Arnall, Pitt argues that the "Danger to our Liberty" lies not in the trading of pensions and places per se but in "luxury, idleness, extravagance" – those character traits that can make men necessitous enough to seek a corrupt dependence.[48] By rooting the problem of political corruption in these personal flaws, Pitt can both acknowledge a danger of corruption and suggest a solution for it without restricting the exercise of Walpole's influence: citizen, heal thyself. As he writes in a 1736 essay, "There is no sure Method, therefore, of preventing Corruption, but by preventing Necessity ... Let them secure private Virtue and they will see all public Virtue rise out of it."[49]

Pitt's effort to discredit the place bill does not lead him to abandon the search for citizen virtue. Rather, he recasts his contemporaries' understanding of what that virtue is. The best citizens, those most able to resist corrupt

---

44 *Daily Gazetteer,* no. 120, 15 November 1735.
45 *Daily Gazetteer,* no. 42, 16 August 1735.
46 *London Journal,* no. 673, 20 May 1732. See also *London Journal,* no. 770, 30 March 1734: "Nor is it possible to invent or frame Laws that will keep Men steadily to the Practice of Wisdom and Virtue ... It is not in the power of Men, or the strongest Laws that ever were or can be invented to purify the Heart, and make a Community religious and virtuous"; *London Journal,* no. 666, 1 April 1732; *Daily Gazetteer,* no. 36, 9 August 1735.
47 *Daily Gazetteer,* no. 120, 15 November 1735.
48 *Daily Gazetteer,* no. 228, 20 March 1736.
49 *Daily Gazetteer,* no. 222, 13 March 1736.

temptations, express in their personal life those qualities that temper the pursuit of luxury and prevent the temptations of necessity. Pitt urges the development of such personal virtues by pointing to their political profit: "If we would ... manage our own Passions and live within our Fortunes, it would be out of the Power of the most designing Government to hurt us."[50] For Bolingbroke, the exercise of civic virtue meant defending the balanced constitution, preserving the citizenry's independence and the nation's liberty by halting the Whigs' corrupt solicitation of votes and supporters. This account of citizen virtue was obviously anathema to Pitt; his professional brief was to defend the Court's exercise of influence against opposition efforts to cut it off. But in rejecting Bolingbroke's account of the good citizen, Pitt does not abandon the idea of virtue altogether. By emphasizing a different root of corruption (luxury not loss of autonomy), Pitt, like Arnall, comes up with a different, and more privately oriented, account of what makes the citizen virtuous. Combating the consequences of luxury does not require the public virtues of love of country, love of constitution, devotion to the public good, but rather the exercise of "Frugality and Industry" in one's private life.[51] These personal virtues, already recognized as excellences of moral character, become the civic virtues of the contemporary populace as well.

But does this account represent a true transformation of *civic* virtue? One could argue that Pitt gives up on political virtue altogether, hoping that moral virtues alone will solve England's problems. But qualities usually considered as morally virtuous can be recommended from two perspectives: first, as the qualities necessary to make a good human being and second, as the qualities necessary to make the individual a good citizen. If frugality, industry, temperance, honesty are recommended for this second end they properly receive the name of political virtues. And if they are recommended as the means by which to preserve a civic mode of life, at least as one was understood in the eighteenth century, they are properly denominated civic virtues.[52] Both Pitt and Arnall intend their version of citizen virtue to accomplish precisely the same end as Bolingbroke's more publicly oriented version and as such it does count as civic virtue, although one that is privately rather than publicly oriented.

Thus Pitt proposes a civic renewal that relies neither on a selfless love of country nor on Bolingbroke's "love of the constitution" but on those other virtues familiar to classical republicanism: temperance and frugality. But rather than expecting such dispositions to be expressed exclusively in the

---

50 *London Journal*, no. 483, 2 November 1728.
51 *London Journal*, no. 770, 30 March 1734.
52 See the discussion in chapter 1.

public realm, Pitt stresses the political benefits of their private exercise. Individuals must be "taught from Infancy to refuse (there lies the Secret) whatever is hurtful in its consequences though it gives present pleasure; it must be done by good Education, Family Government, School-Government, and University-Government... [they must be] early inured and steeled to Temperance and Industry."[53] It is not the statesman who must be frugal with the nation's treasury or the citizen temperate in public debate, but the gentleman, merchant and householder who must express such qualities in their quotidian endeavors. Honesty, industry, frugality will prevent individuals from overextending their financial resources and, living therefore within their means, they will be able to live as well within their conscience.[54] Thus the temptations to public corruption will be eliminated and political liberty secured.

Again, such recommendations represent the transformation, not the abandonment, of civic virtue. To remain free, prosperous, stable and secure, the good state must have virtuous citizens. Nothing else (here Pitt remains wedded to the republican ethos) can hold the naturally corrupting side of government power in check. But defending against corruption and preserving public liberty no longer requires citizens consciously devoted to seeking public welfare. Rather "the only way to prevent Corruption" and preserve public liberty, he says, "is a virtuous Education, good Examples, Strict Order and Government in Families, breeding up Children to Business, and inuring them to Temperance and Labour."[55] Individuals raised in the disciplined virtues of good household and business management will have all the qualities necessary to make them good citizens.

It is perhaps tempting to see the accounts set forth by Pitt and Arnall as an early liberal challenge to the republican politics of public virtue. Against Bolingbroke's classical ideal of the citizen, engaged in autonomous deliberation about the public good, Court Whigs champion the typically bourgeois excellences of frugality and industry, privileging the private over the public sphere for the expression of such virtue. In their appreciation of the private realm and their advocacy of qualities valued in commercial societies, Pitt and Arnall can indeed seem like spokesmen for a new sort of polity that places the priorities of civil society over that of a political *vita activa*. But it is a mistake, I think, in tracing the transformation of virtue, to engage in this sort of liberal versus republican labeling game.

Both Cato and the Court Whigs conceive of civic virtue as privately rather

53 *London Journal,* no. 832, 14 June 1735.
54 So, for the individual living within his fortune, "nothing can corrupt him, for there's nothing to work upon" (*London Journal,* no. 606, 13 March 1731).
55 *London Journal,* no. 666, 1 April 1732.

than publicly oriented. But none of them can properly be described as championing a liberal approach to politics over and against a republican one. In fact, Cato, Pitt and Arnall all ground their politics in assumptions typical of the republican or civic humanist tradition: liberty remains the primary political good, corruption is the greatest threat to its achievement, and the best safeguard against corruption is the civic virtue of the citizens. What changes is not their commitment to virtue but the way in which virtue is conceived. Working within a fundamentally republican framework, they spin out, in different ways and for different reasons, alternatives to the standard politics of public virtue.

It is certainly possible to argue that *Cato's Letters* contains a more attractive and indeed more political account of civic virtue than the one found in the works of Pitt and Arnall. Cato's virtuous citizen remains active in the public sphere, protesting policies that displease him, clamoring for judgment against those who have betrayed the common weal. The image Pitt and Arnall offer of the good citizen is altogether more passive – and for those who equate "civic" with participation, quite alien. How can one express or possess civic virtue simply by being frugal, industrious, temperate? At some point these character traits do lose their status as civic virtues and become simply the qualities that help individuals get along in a commercial world. My point however is that, for better or worse, Court Whigs fasten upon them as the qualities that make individuals responsible public actors, that sustain them in the autonomy necessary for proper deliberation on the public good.

Civic virtue, say Pitt and Arnall, consists in those qualities that help individuals uphold public liberty, individual freedom and good government in the face of the various threats to these goods that necessarily arise in any polity. They agree with their Country opponents that one of the greatest contemporary dangers to virtue and good government is corrupt influence: the inducement of vulnerable individuals, through favors and patronage, to support the government against their considered convictions. But the qualities of character that protect most effectively against this threat are not dispositions oriented or directed towards the public: a love of country or constitution, a tendency to put public good over private interest. Rather the most potent prophylactics for corruption of this sort, and thus the civic virtues most needed in the Augustan polity, are qualities that keep one's private life in order, leaving one independent enough (because not financially necessitous) to participate responsibly in the public realm.

7

◁══════════════════════════════════════▷

A world without virtue: Mandeville's
social and political thought

Both Cato and the Court Whigs find themselves at odds with one version or another of what I have called the republican politics of public virtue. But they do not for this reason abandon civic virtue altogether, nor do they seek to explain how the polity might survive and flourish without excellences of the citizen. For the first attempt in this period to ground the good state independently of citizen virtue, civic or otherwise, we must look not to these authors, nor to others whose commitments might at times seem to merit the name liberal, but to the Augustinian politics of Bernard Mandeville.

Bernard Mandeville's *Fable of the Bees* was the first work of the eighteenth century to provide a comprehensive challenge to the various politics of virtue reviewed in the earlier chapters, and Mandeville's contemporaries fumed at its provocative conclusions. Its contents so scandalized a Middlesex Grand Jury that in 1723 they requested the Sheriff of London to take legal action against its publisher, Edmund Parker.[1] The *Fable*, complained the Grand Jury, recommends "Luxury, Avarice, Pride and all kinds of Vices, as being necessary to Public Welfare" and portrays "Religion and Virtue as prejudicial to Society, and detrimental to the State."[2] This public rebuke naturally attracted a curious, and then outraged, audience for the new edition of a work that when first printed received almost no public notice at all.[3] Far from assuring the book's demise, the Grand Jury's presentment

---

1 The text of the Grand Jury's presentment is in Bernard Mandeville, *The Fable of the Bees: or, Private Vices, Publick Benefits* and *The Fable of the Bees, Part II,* ed. F. B. Kaye, 2 v. (Oxford: Clarendon Press, [1723 and 1729] 1924), I, 383–6. The circumstances surrounding it are discussed in W. A. Speck, "Bernard Mandeville and the Middlesex Grand Jury," *Eighteenth-Century Studies* 11 (1978): 362–74.
2 Mandeville, *Fable,* I, 385.
3 The *Fable* was first advertised in the *Post Boy,* 1–3 July 1714 as "just published." Another edition was advertised in the *Post Man,* 4–7 December 1714 (*Fable,* I, xxxii). Neither

simply provided the prelude to a barrage of criticism that quickly established the *Fable* as one of the most controversial works of its time.[4]

I

The *Fable*'s anonymous author, Bernard Mandeville, was a Dutch physician educated at Leyden, who had settled in England sometime in the 1690s. He enjoyed a substantial medical practice,[5] the patronage of a powerful Whig,[6] and a keen delight in exposing the social pretensions of his adopted

edition attracted much attention. The second edition was advertised as "just published" in the *Daily Post,* 10 April 1723. The Grand Jury presentment was in July. Kaye, who undertook an extensive search of contemporary criticism, found no references to the *Fable* either in published works or private correspondence prior to 1723 (*ibid.,* cxiv). J. A. W. Gunn has more recently noted several oblique references among writers sympathetic to the Court (*Beyond Liberty and Property: The Process of Self-Recognition in Eighteenth-Century Political Thought* [Kingston and Montreal: McGill-Queens University Press, 1983], 106–7).

4 Contemporary criticism of the work came from clerics, moral philosophers, economists and cultural critics. Kaye compiled an annotated list of references to Mandeville's work throughout the eighteenth and nineteenth centuries as well as a summary of the major contemporary criticisms (*Fable,* II, 401–53). One of the few references he missed is one of the earliest (Robert Burrow, *Civil Society and Government Vindicated from the Charge of being Founded on, and Preserv'd by, Dishonest Arts . . .* [London, 1723]). The introduction to John Disney, *A View of Antient Laws against Immorality and Profaneness* (Cambridge, 1729) also contains a lengthy rebuke to the *Fable*'s doctrine not cited by Kaye. See also the citations in Gunn, *Beyond Liberty and Property,* 106–7.

For the assessment of the *Fable* as one of the century's most controversial works, see I, cxlvi and F. A. Hayek, "Dr. Bernard Mandeville," *Proceedings of the British Academy* 52 (1966), 128. Contemporary estimates include Richard Fiddes's, who credited the *Fable* with a "pretty brisk Circulation" (*A General Treatise of Morality* [London, 1724], xi). Mandeville himself wrote of the Grand Jury's presentment, "But this being now-a-Days the wrongest Way in the World to stifle Books, it made it more known and encreas'd the Sale of it" (*A Letter to Dion,* ed. Bonamy Dobrée [Liverpool: University Press of Liverpool (1732) 1954], 29).

Another indication of the *Fable*'s influence is the fact that its epigraph, "Private Vices, Publick Benefits," passed into the language as an excuse for the practice of petty immorality. Witness the following exchange from Hannah More's repository tract, "History of Mr. Fantom, the New-Fashioned Philosopher," first published in the 1790s. Mr. Fantom has just rebuked his servant William for drunkenness, who replies, "Why sir . . . you are a philosopher you know; and I have often overheard you say to your company, that private vices are public benefits; and so I thought that getting drunk was as pleasant a way of doing good to the public as any" (Hannah More, *Works* [London: T. Caddell, 1830], III, 28–9). I am indebted to Susan Pedersen for this reference.

5 Kaye suggests that "positive evidence of Mandeville's [professional] status is contained in a letter from him to Sir Hans Sloane, perhaps the leading physician of the day. This letter shows Mandeville in consultation with the famous court physician and on terms of easy familiarity with him" (*Fable,* I, xxvi). Mandeville also published a respected *Treatise on the Hypochondriack and Hysterick Passions* (London, 1711).

6 The Whig in question was Thomas Parker, one of the managers at the Sacheverell trial, 1710; Lord Chief Justice and member of the Privy Council, 1710–18; Lord Chancellor, 1718–25 (resigned after charges of embezzlement); created Earl of Macclesfield, 1729. For contemporary accounts of this friendship, see *Fable,* I, xxvi, note 4.

countrymen. The *Fable,* a curious amalgam of whimsical satire, skeptical moral philosophy and rigorous economic theory, takes direct aim at what, for Mandeville, was a particularly objectionable self-deception: the cheerful insistence of some English moralists and theologians that the goods of civil society – comfort, prosperity, safety, civility, even sociability itself – were obtained through the exercise of human virtue, rather than its sacrifice. When first published (1714), *The Fable of the Bees* comprised a poem, "The Grumbling Hive," keyed to a series of twenty-two explanatory Remarks and prefaced by "An Enquiry into the Origin of Moral Virtue." The second edition (1723) added a critique of Shaftesbury's *Characteristics* ("A Search into the Nature of Society"), several more Remarks and an attack on charity-schools.[7]

The poem, originally issued separately in 1705, relates the decline and fall of a flourishing beehive that has banished vice and fraud from its community.[8] Supported by the accompanying Remarks, it wittily argues that a nation's strength, stability and prosperity depend upon its having a citizenry swamped in the vices of luxury, avarice, pride and prodigality. This argument, while controversial, was hardly original. But by stretching the definition of "private vices" to include not only the seven deadly sins but selfish passions as well, Mandeville goes on to argue that all moral and social achievements depend importantly on the indulgence of vice. Everything contemporary moralists attribute to the operation of virtue – from national prosperity to a gentleman's honor – is more accurately explained, Mandeville argues, as a particular if convoluted manifestation of self-love. Sociability, courage, lawfulness, politeness, romantic love – all are attributable in some way to man's pride and "self-liking." Seventeenth-century French moralists had similarly probed the "deceitfulness of human virtues" in the individual's moral life; Mandeville extends their arguments about the ubiquity of self-love to cover all spheres of human experience.[9]

---

7 The charity-schools, providing a rudimentary education and vocational training for the children of the poor, were a favorite philanthropy of Anglicans. Mandeville's intemperate sally against this sacrosanct project accounted for much of the 1723 edition's immediate infamy (Speck, "Mandeville," 366–7). John Thorold, who criticizes the *Fable* from an orthodox Christian perspective, spends a fifth of his rebuttal defending charity-schools (*A Short Examination of the Notions Advanc'd in a (Late) Book, Intituled, The Fable of the Bees* [London, 1726], 31–9).

8 The poem began life on 2 April 1705 as a sixpenny quarto of 26 pages (*Fable,* I, xxxiii). It proved popular enough to be "soon after Pirated [and] cry'd about the Streets in a Half-Penny Sheet" of four pages (*Fable,* I, 4).

9 *The Deceitfulness of Human Virtues* (London, 1706) is the title of the English translation of Jacques Esprit's 1678 moral treatise, *La Fausseté des Vertus Humains.* Mandeville's debt to seventeenth-century French moral philosophy is noted, and annotated, by Kaye, who cites Pascal, La Rochefoucauld, Fontenelle, Pierre Bayle, Jacques Esprit, Pierre Nicole and Jacques Abbadie among others as representative authors in this tradition. See the discussion and

He first makes this case in the two essays included in *The Fable of the Bees* (the "Enquiry into the Origin of Moral Virtue" and the "Search into the Nature of Society"), expanding the range of public benefits achieved by private vices to include both moral virtues, as conventionally understood, and the basic elements of man's sociability. He then pursues this argument in two sequels, *The Fable of the Bees, Part II* (1729) and *An Enquiry into the Origin of Honour...* (1732), both written as dialogues between Cleomenes, a supporter of Mandeville, and his cultivated friend Horatio, an admirer of Shaftesbury. *The Fable of the Bees, Part II* sets out in greater detail Mandeville's version of the rise of civil society and his challenge to Shaftesbury's moral theory. The *Enquiry* discusses the suspect genesis of the "virtues" of honor and courage and appends an attack on the modern church's corruption of Christian doctrine. Like the *Fable* itself, these books portray the achievements of civilized nations and peoples solely as the consequence of society's artful manipulation of human weaknesses.[10]

Mandeville calls the target of his books "the Modern Deists and all the Beau Monde."[11] This category includes all those among his contemporaries who not only consider humans naturally virtuous but hold that this virtue advances private interest and public good in tandem. Chief among the offending philosophers is the third Earl of Shaftesbury, whose collected essays on moral theory (*Characteristics of Men, Manners, Opinions, Times, etc.* [1711]) were warmly received a few years before the *Fable*'s first edition.[12]

notes at *Fable,* I, lxx–xciv as well as the index entry at II, 456–7. For a contemporary observation of the link between Mandeville and these French writers, see George Bluet, *An Enquiry Whether a General Practice of Virtue Tends to the Wealth or Poverty, Benefit or Disadvantage of a People* (London, 1725), preface.

10 Although *The Fable of the Bees* is the best known of Mandeville's works, Mandeville pursued his distinctive brand of moral and social criticism in a number of other publications as well. Several of the *Fable*'s themes are anticipated in Mandeville's contributions to the weekly *Female Tatler,* (1709–10), while his mischievous defense of prostitution, already discussed in chapter 3, is elaborated in *A Modest Defense of Publick Stews* (1724). *The Virgin Unmask'd* (1710), *The Mischiefs to be Expected from a Whig Government* (1714) and *Free Thoughts on Religion, the Church, and Natural Happiness* (1720) offer more direct political commentary with a marked Whig bias. *A Letter to Dion* (1732) recapitulates the *Fable*'s themes in a spirited response to Bishop Berkeley's attack (*Alciphron or the Minute Philosopher,* in George Berkeley, *Works,* ed. A. A. Luce and T. E. Jessop [London: Thames Nelson and Sons Ltd., 1950]).

11 Mandeville, *Fable,* II, 102.

12 M. M. Goldsmith in analyzing Mandeville's contributions to the *Female Tatler* (1709) suggests that it may have been Richard Steele's *Tatler* that first "stung Mandeville... into expounding a general account of society contrary to the theory of public and private virtue" (*Private Vices, Public Benefits: Bernard Mandeville's Social and Poltical Thought* [Cambridge University Press, 1985], 37). By 1723 however, Shaftesbury is Mandeville's primary target, while "the Incomparable Sir Richard Steele" receives more subdued, if still ironic, treatment (*Fable,* I, 52). Mandeville continues his attack on the *Characteristics* at devastating length in the *Fable, Part II.* The first dialogue in particular offers a masterful send-up of

Of the *Characteristics* Mandeville writes, "The attentive Reader . . . will soon perceive that two Systems cannot be more opposite than his Lordship's and mine." What Mandeville objects to in moral theories such as Shaftesbury's are their false notions that virtue is inseparably connected to public happiness and that individuals can achieve this virtue "without any Trouble or Violence upon themselves."[13] In Mandeville's opinion, such roseate propositions bowdlerize human nature and sugarcoat the source of public good.

The Fable of the Bees argues that virtue properly understood is the exception, not the rule, of human experience. "To perform a meritorious Action," Mandeville writes, "it is not sufficient barely to conquer a Passion, unless it likewise be done from a laudable Principle . . . [i.e.] a rational Ambition of being Good." Such rational action is beyond the powers of almost everyone because "it is impossible that Man, mere fallen Man, should act with any other View but to please himself."[14] Here Mandeville adopts an orthodox Christian perspective: without the intervention of preternatural grace, humans must be considered irredeemably selfish and thus inevitably lacking in virtue. This pessimistic understanding of human nature banishes not only true "rational" virtue as beyond the capacities of corrupt man but also the inborn "benevolence" Shaftesbury claimed for humanity. Such other-regarding affections, according to Mandeville, simply do not exist.

For these reasons Mandeville rejects the moral doctrines collectively known as philosophical optimism. Shaftesbury and his ilk are guilty not only of transmogrifying the rank, raw passions of an animal nature into benevolent affections. They compound their sin by calling these nonexistent benevolent affections "virtue" and portraying this virtue as the basis of society.

Mandeville intends his social theory as a bracing corrective to this panglossian illusion. Its primary concern is to show that the benevolent and virtuous affections cherished by philosophical optimists as the bedrock of society are both illusory and superfluous. But in demonstrating that the imaginary virtue of these moralists makes no contribution to the welfare of the community, Mandeville also concedes – indeed, insists on – the political and social irrelevance of true virtue, virtue grounded in the rational suppression of selfish passions. It turns out, in fact, that our society coheres, our polity flourishes, not through any excellences of character on the part of citizen or statesman but from an intricate system of pressure, deception and education that, unknown to those it manipulates, places selfish passions at

"the lovely System of Lord Shaftsbury [sic]" which, Mandeville says, "judge[s] of Men's Actions . . . in a Manner diametrically opposed to that of *The Fable of the Bees*" (*Fable,* II, 43).

13 Mandeville, *Fable,* I, 324, 323.

14 *Ibid.,* 260, 348.

the service of common good. Where philosophical optimists extol the value of virtue, Mandeville insists on the efficacy of sin, selfishness and "natural evil," summarizing his doctrine in the infamous subtitle, "Private Vices, Publick Benefits."

It is difficult to determine the spirit in which Mandeville outlines this paradox of the modern world. Mandeville himself claims that his work is not morally subversive. "When I say that Societies cannot be rais'd to Wealth and Power, and the Top of Earthly Glory without Vices, I don't think that by so saying I bid Men be Vicious . . . If I have shewn the way to worldly Greatness, I have always without Hesitation preferr'd the Road that leads to Virtue."[15] Contemporary readers suspected the sincerity of this declaration and accused Mandeville of setting an impossibly high standard of virtue in order that people might indulge all the more guiltlessly in vice. Thus George Bluet, after comparing Mandeville to the moral skeptic Jacques Esprit and to the "Duke of Rochefocault," complained, "He has much outdone the Original. It is not only that most things are not virtuous which the World takes for such, but the Thing itself, we are told, is ridiculous in theory and mischievous in Practice."[16] More recently, scholars have argued that Mandeville placed his skepticism about virtue at the service of the Whig administration, offering his theory of the public benefits of private vices in order to defend "the Court and its luxury" from Country critics.[17]

Neither of those approaches adequately captures the ambiguity of Mandeville's case for the virtue-less polity. Mandeville affirms the irrelevance of virtue to the good polity not for partisan political reasons nor for subversive moral ones. His conclusions derive instead from following out the implications of a proposition most compellingly formulated by Augustine: natural man is constitutionally incapable of virtue's achievement. Mandeville argues, as did the fifth-century bishop, that while virtue is real, it is not and never was of this world. For Mandeville, any adequate explanation of social phenomena must begin with this truth, sketching the for-

15 *Ibid.,* 231.
16 Bluet, *Enquiry,* preface.
17 Gunn, *Beyond Liberty and Property,* 106. See also Isaac Kramnick, *Bolingbroke and His Circle: The Politics of Nostalgia in the Age of Walpole* (Cambridge: Harvard University Press, 1968), 201–4. Much of the case for Mandeville as a Court Whig rests on the contention that Court Whig writers, like Mandeville, reject the need for or possibility of virtue in the modern polity. But, as I argue in chapter 6, Court Whigs generally do not take this line. It should also be noted that few politicians would welcome the sort of "defense" of their activities that Mandeville's *Fable* provides. Mandeville's more strictly political writings are well dealt with in H. T. Dickinson, "The Politics of Bernard Mandeville," in Irwin Primer, ed., *Mandeville Studies: New Explorations in the Art and Thought of Bernard Mandeville* (The Hague: Martinus Nijhoff, 1975), and Goldsmith, *Private Vices, Public Benefits.* In these works, a case for Court Whig sympathies can be better made.

tunes of civil society by reference to the selfish passions alone. We must understand our world as unalterably profane, a *civitas terrena* in which true virtue can find no purchase or purpose, although it rises to heights of glory and power as great as republican Rome's.[18] This conviction that we must accept a vast gulf between worldly success and otherworldly virtue informs the whole of Mandeville's work. The unsettling nature of its presentation comes from the fact that, unlike Augustine, Mandeville writes as a contented resident of the City of Man – accepting, indeed celebrating, a world in which "a most beautiful Superstructure may be rais'd upon a rotten and despicable Foundation."[19]

The task that Mandeville sets himself, as a more or less renegade disciple of Augustine, is to explain the complex phenomena of social experience solely in terms of the individual's most basic selfish impulses. To this end, he takes a certain perverse pleasure in examining the disreputable sources of highly praised behavior (from a young girl's chastity to a soldier's courage) and demonstrating the redeeming features of social and moral evil (from prostitution to theft and miserliness).[20] But the centerpiece of Mandeville's attack on the philosophical optimist understanding of the world is his demonstration of the selfish sources of national prosperity, personal morality and human sociability. In this demonstration Mandeville preserves intact the qualities contemporaries consider intrinsic to the good state: the citizens of his polity are as sociable, civil and industrious as any philosophical optimist could wish. But what Shaftesbury attributes to virtue, Mandeville credits to the asocial passions. In detailing the way in which such "private vices" produce "publick benefits," Mandeville sketches the outline and explains the resiliency of a polity that thrives without the benefit of any sort of virtue, civic or moral.

The most familiar and straightforward example of how vices come to benefit a society concerns the prosperity of "great Trading nations." Building on the uncontroversial premise that a nation's prosperity depends on a large populace gainfully employed, Mandeville wittily sustains his contention that asocial appetites – in particular, the desire to outdo one's neighbor and live ever more comfortably – best create the consumer demand that fuels a modern economy. Because "Humility, Content, Meekness" and modesty are virtues that stifle desire, "they may render a small Nation Good, but they can never make a Great one."[21] Frugality likewise is "a mean starving Virtue . . .

18 Cf. Augustine, *The City of God,* tr. Marcus Dods (New York: Modern Library, 1950), esp. Book V, sections 13–22. See also Herbert A. Deane, *The Political and Social Ideas of St. Augustine* (New York: Columbia University Press, 1963), chapters 1–4.
19 Mandeville, *Fable,* II, 64.
20 See Remarks C, R, H, B and I respectively.
21 Mandeville, *Fable,* I, 228, 367.

that employs no Hands, and therefore [is] very useless in a trading Country."
Instead of thriving on the goodness of human beings, the economy draws its
strength from their weaknesses: "Pride and Luxury are the great Promoters
of Trade."[22]

This link between vices and prosperity was a familiar one to political
economists. Why then did Mandeville's argument so greatly distress contemporary moralists?[23] One reason may be that political economists, in their
dispassionate observation of the current source of England's wealth, did not
particularly threaten the moralists' assumption that in a better world economic prosperity and a virtuous citizenry might go hand in hand.
Mandeville's work allowed none of this equivocation. "Great Wealth and
Foreign Treasure will ever scorn to come among Men, unless you'll admit
their inseparable Companions, Avarice and Luxury: Where Trade is considerable Fraud will intrude."[24] Mandeville's claim is not only that England currently lacks the virtues praised by his contemporaries, but that their cultivation will harm, not help, national welfare. His predecessors did not go out of
their way to make this point. Mandeville positively revels in his argument
that exchanging avarice, pride and luxury for the virtues of frugality and
temperance will destroy the conditions for national prosperity.

Mandeville does not however recommend unrestrained gratification of a
nation's vices as the route to public riches. Rather he insists that what
opponents characterize as a moral problem – a taste for luxury that impover-
ishes the body politic, enervates the populace and corrupts statesmen – is in
reality a political one. "These are indeed terrible Things," Mandeville says,
"but what is put to the Account of Luxury belongs to Male-Administration
[sic] and is the Fault of bad Politicks." As long as politicians "keep a watchful
Eye over the Balance of Trade in general," the populace may indulge in
foreign luxury as much as they wish.[25] Pitt's prescription for the problem of
luxury was a citizenry schooled in the virtues of self-restraint. Mandeville
argues that as long as trade policies assure that the state as a whole does not
import more than it exports, the citizenry's selfishness and greed may be
safely indulged.

22 *Ibid.,* 104–5, 67.
23 Contemporary critiques that attacked Mandeville's economics include Bluet, *Enquiry,* sections 1 and 3; Archibald Campbell, *An Enquiry into the Original of Moral Virtue* (London,
1728), Treatise III, esp. 488; Francis Hutcheson, Letters in the *Dublin Journal* (1726) in
Reflections upon Laughter and Remarks upon the Fable of the Bees (Glasgow, 1750),
Letter I, esp. 53. Contemporary arguments similar to Mandeville's are described in Joyce
Appleby, *Economic Thought and Ideology in Seventeenth-Century England* (Princeton:
Princeton University Press, 1978), 114–15, 169–71, 256–8.
24 Mandeville, *Fable,* I, 185.
25 *Ibid.,* 115, 116.

II

Demonstrating that national prosperity is best secured not by the practice of virtue but by the satisfaction of asocial passions is Mandeville's easiest task. But trade alone does not a polity make. For Mandeville to explain the entirety of civil relations by means of asocial passions, he has also to show the vicious sources of morality, good manners and honorable behavior. Mandeville has little to say directly about civic virtue or its place in the polity. But if Mandeville succeeds in grounding these social practices independently of benevolent affections, he will have constructed a society of individuals whose psychology is such as to make any sort of virtue, public or private, political or moral, impossible. In these circumstances, the polity does not cohere or thrive because of the virtues of the citizens but because its leaders effectively manage what is most unvirtuous about them.

The philosophical optimists held that people are virtuous because it is their nature to be so – a natural benevolence,[26] an inborn "moral sense,"[27] an abundance of social affections are all suggested as the basis of the moral behavior of civilized beings. Mandeville argues, against this theory, that moral virtue, or what passes for moral virtue in this world, is not a product of nature or reason but of guile, self-deception and the most fundamental animal passions. Just as luxury and avarice sustain modern society's economic activity, the vices of pride and self-love (not the workings of nature and reason) secure the moral basis of community.

Mandeville suggests two ways in which people learn what moral virtue is. The first is through "True Religion"; Christianity teaches us that virtue requires conquering our corrupt passions, either rationally, or more effectively, through grace.[28] Mandeville dwells only momentarily on this source of moral knowledge in the "Enquiry." His focus is on how the majority of the world's population, deprived of or uninterested in God's revelation, manage to formulate a conception of virtue and approximate their practice to it.

---

26 See for example Anthony Ashley Cooper, Third Earl of Shaftesbury, *Characteristics of Men, Manners, Opinions, Times, etc.*, ed. John M. Robertson (Gloucester, MA: Peter Smith, [1711] 1963), I, 258 and Henry Grove, *Spectator*, no. 588, 1 September 1714. Stanley Grean, *Shaftesbury's Philosophy of Religion and Ethics* (Athens: Ohio University Press, 1967), chapter 12 provides a careful reconstruction of Shaftesbury's somewhat fuzzy doctrine of virtue. Grove presents his case for a natural "principle of benevolence" in opposition to the philosophies of Epicurus and Hobbes; it is worth noting however that the *Fable*'s first edition was published only two months prior to Grove's essay.

27 Francis Hutcheson, *An Inquiry into the Original of our Ideas of Beauty and Virtue; in Two Treatises. In Which the Principles of . . . Shaftesbury are . . . Defended against . . . the Fable of the Bees* (London, 1725); Francis Hutcheson, *Illustrations on the Moral Sense*, ed. Bernard Peach (Cambridge: Harvard University Press, [1728] 1971).

28 Mandeville, *Fable*, I, 57.

Mandeville thus intends the "Enquiry" as an examination of how individuals understood only as a "compound of various Passions . . . might yet by [their] own Imperfections be taught to distinguish between Virtue and Vice."[29] His account is imaginative, amusing and offensive to almost all Augustan schools of moral philosophy.

Mandeville begins by describing humans as the only animals capable of true sociability, yet as so "selfish and headstrong, as well as cunning" that sociability must be preceded by "the Curb of Government." How was the bridle of government successfully slipped onto humanity? Mandeville's argument assumes a "State of Nature" in which people are already divided between "Lawgivers and other wise Men, that have laboured for the Establishment of Society" and the populace at large who will presumably follow the lawgivers' orders. To complain, as some of Mandeville's contemporaries did, that no such legislators ever existed makes good historical sense but is somewhat beside the point. Mandeville is using these faceless authorities to frame a fundamental anthropological insight: individuals develop the idea of moral virtue not in the abstract but only as socialized, politicized beings who are subject to the pressures of maintaining a cohesive community life. The origin of moral consciousness in this situation is perhaps most accurately described as a product of abstract social forces; Mandeville however increases the charm, originality and power of his account by ascribing the process to "skilful Politicians."[30]

Mandeville imagines the problem those that "laboured for the Establishment of Society" set themselves at the dawn of history. They learn quickly that "Force alone" will not make men or women "tractable." "The Chief Thing, therefore, which [they] . . . have endeavour'd, has been to make the People they were to govern, believe, that it was more beneficial for every Body to conquer than indulge his Appetites, and much better to mind the Publick than what seem'd his private Interest." After investigating human psychology, these would-be civilizers conclude that the best way to encourage such moral behavior is to reward it. Flattery, pleasing to everyone and in inexhaustible supply, is the perfect coin. "Making use of this bewitching Engine," politicians and moralists begin to preach the myth of human rationality while developing their charges' sense of pride and shame.[31] Because they respond so effectively to flattery, these passions are the "seeds of most Virtues," the "natural frailties" by which individuals are first enticed to sociable behavior and through which they continue to be influenced. Just as parents prod a child to good behavior with "extravagant Praises," so moralists "draw

29 *Ibid.*, 39–40.
30 *Ibid.*, 42, 41, 47.
31 *Ibid.*, 42, 43.

Men like Angels, in hopes that the Pride at least of Some will put 'em upon copying after the beautiful Originals which they are represented to be."[32] If pride fails, the shame of falling short of these grandiose portraits may prompt the self-renunciation that is the hallmark of moral virtue.

This moral education creates the intellectual and emotional desire actually to restrain one's asocial appetites along with the belief that the self-restraint is achieved through some laudable or rational principle.[33] In fact, newly civilized individuals are so entirely persuaded by the flattery lavished upon them, that they agree to define moral virtue as "the Conquest of [one's] own Passions out of a Rational Ambition of being good."[34] This definition is in fact the correct understanding of virtue, so Mandeville has demonstrated his first point: without any supernatural guide to the nature of good and evil, individuals may still learn to distinguish between vice and virtue.

However, correctly defining virtue and satisfactorily performing it are two different things. Although the newly "moral" creature does not realize the deception, "the Self-Denial the Man of Honour submits to in one Appetite, is immediately rewarded by the Satisfaction he receives from another, and what he abates of his Avarice, or any other Passion, is doubly repaid to his Pride."[35] Individuals control their asocial appetites only for the selfish gratification of believing themselves to be rational beings capable of sacrificing private interests for the good of the whole, an illusion fostered by the "skilful Politicians" concerned to render them sociable. Because people come to an accurate definition of virtue only through these politicians' manipulation of their self-love, "Moral Virtues," says Mandeville, "are the Political Offspring which Flattery begot upon Pride."[36]

Citing this epigram, critics accused Mandeville of denying the reality of virtue. In fact, Mandeville was denying only the ability to perform it successfully. Without the gift of God's grace, human beings can come to know and value true virtue only through a process that condemns them first to the performance of a counterfeit virtue based on manipulation of the passions and second to the vain belief that they have achieved the real thing. Mandeville's account of morality then does not focus on the reality or possibility of true virtue. Rather it highlights the way historical forces, personalized as "sagacious Moralists" and politicians, fashion the moral building blocks of the civilized world and do so from individuals' asocial passions, rather than from their reason.

32 *Ibid.*, 67, 53, 52.
33 *Ibid.*, 45.
34 *Ibid.*, 48–9.
35 *Ibid.*, 222.
36 *Ibid.*, 51.

In *The Fable of the Bees, Part II,* Mandeville considers the origin of politeness, which he defines as the indispensable art of "making ourselves acceptable to others, with as little Prejudice to ourselves as is possible."[37] Mandeville once again approaches his object of study anthropologically: how might naturally selfish people have learned to value civility, deference and common courtesy? He brushes aside any suggestion that an inborn affection such as benevolence might account for moral or sociable behavior. The true source of politeness is the same passion that makes politeness so necessary: self-liking.[38] Here again Mandeville describes the genesis of the complex social good civility from the various mutations of one selfish passion. His story plays upon the dysfunctional aspects of indulging too openly in a naturally overweening self-love.

Mandeville begins by positing an ingrained tendency of individuals to overvalue themselves, a tendency born of the passion of self-liking. Because of this trait, "all untaught Men will ever be hateful to one another," constantly offending others with their vain estimates of self-worth.[39] Finally, self-interest will lead a handful of persons to experiment with what are now known as good manners. "The most crafty and designing will everywhere be the first, that for Interest-sake will learn to conceal this Passion of Pride." The beneficial effects of curbing one's pride, at least in public, are so apparent that Mandeville speculates individuals will soon "grow impudent enough, not only to deny the high Value they have for themselves, but likewise to pretend that they have greater Value for others, than they have for themselves."[40] As the social benefits of this "Pitch of Insincerity" become apparent, parents will teach this hypocritical behavior "to their Offspring . . . by which Means, in two or three Centuries, good Manners must be brought to great Perfection."[41]

Unlike moral virtue, the route to politeness is a spontaneous discovery: a matter of self-interest not manipulation. Still it involves both the redirection of selfish passions and a psychological self-deception so effective that civilized individuals believe good manners to be a sign of natural benevolence or unselfishness. Here is where Mandeville parts company with Shaftesbury,

37 Mandeville, *Fable,* II, 147.
38 Mandeville here reverses his position that pride and shame are the "seeds of most Virtues," the fundamental passions that drive humans' actions and shape their personality (*Fable,* I, 67). By the publication of *Fable of the Bees, Part II,* Mandeville has decided that sociability and morality stem from a more basic passion of self-liking, invested in every living animal, of which pride and shame are two of many manifestations.
39 Mandeville, *Fable,* II, 138.
40 *Ibid.,* 145.
41 *Ibid.,* 145–6.

Addison and "polite journalists": "To be at once well-bred and sincere, is no less than a Contradiction," he asserts.[42]

Mandeville's final example of how selfish passions produce moral behavior concerns the aristocratic notion of honor. Like moral virtue, honor is yet another "Offspring of Flattery upon Pride," another political invention that lures individuals into social behavior by falsely extolling the excellence of the species. Mandeville's explanation of its genesis in *An Enquiry into the Origin of Honour* (1732) is brief and typically iconoclastic. As with his derivation of moral virtue, the problem that lies behind the origin of honor is one of social cohesion: how to persuade selfish and self-interested individuals to live up to obligations, contracts and promises, even when such commitments inconvenience immediate desires.

Mandeville begins by dismissing religion as inadequate to this end. Without the infusion of divine grace, he argues, belief in the rewards and punishments of an afterlife remains mere superstition, too weak to stifle our impulse to self-gratification. "Whatever Fear or Reverence [Man] might have for an invisible Cause, that Thought [is] often jostled out by others, more nearly related to himself."[43] Politicians must seek a more effective incentive to honor one's promises than the dangers of hell. Once again, Mandeville phrases his anthropology in personalized terms, emphasizing the manipulative character of the process he describes. Just as moralists at the dawn of history sought to control human appetites with a reward ready at hand and inexhaustible (and chose flattery), so ancient civilizers struggling to stabilize civil society looked "for Something in Man himself, to keep him in Awe." If persons could be persuaded to take themselves as "an Object of Reverence," the "Dread of Shame" might effectively control their behavior when the fear of divine power did not. Once again, the passion of self-liking plays the crucial role.[44]

Mandeville concludes, of course, that Augustan gentlemen should not flatter themselves with being men of honor. The performance of honorable actions indicates only the success of cultural forces in transferring each person's reverence and awe from a divine being to an exalted image of humanity itself.[45] Honorable actions, although valuable, are not virtuous because they stem from an effort to satisfy the passion of pride rather than conquer it.

42 Mandeville, *Fable,* I, 185. For the contrast to polite journalism, consider Richard Steele's view that the well-bred man is one for whom all public and private acts "have their rise ... from great and noble motives" (*The Spectator,* 4 v. [London: J. M. Dent and Sons, 1957], no. 75, 26 May 1711).

43 Bernard Mandeville, *An Enquiry into the Origin of Honour, and the Usefulness of Christianity in War* (London: Frank Carr and Co., [1732] 1971), 39–40.

44 *Ibid.*

45 *Ibid.,* 42.

Mandeville's polity thus grounds the familiar social and moral virtues not in human excellences but in human weakness, offering an account similar to his analysis of the sources of economic prosperity. He emphasizes first, the malleability of the selfish passions (the myriad directions in which pride will push a person) and second, the vital role of "politicians" in directing this manipulation. Mandeville extends both themes further in his final example of "private vices, publick benefits" – the development of human sociability.

III

Mandeville's work provides two complementary accounts of the origin of civil society. In "A Search into the Nature of Society," an essay added to the 1723 edition of *The Fable of the Bees,* Mandeville explains how presocial individuals, considered as purely selfish beings, might yet be brought to form stable communities. In *The Fable of the Bees, Part II,* Mandeville focuses more specifically on how such presocial persons might come to have a principled respect for private property and personal liberty, the preconditions of harmonious community life. In both cases, Mandeville stresses the role of rudimentary political authority in manipulating or structuring humanity's asocial passions.

"A Search into the Nature of Society" is primarily an attack on Shaftesbury's notion that people are brought together into communities by the operation of social affections or naturally amiable qualities.[46] Mandeville argues here and in Remark R that even if such affections existed (which they do not), they could ground only a presocial "State of slothful Ease and stupid Innocence."[47] Selfish desires alone prompt the struggle to better our own condition, encouraging inventions, technical progress and rudimentary communities. Unfortunately, such desires, while absolutely essential to society's development, also make people angry, jealous and desirous of dominating others, thus threatening any long-term cooperation. How then do such quarrelsome brutes put aside their differences and become sociable? In his moral genealogies, Mandeville details how "sagacious moralists" use the asocial passion of pride to persuade individuals to the practice of virtue and honor. He posits an analogous process at the level of social organization in which politicians secure the "Peace and Quiet of a Society" by exploiting the asocial passion of fear. When the individual's social environment is properly structured through the authoritative imposition of rules and legal sanctions,

46 Shaftesbury, *Characteristics,* I, 75–6, 315. See also the account in Green, *Shaftesbury's Philosophy,* 152–63.
47 Mandeville, *Fable,* I, 184.

"he'll be taught by his Fears to destroy his Anger."[48] Social cooperation will become a matter of self-interest.

Mandeville thus belies Shaftesbury's argument that Hobbesian man could never form a stable society.[49] Certainly, selfish passions unmediated by political control would be as useless to the formation and growth of civil society as Shaftesbury's imaginary benevolent affections. But with the help of political authority, the acquisitive passions that seem the greatest threat to the civilizing process can become its greatest resource.

In *The Fable of the Bees, Part II*, Mandeville returns to the question of the origin of society, again relying on politicians to provide the discipline necessary to socialize man. Here he identifies natural man's ignorance of and disdain for the principles of justice as the major obstacle to the formation of civil society and argues that only an external political authority can succeed in teaching primitive peoples the preconditions of peaceful living: respect for private property and one another's liberty. But for political authority to do its work, individuals must first be brought to submit to government. So Mandeville details a four-step process by which anarchic savages, endowed only with a love for life and their own well-being, might be made governable and thus sociable.

In the decisive reversal of these two qualities, Mandeville challenges a basic tenet of liberal consent theory. Consent theory, of course, holds that individuals not yet brought under political rule might still be sociable enough to agree to consent together to a particular form of government. For Mandeville, the sociability that would allow a discussion of one's political fate does not precede but follows from the (necessarily arbitrary) establishment of political authority. The argument in *The Fable of the Bees, Part II* is significant for another reason as well. Mandeville's earlier writings assume the existence of politicians ready and able to impose "various Laws ... strictly executed."[50] Here for the first time Mandeville provides an account of how the politicians and civilizers on which many of his arguments rest might have themselves arisen.

Mandeville begins his story with the brute passion of fear. "Common Danger, which unites the greatest Enemies" is the first impetus to community.[51] Terror of wild animals drives individuals to combine and spurs the invention of weapons, tools and shelters. But close contact between such selfish people soon activates the "stanch Principle of Pride and Ambition," and those who had once huddled together in fear begin quarreling among

---

48 *Ibid.,* 206.
49 Shaftesbury, *Characteristics,* I, 73.
50 Mandeville, *Fable,* I, 206.
51 Mandeville, *Fable,* II, 230.

themselves. These clashes in turn prompt people to protect themselves by forming "Bands and Companies" under the leadership of the strongest men or families.[52] These rudimentary communities are the second step on the way to civil society proper. Mandeville insists however that the prospect for peace and sociability remains uncertain. Fear and force rule these "precarious and unsettled" packs until, propelled by the natural desire to dominate, the packs' leaders begin to investigate the causes of the strife that tears apart their followers.

Humanity now enters the third stage of establishing sociability. Through this self-interested investigation of the sources of social discord, the first politicians – the leaders of these bands of savages – painstakingly formulate the basic principles of justice and right, promulgating them as rules designed to keep the peace.[53] Mandeville concludes his account with the "Invention of Letters," without which "no Laws can be long effective." By providing the ability to codify and preserve accurately society's laws, writing assures the principled enforcement of the rules of justice. The result is rapid progress into a civilized society. "When once Men come to be govern'd by written Laws, all the rest comes on apace. Now Property, and Safety of Life and Limb, may be secured: This naturally will forward the Love of Peace and make it spread."[54] The next step is a cooperative division of labor. Mandeville has now brought the savage from battling to bartering without once assuming a benevolent instinct or praiseworthy motive.

Reading Mandeville's major works as an extended critique of philosophical optimism helps explain the spirit in which Mandeville argues for the viability of a virtue-less polity. Mandeville does not dispute the reality of moral or political excellences. In fact, he insists throughout his work that there is such a thing as moral virtue that it would indeed be praiseworthy to have. Rather, he opposes what he considers a false and simplistic doctrine of the nature of humans and society – one that distorts social reality by claiming that virtue is both possible and necessary in a world he considers irredeemably profane. His major works attempt to correct the errors of this doctrine by demonstrating first, that a virtue based on benevolent instincts is illusory and second, that true virtue (the rational conquest of the passions) is unnecessary to the achievement of a thriving commonwealth. Instead, he argues, the political manipulation of "private vices" (understood generally as selfish passions and asocial appetites) underwrites the three basic building blocks of the thriving polity: national prosperity, personal morality and basic sociability.

52 *Ibid.,* 266, 267.
53 *Ibid.,* 268.
54 *Ibid.,* 283–4.

Mandeville rounds out his attack on philosophical optimism by explaining why such a doctrine retains such a powerful hold on civilized society. As with the sources of economic prosperity, moral behavior and sociability, there are two contributing factors: the malleability of the asocial passions and the willingness of cunning politicians to take advantage of them. Thus, politicians will forever preach the possibility and necessity of virtue for such rhetoric inspires the people to a mimicry of true virtue based on the satisfaction of pride. The moralists who insist, sincerely but incorrectly, on the importance of virtue or honorable behavior in public life are the innocent dupes of such men. They are living proof of how effectively politicians and cultural forces in general can deceive human beings as to their true nature.

Mandeville then is quite prepared to conceive of and argue for a polity that does without the virtue of citizens altogether. But this emphatic political conclusion does not derive from an attack on a particular understanding of the virtuous citizen; he does not target the Country politics of virtue, for example. Rather Mandeville banishes virtue from the polity in order to banish philosophical optimism from moral philosophy. As such, his work lies outside the dynamic of transformation I have traced in the previous chapters.

Mandeville is not striving to adapt a religious or republican understanding of civic virtue to changed political or social circumstances. Nor is he replying directly to a politics of public virtue. His work may have been deployed by some Court writers to excuse the seemingly corrupt practices of Walpole's ministers. But as I have already argued, Mandeville himself had other targets in mind when preparing his publications. Mandeville's corrosive politics, his willingness to frame an account of a community in which citizens are not asked to be good because they will simply be managed, is fueled by his profound antipathy to a particularly rosy view of human nature increasingly popular among his contemporaries. His work is significant not as the precursor of Smithian liberalism nor as the last gasp of classical republicanism but rather as a demonstration of how different the politics of a truly virtue-less polity would be from anything republicans or liberals of the eighteenth century might be said to be proposing.

IV

One of the significant differences between Mandeville's work and both republican and early liberal theory is the role assigned to figures of cultural and political authority: the "skilful Politicians" and "sagacious Moralists" so frequently mentioned in Mandeville's analyses. These terms often stand for the anthropomorphized forces of civilization: those social and political institutions, persons and traditions that successfully de-nature individuals, channeling their most basic passions in a way that serves the ends of society not self.[55] But at times Mandeville means precisely what he says: "Private Vices *by the dextrous Management of a skilful Politician* may be turned into Publick Benefits."[56] This climactic dictum, Mandeville's long-withheld elaboration of what he means by the *Fable*'s notorious subtitle, not only banishes the need for virtue from the life of the ordinary citizen. It announces new expectations for the statesman as well.

To serve the public welfare fully, politicians must grasp the essential nature of human beings: their pride, their vulnerability to shame and flattery, their desperate desire to outstrip their neighbors. They must, Mandeville says, be "thoroughly acquainted with the Passions, Appetites, Strengths and Weaknesses of [man's] Frame." Through this psychological knowledge, not through any rarefied virtue of his own, the politician fulfills his crucial social role: turning man's "greatest Frailties to the Advantage of the Publick." The statesman must use the vices of the citizenry to create a strong, peaceable and flourishing people.

Mandeville reinforces this managerial rather than moral understanding of the statesman's function by insisting on the value of an almost encyclopedic knowledge of the material determinants of political action. In *The Virgin Unmask'd* for example, Mandeville sets out the following qualifications for one "that would meddle with . . . State-Affairs."

[He] ought to have not only read, but digested all manner of History . . . [He] ought to be acquainted with other Countries, as well as he is with his own, to know the great Cities, their Commerce, the Sea-ports, their Shipping, the Fortifications, Artillery, Stores, and Ammunition; all the Towns of Note, the Number of Villages, and People they contain; the Soil, the Climate, the Extent and Product of every Province . . . he ought likewise to know the Prince, and all his Court . . .their Abilities, Circumstances, and Inclinations, all their Vertues and Vices.[57]

This masterful grasp of all possible influences on the political decisions of allies and rivals enables a statesman wisely "to judge of the Event of Things to come," a prerequisite for successful policy decisions.[58] Like the psychological insight recommended in the *Fable*, it is a knowledge accessible even to those consumed by corrupt machinations and factional intrigue.

Because Mandeville believes that only the careful channeling of human

55 Mandeville, *Fable*, II, 139; Mandeville, *Enquiry into the Origin of Honour*, 40–1.
56 Mandeville, *Fable*, I, 369, emphasis added.
57 Bernard Mandeville, *The Virgin Unmask'd* (Delmar, NY: Scholars' Facsimiles and Reprints, [1710] 1975), 133–4.
58 *Ibid.,* 133.

passions can produce the public good, he breaks with both liberal and republican notions of the statesman's responsibilities and character. Country thinkers, of course, considered civic virtue a vital attribute of any politician, assuring his ability to deliberate on the public good without the interference of private interest or advantage. Mandeville dismisses this classical republican preference for virtuous politicians as misguided and unnecessary. Politicians, like all men, are selfish, vain and thoroughly committed to advancing their private desires. But for Mandeville these shortcomings do not affect an individual's ability to further the public good; the politician needs not moral wisdom or civic virtue but technical knowledge and psychological insight.[59]

Mandeville's contention that the good state can thrive independently of the virtue of its citizens and statesmen is a far less shocking notion to modern readers than it was to Mandeville's contemporaries. Few of us may relish as much as Mandeville the chance to claim that private vices lead to public benefits. But we accept that components of the social order or of political life in themselves not particularly praiseworthy can be combined in a way that assures their contribution to the public good. For Americans, the quintessential expression of this public philosophy comes in *Federalist* 10, where Madison argues that an extensive representation encompassing numerous self-interested factions may be just as good a guarantor of public liberty as the illusory ideal of a legislature filled purely with "enlightened statesmen." Another familiar incarnation of this proposition is Adam Smith's notion of the "invisible hand." This term encapsulates the social phenomenon by which self-interested individuals may pursue their own economic ends and yet, through the mediating mechanism of the market, advance national prosperity and public good as well.[60] Because these teachings, as found in the writings of Madison and Smith, are often labeled as liberal, Mandeville's case for the connection between private vices and public benefits may also seem to epitomize a typically liberal approach towards the place of virtue in political life. But appearances in this case are deceiving.

59 One might ask how far Mandeville departs from Cato in this assessment of the politician's role. The difference between the two is that Mandeville takes the moral shortcomings of men in power to imply the impossibility of virtue, discussing what such statesmen might achieve without it; Cato remains committed to a statesman and people recognizably virtuous in classical republican terms even if this behavior is grounded in private interest. J. C. Maxwell, picking up on this radical shift in expectations, provides a suggestive discussion of the Mandevillian statesman as utilitarian ("Ethics and Politics in Mandeville," *Philosophy* 26 [1951]: 242–52).

60 Alexander Hamilton, et al. *The Federalist Papers* (New York: New American Library, 1961), 80. Smith uses his famous phrase in *The Theory of Moral Sentiments*, Part IV, chapter 1 (Indianapolis, IN: LibertyClassics, [1759] 1976), 304 and in *An Inquiry into the Nature and Causes of the Wealth of Nations*, Book IV, chapter 2 (New York: Modern Library, [1776] 1937), 423.

Perhaps the most notable difference between Mandeville's skeptical political philosophy and the classical liberal ideas taking shape at the same time
lies with their contrasting conceptions of human nature. Locke's writings
are typically understood as describing and defending a politics structured
around individuals capable of rational political deliberation and choice.
These individuals are willing and able to moderate their passions both to
advance their own interests and to nurture a broader public good.[61] Yet
even rational individuals cannot be expected to adjudicate fairly when their
desires and interests bring them into conflict with others. Conceiving of the
individual in this manner encourages what we have come to call a liberal
understanding of the state's role in civil society: the state provides the stable
framework within which such self-interested men may harmoniously and
constructively pursue their independent ideals of the good.

Mandeville holds a more pessimistic view of political individuals. Mandeville understands human beings as motivated by passions only, passions
which can be manipulated and directed but never controlled or supplanted.
Such persons are radically ill-suited to a polity that allows them to pursue
their own interests and conceptions of the good with a minimum of con-
straint. Indeed, they cannot even be said to have "interests," in the sense of
rationally and independently generated priorities that guide selfish individuals and moderate their passions.[62] As Mandeville states in his introduction to
the *Fable,* "I believe Man ... to be a compound of various Passions, that all of
them, as they are provoked and come uppermost, govern him by turns,
whether he will or no."[63] Without cultural constraints and instruction, such
passions will issue in asocial and unproductive behavior that make individuals unfit for civil society. The state must thus provide more than the framework within which selfish individuals pursue their ends; it must through
laws, education and deception intervene more actively to shape the desires
of the citizens, arranging matters so that private vices will produce public
benefits.[64]

Mandeville's work is also profoundly unsympathetic to a liberalism that

61 See John Colman, *John Locke's Moral Philosophy* (Edinburgh: Edinburgh University Press,
1983), esp. chapter 8; Charles Vereker, *Eighteenth-Century Optimism* (Liverpool: Liverpool University Press, 1967), 78–85.
62 For the development of this understanding of interest in the eighteenth century, see Albert
O. Hirschman, *The Passions and the Interests: Political Arguments for Capitalism before
its Triumph* (Princeton: Princeton University Press, 1977), 14–55.
63 Mandeville, *Fable,* I, 39.
64 This is not to argue that either early or contemporary liberals ignore the importance of laws
or even of education in shaping the rational citizen. But they do conceive of any political or
structural framework as nurturing a *rational* citizen whose desires at some point may be
considered independently justified and legitimated, just because they are his or her own.
Mandeville's more skeptical psychology of passionate man rejects this alternative.

would limit both state power and citizen obligation by explaining the creation of civil society as a contractual act. Locke presented the entrance into civil society as a rational choice in which a sociable, if discordant, populace join in entrusting government to an authority who will better enforce the codes by which the society is already living. Individuals in the state of nature are conversant not only with fellow-beings but with moral truth and the laws of nature. Concerned to rebut the philosophical optimists' claim that sociability arises from a natural affection for fellow creatures, Mandeville's work ends up challenging the contract theorists' assumption that some form of civil society precedes the establishment of political authority.

To Mandeville, only the fact of government, of "cunning Management" by moralists and politicians, can make individuals sociable enough to interact with others for more than a fleeting instant. "If by Society we only mean a Number of People, that without Rule or Government should keep together out of a natural Affection . . . then there is not in the World a more unfit Creature for Society than Man."[65] Without the discipline of the laws and the punishments of politicians, the prepolitical individual lacks both the moral knowledge and emotional restraint to unite with others for more than arbitrary and unpredictable periods of mutual convenience. To speak, even philosophically, of a state of nature from which individuals might offer a limited consent to the conventions of political community is, for Mandeville, to misconstrue profoundly the basis of governmental authority. Force and fraud are the only possible tools with which to leverage humanity out of its natural state.

In the same vein, Mandeville's primitive peoples are not bearers of natural rights. To Mandeville the calculus of prepolitical (and presocial) human beings proceeds not in terms of rights and reason, but purely in terms of passions and desires. His account of the state of nature mentions rights only to say that prepolitical individuals have no conception of them. "Man would have everything he likes, without considering, whether he has any Right to it or not."[66] Rights in Mandeville's theory have a similar status to moral virtue. That is, both enter social consciousness only when politicians invent a device for social concord that matches what Mandeville believes to count objectively as "right" or "virtue." Just as individuals acknowledge moral virtue only when they are enticed into doing so by the manipulation of moralists, so they gain rights only when selfish leaders, seeking a more effective way to control their followers, discover that the concept of rights provides a useful guarantee of social order. For Mandeville, the rights of man do exist, but they are not the natural properties of the individual.

65 Mandeville, *Fable,* I, 347.
66 Mandeville, *Fable,* II, 270–1.

Mandeville's accounts of human nature, the origin of civil society and the genealogy of morality thus sit uneasily with the assumptions of Lockean liberalism. Locke's rights-based liberalism is a philosophy for and about the self-made man, but Mandeville treats the citizen as literally and necessarily molded by others, in particular, by established political authority. Rational individualism, the social contract and natural rights have no place in his skeptical political philosophy. Mandeville's rejection of virtue thus becomes more than a potent critique of philosophical optimism. It is also a challenge, albeit unintentional, to the emerging tenets of liberal individualism.

Much modern scholarship displays a lingering suspicion that liberalism and virtue, commerce and virtue are at bottom incompatible. In this view, the triumph of liberal ideology combined with a prosperous market economy profoundly circumscribed the practice of any sort of civic virtue, publicly or privately oriented. Citizens begin to approach the public realm as purely private individuals, lacking those character traits which would sustain and enhance a civic mode of life and ignorant of the means by which such traits might be developed.

The arguments of this book do not themselves justify dismissing this suspicion as unfounded. To show that the first outright rejection of virtue in political life (Mandeville's *Fable*) had little to do with the triumph of liberal ideology is not to demonstrate that liberalism is compatible with the practice of civic virtue. Similarly, to demonstrate that the difficulties encountered by the various politics of public virtue had little to do with the challenges posed by the development of commercial society does not in itself prove wealth and virtue always compatible.

What the account presented here does suggest is that the problems of pursuing a politics of public virtue arose prior to and independently of the large-scale social forces usually held responsible. In the exchange between Bolingbroke and the Court Whigs for example, polemical politics provided the setting in which a new vision of the good citizen entered public consciousness. And Cato found an egoistic view of human psychology persuasive enough to attempt a new account of the nature and grounds of civic virtue. Likewise, Mandeville argued for the irrelevance and impossibility of true public spiritedness not as part of a liberal vanguard nor as a disgruntled critic of Country polemics. Rather his conclusions followed from the pursuit of his primary goal – a criticism of the rosy doctrines of philosophical optimism. But if the decline of the politics of public virtue, the eclipse of republican political values, is not tied in the first instance to the emergence of liberal ideals or to the establishment of the stock market and a system of public credit, where precisely does the difficulty lie? I suggest an alternate answer to this problem in the concluding chapter.

8

◁══════════════════════════════════════▷

Virtue transformed

One can set no precise date at which the importance of a politics of public virtue was first questioned or last appreciated in English political thought. Still, the first half of the eighteenth century in England marks a particularly significant moment in society's perennial political engagement with the question of virtue. For at this time, an enthusiastic revival of the politics of public virtue (prompted by the triumph of 1688 and the transformation of political culture that followed from it) coincided with the emergence of features of the modern state that have often been held to make the practice of civic virtue more difficult if not impossible.[1] We know from seventeenth-century history (the failed puritan and republican initiatives of the Civil War and interregnum) that the politics of public virtue did not fare so well prior to the Augustan age.[2] But what were its fortunes at this, the dawn of the modern era? The short answer is equally poor. Not only did the various advocates of public virtue fail to secure governmental support for their understandings of the good citizen; their own political argument as well as that of their opponents transformed the public debate about the nature and necessity of political virtue.

There existed at the end of the seventeenth century a virtually unanimous consensus that public virtue of some sort was necessary to ground the good state. Both religious and political teachings reinforced the idea that good citizens must be loyal lovers of their country, willing and able to set aside their personal desires to advance the public good. But following the Revolu-

---

1 See chapter 2, pp. 29–32.
2 On the puritan politics of virtue, see Donald Pennington and Keith Thomas, *Puritans and Revolutionaries* (Oxford: Clarendon Press, 1978) and K. E. Wrightson, "The Puritan Reformation of Manners with Special Reference to the Counties of Lancashire and Essex, 1640–1660," unpublished Ph.D. dissertation, Cambridge University, 1974.

tion of 1688, these platitudes were taken seriously and the politics of public virtue pursued in political earnest. Then, the ideological terrain changed dramatically. Political argument quickly expanded to include not only alternative, privately oriented conceptions of political virtue but also, more tentatively, the notion that citizen excellences were not relevant at all to a community's flourishing. By the middle of the century, the notion of publicly oriented civic virtue as the quality most appropriate to the good citizen was not eclipsed entirely, but the issue of its possibility was no longer at the center of political argument or political activity.

How are we to explain this precipitous decline? Historians of this period tend to account for it in terms of the new social and economic circumstances confronted by Augustan citizens. The new world of market speculation and public credit is said to have transformed English society in such a way as to close down, directly or indirectly, the possibilities for public, civic virtue. J. G. A. Pocock argues, for example, that for those concerned with the moral grounding of the political order, two alternatives existed. One could reaffirm, as critique, a now "archaic" ideal of civic virtue as the proper and necessary protection for English liberties and prosperity.[3] Because this option amounted to an attack on the Whig regime that had sponsored the policies now thought to have made virtue obsolete, those more comfortable with the new social order sought to offer a more positive characterization of it. Their work affirmed the substantial moral achievements that could be expected of the individual involved in both "commerce and culture."[4] In this vision, the virtues of sociability substitute for civic virtues in making the polity cohere and thrive. The gentleman of manners, the polite individual, takes the place of the virtuous citizen. As Pocock describes the dynamic, this new collection of values, grounded in an appreciation for the new commercial polity, contends with and ultimately displaces the Country politics of public virtue.[5]

The difficulty with this account is twofold. First, it fails to capture the full array of intellectual alternatives pursued by Englishmen confronting the problem of political virtue. Second, it assigns advocates of civic virtue a purely critical role; the politics of public virtue they defend are intended less to promote virtue within the Augustan citizenry than to indicate how far from the path of true virtue the Augustan polity has strayed.

A fuller picture would make allowance for three sorts of responses to the social and economic changes confronting English society in the early eigh-

---

3 J. G. A. Pocock, *Virtue, Commerce, and History: Essays on Political Thought and History, Chiefly in the Eighteenth Century* (Cambridge University Press, 1985), 48.
4 *Ibid.,* 147.
5 See chapter 2, pp. 32–4.

teenth century. Some political thinkers continue to affirm what would be called a pure politics of public virtue, one that makes no accommodation with the new economic and political order then emerging. The Scotsman Andrew Fletcher is a case in point. To remedy the problems besetting eighteenth-century Scotland, he prescribes the institutions of a classical republic; Scotland should return to an economy of slave labor and the politics of an armed militia. Fletcher's work certainly makes the case for a robust republican civic virtue, but his failure to reach any realistic accommodation with the commercialized society to which he directed his proposals renders his politics of virtue completely marginal.[6] If all defenders of public virtue were like Fletcher, one would have to say that events had outstripped their political imagination. Their work would be less critique than utopian reverie, unconnected to the political realities of their time.

But Fletcher's steadfast defense of a truly antiquated public virtue borders on the idiosyncratic. This version of public virtue is certainly an innocent victim of new times, an idea overtaken by developments with which it could not cope. Such a verdict is misplaced, however, for the vast majority of reflection on citizen virtue in this period.

Most of those who value or speak for citizen virtue at this time sensibly tailor their case to contemporary concerns and circumstances. If making room for political virtue entails moving beyond conventional conceptions of or traditional arguments for its practice, they are prepared to do so. Their politics of virtue are not critical but constructive, and their arguments are adaptive. It is here, in the adjustments and adaptation of political argument to the realities of eighteenth-century politics and culture, not simply in the impingements of the outside world, that the transformation of virtue begins.

Those who adapt a politics of public virtue can again be more or less divided into two camps. On the one hand are writers who advocate familiar forms of political virtue while updating or adapting the account of this virtue to strengthen the case for its importance to the English public. In each case, however, their effort to fit such politics to modern circumstances serves less to strengthen the prospects for public virtue than to undermine the case for its political necessity.

The Societies for Reformation of Manners provide a case in point. These moral reform groups, allied with Low Church Anglicans and sympathetic dissenters, described the good citizen, the virtuous citizen, as one who conformed to conventional religious standards of moral behavior; abstaining

6 Andrew Fletcher, *A Discourse of Government with Relation to Militias* and *Two Discourses Concerning the Affairs of Scotland Written in the Year 1698* in David Daiches, ed., *Selected Political Writings and Speeches* (Edinburgh: Scottish Academic Press, 1979).

from an array of common sins made individuals not only good persons but good citizens as well. To portray the activity of moral reform as a means to the promotion of political virtue was a significant departure from previous justifications for the reformation of manners. But in opting for a political justification of what was essentially a religious ideal, the Societies, and the Anglican ministers who supported them, implicitly accommodated the political temper of their time, invoking the least controversial criterion for political action, the temporal welfare of the state, to justify prosecution of public and private immorality. At the same time, however, this approach to the justification of moral reform invited a devastating line of critique: a denial that the sins of drunkenness, lewdness, profanity and blasphemy posed a substantial danger to the public welfare.

The problem here is not that the church, wedded to traditional theocentric claims for a religious reformation of manners, gets left behind by the rise of a secular ideology articulated outside its fold. Anglican ministers themselves chose to stake their case for a political virtue of personal morality on the temporal dangers of immortality. Moral reformers lost out not to a new view of the political world but to arguments that engaged their case on its own terms: arguments that offered a more persuasive account of what behavior threatened the peace and prosperity of modern society – and thus what behavior could legitimately come within the scope of legislative action.

Bolingbroke too updates a familiar language of virtue with similarly striking consequences. His periodical, *The Craftsman,* was the voice of the Country opposition. Over and over again, it damned Walpole and his allies on recognizably republican grounds: the economic and political practices pursued by Walpole and his allies were fundamentally corrupt and corrupting, threatening to English liberties and a dangerous prelude to an age of tyranny. But to wrest such a conclusion from the facts of English political life required reworking the classical republican account of what civic virtue and its corruption consisted in. Bolingbroke's work preserves the public sense of the republican understanding of civic virtue: citizens are virtuous because of their devotion to some common good beyond themselves. But the nature of this good is narrowed to the single entity of the balanced constitution. The good citizen is one who defends the balanced constitution as Bolingbroke defines it, nothing more, nothing less.

It is a sign of Bolingbroke's brilliance as a political writer that his works, with this subtle variation on republican themes, managed to persuade so many that the political and financial innovations introduced by the Whigs placed the nation's freedom at risk. But this very success led others, less enamored of the Country reform program, to challenge Bolingbroke's account of the imminent collapse of civic virtue, articulating a new, privately oriented understanding of the good citizen grounded in personal temperance and frugality. One should not, however, use England's financial revolution nor the problems that this financial revolution posed to reigning paradigms of political thought to explain the genesis of this new account of virtue. Its source was not finance, but politics. Both Bolingbroke's reconceptualization of republican virtue and the Court Whigs' response to it were prompted by the interests of partisan politics, by the contention between political factions for which Whig financial and political policies provided a convenient target.

Those willing to defend more traditional forms of citizen virtue thus found their efforts subjected to a frustrating paradox. As they sought to accommodate their ideology to the realities of eighteenth-century politics and culture, they succeeded only in undermining their case for the importance of a publicly oriented virtue and encouraging what I have called a more private conception of political virtue to take hold. The other facet of the dynamic I trace is found precisely in this articulation of privately oriented understandings of political virtue. Authors whose work falls within this category remain eager to make the case for the possibility and relevance of civic virtue to the modern world. Yet, for different reasons, they remain reluctant to enlist under the banners of the various politics of public virtue. In their place, they offer understandings of citizen virtue that are more privately oriented, best cultivated independently of state action and most immediately manifest in the private rather than the public sphere of life.

Cato's Letters represents one of the most interesting of these efforts to recast a traditional politics of virtue in a mold more suited to the sensibilities and expectations of eighteenth-century society. Despite evident republican sympathies, Cato does not see a role in the contemporary polity for the sorts of "Heroick" virtues – a selfless love of one's own country, a patriotic passion to preserve the nation's freedom – usually recommended by republican texts. Human nature is simply too selfish and corrupt for citizens to be counted on to behave in such a fashion. But rather than abandon the ideal of civic virtue, Cato reconceives it in a way that makes it accessible to a world of private-minded citizens. In Cato's world, concern for personal welfare can and does underwrite virtuous political activity. "The Whole People, by consulting their own Interest, consult the Publick, and act for the Publick by acting for themselves."[7]

Here again we can trace a transformation in the public understanding of

7 John Trenchard and Thomas Gordon, *Cato's Letters,* 4 v., 3d ed., facsimile reprint in 2 v. (New York: Russell and Russell, [1733] 1969), II, 41.

virtue not to outside forces but to political argument about virtue itself. We tend to think of self-interest as the political economist's substitute for virtue, a new sort of accommodation with the political order imposed over and against a more patriotic republican ideal. In this scenario, the republican ideal can come across as a noble victim thrust aside by a coarse modern upstart. *Cato's Letters* shows that the case for the political palatability of the self-interested citizen originates within republican discourse itself and that it was seen as enhancing, not replacing, the practice of civic virtue.[8]

James Pitt provides another example of an eighteenth-century theorist who turns away from publicly oriented civic virtue without putting an apolitical social virtue in its place. Like Cato, Pitt and his Court Whig colleague Arnall argue for a privately oriented civic virtue in which citizens come to serve their country and preserve its liberties through attention to their own rather than their country's good. For Pitt and Arnall, the key to civic virtue lies in the personal habits of frugality, industry and honesty. Only those citizens able, through the exercise of these dispositions, to keep their fiscal house in order will possess the moral fiber to resist the corrupt temptations of an overreaching Court. Such an account can indeed read like an advocacy of social rather than political virtue. The point to keep in mind, though, is that Pitt and Arnall fully intend the individuals distinguished by these attributes to use them to perfect their civic contributions. These qualities are not simply recommended as the way to more civilized social interaction or more comfortable personal circumstances.

As we can conclude from this brief review, making a persuasive case for a politics of public virtue compatible with the political and cultural norms of eighteenth-century England was not an easy task. Some of those engaged in Augustan politics abandoned the effort altogether in favor of a politics of privately oriented civic virtue (Cato and the Court Whigs), while those who sought to preserve a place for more traditional understandings of public virtue (SRMs and Bolingbroke) found their newly constructed arguments rejected or turned against them. This twofold dynamic suggests that it is in some sense correct to say that the encounter with modernity – in the form of eighteenth-century English politics and culture – made things difficult for all politics of public virtue. But we must be careful of just where we say the difficulties lie. In particular, what many observers might consider the crucial challenge to the ideology of public virtue – the newly commercial nature of society – figures only tangentially in the case studies presented here.

8 I do not presume to trace later arguments for the political utility of self-interest back to *Cato's Letters,* although the work was well known throughout the century. My point here is that the conceptual alternative existed within the republican tradition, whether seized upon by contemporaries or not.

For Low Church Anglicans, a new understanding of the civil magistrate's role, one forged in the struggle for religious toleration, prompts the shift from a theocentric to a secular defense of a religious politics of virtue. By the time the SRMs become active, it has become easier to win acceptance for a reformation of manners because it furthers the public welfare than because it conforms to God's will. Cato defects from traditional republican views of civic virtue primarily because he cannot reconcile them with his pessimistic psychology of human nature. Finally, Bolingbroke and the Court Whigs suggest a third factor that precipitates change within the Augustan politics of public virtue. Their work explicitly addresses the supposed dangers of the newly commercialized society and the expansive governmental apparatus that grows with it. But it would be a mistake to assign these factors a primary role in these authors' transformation of virtue. The writings of both Bolingbroke and his Court Whig opponents adapt, and ultimately compromise, the republican conception of civic virtue in the service of partisan political ends. Bolingbroke reconstitutes the republican understanding of virtue, describing it narrowly as loyalty to a particular "balanced" form of constitution, so that he may denounce Walpole and the Whig ministry as dangerously corrupt. Court Whigs then counter Bolingbroke's rewriting of the republican tradition and defend their patron's reputation with an innovation of their own: an account of civic virtue that grounds the character of the good citizen not in love of country or constitution but in frugality and industry. Like Cato, the Court Whigs advance an understanding of political virtue that, by withdrawing it from the public realm, makes it both more accessible and more attractive to the citizens of an increasingly pluralistic and democratic society. But this privatization of virtue is best seen as the result of pitched partisan battles rather than some concession to the supposed constraints of commercial society.

If commerce, or more specifically, the twined institutions of stock market and public debt, are not to blame for virtue's transformation, what of liberalism? Did the emergence and gradual adoption of liberal ideals, at least those of the Lockean variant on offer in Augustan England, threaten the politics of virtue more broadly?

Certainly, the increasing acceptance of what we usually think of as a liberal view of the ends of the state did play some role in encouraging the turn towards a more privately oriented conception of civic virtue. The accounts of citizen virtue offered by both Cato and the Court Whigs, for example, are especially suited to helping a liberal sort of government flourish, one in which the business of government is seen as advancing the rights of citizens, securing their liberty, property and prosperity. And the SRMs' shift from a theocentric to a secular justification of moral reform depends importantly on the reformers' acceptance of a liberal account of the scope of magisterial power.

Liberal commitments do not make the politics of public virtue impossible; nor does liberalism itself turn against and repudiate the idea of the virtuous citizen. But what we now think of as a liberal conception of the ends of the state does provide intellectual resources that encourage the articulation of privately oriented alternatives to traditional, public conceptions of political virtue. In this sense, liberal ideals do play a role in the transformation (though not the eclipse) of civic virtue.

But perhaps liberalism with its historical emphasis on the self-interested pursuit of personal happiness, the protection of individual liberties and the privileged nature of nonpolitical aspects of social life strikes at the politics of virtue more deeply. It is tempting in this context to take Bernard Mandeville's corrosive policy recommendations as indicative of the threat that liberal ideals hold for the polity, to see him as the only writer with the courage to carry through the Court Whig argument for the privatization of civic virtue to its logical conclusion: the elimination of the polity's reliance on virtue altogether. Yet, without too much exaggeration we might call Mandeville the last Augustinian in England rather than an early liberal. Mandeville's rejection of the necessity and desirability of virtue in the modern world stems from a pessimism about human nature even deeper than Cato's. And his political prescriptions for managing in such a world have more in common with the classical republican's emphasis on the constitutional ordering of the masses' political desire than with the modern liberal's faith in the rational consent of the self-interested individual.

There is no easy route, then, from the privatization of civic virtue embraced by Cato and the Court Whigs to the virtue-less polity of Bernard Mandeville. These authors offer two separate answers to the challenges of the modern world, one liberal and the other illiberal. Cato and the Court Whigs, intentionally or not, champion what we have come to think of as a liberal personality; their ideal citizens are not only acutely aware of their personal interests, but also publicly engaged in the effort to defend the circumstances of their freedom and prosperity. Mandeville offers only passion-driven ciphers, shaped by the decisions of the men who happen to rule them.

Thus Mandeville's work reinforces one of the first conclusions of this study, if only in a backhanded way: there is nothing in the historical record to suggest that the practice of civic virtue is beyond the competence of a polity characterized by predominantly liberal commitments. For it is those writers who insist on the importance of civic virtue, albeit in a privatized form, who sustain a liberal view of human nature and politics. Mandeville, who shocked his contemporaries by disparaging the pursuit of public and private virtue, embraces a manipulative, illiberal conception of the political realm.

There is little in the specific circumstances in which the politics of public virtue faltered to suggest that the rise of liberalism or the emergence of commercial society makes the achievement of public civic virtue impossible. Were, then, the defeats of eighteenth-century proponents of public virtue purely contingent? This conclusion is also mistaken. Rather, in accounting for the difficulties of public virtue in Augustan England, we must focus our attention on the explicitly political dimension of the politics of public virtue. Advocates of public virtue in eighteenth-century England played to win in the political arena, seeking legislation and public action that embodied their favorite initiatives, and they lost. Every effort to further their case in politics or political argument was decisively rebuffed – not by claims for the irrelevance of civic virtue but by arguments in favor of an alternative, competing conception of the good citizen. Those who sought to impose the various politics of public virtue on their compatriots failed in the give and take of robust political debate to convince either those in or out of power of the correctness of their cause.

Why was this so? Why, despite the consensus on the importance of a virtuous citizenry, did eighteenth-century advocates of public virtue get almost nowhere with their political agenda? To answer this question, I want to step back from the historical record slightly and reflect upon the realities of the political process in certain sorts of nondespotic regimes. The problem, I want to argue, is that a successful politics of public virtue requires circumstances not present in Augustan England – not because the country was tainted or corrupted by commercial values or liberal ideals, but because it was a free polity characterized both by a substantial degree of citizen participation in government and by the existence of that space between the political realm and the individual that we now call civil society.

Such circumstances bode ill for the successful establishment of any politics of public virtue. The existence of civil society, with the possibility it creates for multiple allegiances and sources of emotional attachment separate from state and family, necessarily undermines efforts to make politics and the public good the focus of individuals' public action. And democratic government, of however limited a sort, poses a daunting obstacle – a majority in the legislature to be precise – to any program for the renewal of virtue. Once the needs and desires of the citizens become the focus of political deliberation, as they will be in any nation that cedes the populace some role in government, this majority will necessarily remain elusive. To speak in broad terms, absent war or an extraordinary level of social indoctrination provided for by the fundamental laws of a polity, individuals in regimes that make a claim to political liberty are not going to opt for a political or social life in which the needs of the whole are made precedent to their own struggles to achieve meaningful, decent, secure lives.[9]

To put it another way: the existence of civil society and a functioning representative government virtually guarantees the absence of a commanding legislator able to reshape the citizenry's hopes and desires in accordance with public needs. And without such a legislator to put in place a constitutional order that radically reorients individual aspirations, directing them above all else to the polity's well-being, no robust politics of public virtue can make much headway. Classical republican theorists understood this limitation clearly.[10] The strictures and expectations it places on a citizenry are simply not sufficiently appealing to the unconverted to win the support required to put it into action.

One might object that this is precisely the point: living in a commercialized society, living by liberal ideals, makes one the sort of person unable or unwilling to embrace a politics of public virtue. My contention however is that the operative factors lie elsewhere: in *any* society that gives persons both a say in politics and a life in civil society, the politics of public virtue will find few takers. Citizens of these pluralist polities (most of which may also be liberal and/or commercial republics) will not find the mode of citizenship called for by the politics of virtue attractive.

When people have a say over their own lives they do not usually choose to dedicate those lives to the public and its good. The exception, at least in theory, are those small, homogeneous republics quite unlike the constitu-

---

9 Small religious or utopian communities are the partial exception to this rule, but the circumstances of their members are very different from those of citizens of an established nation-state such as Great Britain. Obviously, one would not want to call early eighteenth-century Britain a representative democracy. J. H. Plumb provides the classic account of how formal political participation actually decreased during the period between 1714 and 1760 (*The Growth of Political Stability in England, 1660–1730* [London: Macmillan, 1967]). Yet the franchise was still broad enough, the voters heterogeneous enough, for my argument to hold here as well as in more open and explicitly democratic regimes. And the potential, more fully realized later in the century, for public protest and participation gave the regime a somewhat less oligarchic character than the closed character of parliament suggests. See, for example, Geoffrey Holmes, *The Trial of Doctor Sacheverell* (London: Eyre Methuen, 1973); Paul Langford, *The Excise Crisis: Society and Politics in the Age of Walpole* (Oxford: Clarendon Press, 1975); and, at a slightly later date, John Brewer, *Party Ideology and Popular Politics at the Accession of George III* (Cambridge University Press, 1976).

10 For the necessity of a legislator in founding any regime of virtue, see Machiavelli, *The Discourses*, Book I, chapter 9; Harrington, *Oceana* in *The Political Works*, ed. J. G. A. Pocock (Cambridge University Press, 1977) and Rousseau, *On the Social Contract*, Book II, chapter 7. The potentially disastrous effects of such an effort can be gathered from any history of the French Revolution; see Simon Schama, *Citizens: A Chronicle of the French Revolution* (New York: Alfred A. Knopf, 1989), especially part four.

tional monarchy of Augustan England. It is this political fact rather than broad trends in social or economic development that was immediately responsible for the failure of various religious and republican politics of public virtue in the early eighteenth century.

The difficulty involved in bringing any nondespotic regime to affirm a program meant to cultivate public forms of political virtue does not however mean that the modern polity must learn to cope without any sort of political or civic virtue at all. There exist conceptions of civic virtue far more suited to democratic, pluralistic, self-governing politics than the all-encompassing publicly oriented ones represented by Bolingbroke or the SRMs.

Court Whigs champion a civic virtue of this sort in their account of the good citizen as the frugal, industrious budget balancer. As they see it, English citizens are generally competent deliberators on the public good – for who would not want to support the circumstances that secured their property, offered hopes of greater prosperity and guaranteed their security? Penury however can jeopardize the citizen's virtue, making him vulnerable to the assaults of a venal executive. The nation's well-being rests therefore with citizens disposed to manage their affairs thriftily, industriously, virtuously. In this scenario, individuals attend to the public good not from selfless, patriotic motives but because they want to secure the circumstances under which they and their families can flourish. The threat to good political judgment, the pathology that republicans call corruption, arises not from self-interest per se but from circumstances that detach the interests of the individual from the interests of the whole (in this case, a desperate financial situation).

This particular understanding of the good citizen embodies the features that make a privately oriented conception of civic virtue a plausible and desirable alternative to public virtue. By making thrift, honesty and industry the characteristics of a good citizen, the Court Whigs ground civic virtue not in the abandonment of self-interest but in the close correlation or molding of self-interest to the public good. The primary attraction of this acceptance of self-interest lies in its contained ambition. Rather than attempting to remake humans in a new, improved, more selfless version, Court Whigs describe citizens who contribute to the good polity in spite or even because of a lively sense of self-interest. This lack of hubris also places a politics of civic virtue within practical reach: one need neither convince a nation of the particular means best suited to weaning men and women from their egoism nor lobby the legislature (filled itself with self-interested actors) for the institution and funding of such programs.

The Court Whig account of civic virtue also places implicit limits on any governmental role in the cultivation of civic virtue. Pitt and Arnall expect traditional sources of moral education – family, church and schools – to play the primary role in developing the habits and dispositions they praise as civically virtuous. This tendency to leave the cultivation of virtue to forces largely outside the political arena has two advantages. It is easier to pursue a politics of this sort for one need not get involved in lengthy and divisive legislative debates about the proper allocation of state resources. It is also more attractive, because it provides for an education in virtue without the intrusion of officious bureaucrats or the coercive threats of the criminal law.

However, the specific civic virtues identified by Pitt and Arnall hardly provide the basis for a serious modern politics of virtue. One problem is simply the polemical context in which Pitt and Arnall develop their account of the good citizen. A private virtue grounded in responsible fiscal behavior is the most forceful answer they can provide to the bogey of public corruption called forth in Bolingbroke's political writings. It is not necessarily the best account of the dispositions actually required to make Englishmen into good citizens.

A second difficulty is that, as a politics of virtue, the Court Whig prescription says little about how best to nurture the deliberative abilities of the good citizen. Court Whigs take for granted the institutions and habits that make for effective public deliberation on the part of English citizens. Their concern is to prevent the corruption that would interfere with what they see as the natural development of civic virtue. A modern politics of virtue needs to focus more specifically on what it means to act well politically and how best to elicit such behavior from individuals.

In this context, *Cato's Letters* offers a more pertinent example of what a privately oriented civic virtue might look like. Cato's good citizen very much resembles the good judge of the modern liberal vision.[11] He keeps vigilant watch on the behavior of elected officials, inspects public policies for any unjust or tyrannical designs and protests government activity that harms the public good. However, the motivation for this civic service is not an abstract belief in or commitment to the ideals of a liberal polity, but a very concrete sense of the benefits to which each individual is entitled in a free society. Government, says Cato, should further the public interest, and the best judge of the government's success or failure is the citizens' own experience. Thus, "every Ploughman knows a good Government from a bad

---

11 See, for example, Stephen Macedo, *Liberal Virtues: Citizenship, Virtue and Community in Liberal Constitutionalism* (Oxford: Clarendon Press, 1990); Rogers M. Smith, *Liberalism and American Constitutional Law* (Cambridge: Harvard University Press, 1985); Elaine Spitz, "Citizenship and Liberal Institutions," in Alfonso J. Damico, ed., *Liberals on Liberalism* (Totowa, NJ: Rowman and Littlefield, 1986).

one, from the Effects of it; he knows whether the Fruits of his Labour be his own, and whether he enjoy them in Peace and Security."[12] As with the Court Whigs, the citizens' self-interest is seen not as an obstacle to civic virtue but as the source of positive contributions to the public good.

For such an arrangement to work, however, at least two political circumstances must hold. First, there must exist a genuine fit between the private interest of the individuals from whom civic virtue is being asked and the public good. One reason the classical republican tradition places such emphasis on overcoming private interest or subordinating it to the public good is that historically it spoke primarily to those whose private interests were at odds with the public good: the ambitious elite whose desire for power and prestige had to be reconciled with the republicans' hope for a free polity. Those whom Cato calls "the People at large" are devoid of these dangerous ambitions. They are far more interested in keeping government faithful to its constitutional principles, just and efficient in its operations, not because they are loyal to a public morality or political ideal but precisely because such a government best allows them to secure their personal welfare. Once the political realm expands to include those individuals for whom the fit between personal and public good is tighter than with elites, as it will in any democratic polity of either the liberal or republican variety, Cato's claim to ground civic virtue in the citizen's assessment of his or her self-interest makes good sense.

Second, individuals in a mass democracy must be able to see themselves (when appropriate) as citizens and reason about their self-interest on this basis. When called upon to participate in public political deliberation, they must be able to put aside self-interest narrowly conceived, in which the horizons of interest stop at one's front doorstep, and consider instead what is in one's self-interest as a member of the political community. Bruce Ackerman distinguishes in this vein between "the perfect privatist [who] when confronting the question of 'what is good for the country?' . . . acts as if this inquiry can be reduced to the question, 'what is good for me?' " and the "private citizen" whose inquiries center on "the effort to define a public policy that best fulfills the 'rights of citizens and the permanent interests of the community.' "[13]

Civic virtue of the sort Cato has in mind thus requires individuals who understand themselves as citizens and take seriously the rights and responsibilities this role implies. Not only must they possess an understanding of their polity's constitution, so as to judge when and if its principles are being

---

12 Trenchard and Gordon, *Letters,* II, 35.
13 Bruce A. Ackerman, "The Storrs Lectures: Discovering the Constitution," *Yale Law Journal* 93 (1984), 1033.

violated, but they must understand themselves as possessing rights and privileges worth defending through political action. (The best possible citizen would also be driven to assure that not only he or she, but all individuals had their rights respected and justice done to them. But, such an expansive disposition is not strictly necessary to Cato's vision of virtue, although it suits perhaps the "friend of liberty" like Cato himself.[14] For Cato, the selfish impulse to protect and satisfy ones own interest is sufficient to assure a flourishing state.)

Cato's vision of the good citizen also assumes a substantial amount of education in citizenship, a precondition the *Letters* do not make at all obvious. But unlike the sort of civic education called for by proponents of public virtue, the education necessary makes no unusual demands on the basic impulses of human nature (the scope of self-interest is to be expanded, not narrowed) nor does it require an inordinate involvement on the part of public institutions. The need is to introduce individuals to the practice of citizenship, to provide a sense that they can and should pursue their own interests within its disciplines. The various institutions and fora through which this education occurs are largely in place. For Cato, journals, pamphlets, newspapers and public, political argument play the crucial role in fostering the sort of opposition mentality necessary for challenging an entrenched and corrupt governmental elite. Modern societies might include the media, the schools, religious institutions, voluntary associations, local political organizations and assemblies, as well as family, as all able to reinforce the understanding of self as a bearer of political rights that deserve realization.[15] And as with the Court Whig version of civic virtue, the realization of this vision of the good citizen is not held hostage to the political process, for its cultivation does not depend upon the agreement of national or local legislatures to major institutional or political reforms.

The most serious problem with Cato's account of civic virtue is its limited sense of the political activities appropriate to good citizens. Their role remains primarily that of watchdog: to react to danger, to alert the community to malfeasance and pressure the government for its correction. To the extent that modern democracies aspire as well to a polity in which citizens shape and reshape the political agenda, decide what ends the government should pursue as well as judge how well it pursues them, more is needed. Neither Cato nor the Court Whigs then provide a transparent model for

14 See chapter 4, p. 84–5.
15 To say that these institutions are able to nurture an understanding of self that disposes to civic virtue is not to say that in all cases they do. One would need to know more about the circumstances that encourage the institutions of civil society to reinforce the political ideals of the regime (for good or for bad).

modern citizens interested in pursuing a politics of public virtue. Nor should one expect them to do so. But they do suggest that citizens can embrace civic excellences, and participate in political life in a way reflective of civic virtues, without exhibiting the self-sacrificing devotion to public ends characteristic of publicly oriented civic virtue.[16] Some may find it hard to abandon the seductive vision of a truly public civic virtue, of citizens who manage to make the public, the whole of which they are a part, the center of their reflections and affections. One can and at times should hold out the image of this sort of virtue as an imposing critical standard against which the various accommodations men and women make with public life may be measured. But we should not and cannot mourn the passing of a politics of public virtue, for this implies that the conditions where it could have flourished once existed and have been superseded. In fact, a politics of public virtue was never a live option in any community not supremely aristocratic in nature. To put this another way: public virtue is not the victim of liberalism or of commercial society, snagged and left behind at some watershed of modernity. The difficulty with the politics of public virtue is, as the eighteenth-century examples demonstrate, political. The programs by which a truly publicly oriented civic virtue might be nurtured in any citizenry are simply too controversial, too intrusive, too psychologically problematic to gain the lasting assent of those who make the polity's laws – or of those who must live under them.

Fortunately, whatever the context, the eclipse of public virtue does not consign the democratic citizen to the manipulative politics of a virtue-less polity, to a mechanics of passion or interest in which political elites elicit the desired behavior through the careful structuring of incentives and institutions (Mandeville's brave new world). To those willing to bracket the pursuit of public virtue for a better and different world there remain compelling civic virtues available to the modern citizen, virtues nurtured largely independently of government action and expressed in consonance with one's self-interest. The challenge for modern advocates of virtue therefore goes beyond simply shepherding their vision of the good citizen through the vagaries of political debate. They must transform that debate from an impossible emphasis on public virtue to a focus on the sorts of privately oriented civic virtue that can and hopefully will ground responsible political deliberation and action.

16 See chapter 1, pp. 7–11.

Bibliography

Ackerman, Bruce. "The Storrs Lectures: Discovering the Constitution." *Yale Law Journal* 93 (1984): 1013–72.

"An Account of the Reputed Writers in the News-Papers." *Gentleman's Magazine* 3 (1733): 91.

Allison, C. F. *The Rise of Moralism: The Proclamation of the Gospel from Hooker to Baxter.* London: Society for Promoting Christian Knowledge, 1966.

Appleby, Joyce Oldham. *Economic Thought and Ideology in Seventeenth-Century England.* Princeton: Princeton University Press, 1978.

Aquinas. *Selected Political Writings.* Ed. A.P. D'Entrèves. Oxford: Basil Blackwell, 1948.

Arendt, Hannah. *Between Past and Future: Eight Exercises in Political Thought.* New York: Penguin Books, 1961.

The Human Condition. Chicago: University of Chicago Press, 1958.

Aristotle. *The Politics.* Ed. and tr. Ernest Barker. Oxford: Oxford University Press, 1958.

Arnall, William. *Clodius and Cicero.* London, 1727.

The Free Briton: Or, The Opinion of the People. Number II. London, 1727.

Ashcraft, Richard and M. M. Goldsmith. "Locke, Revolution Principles, and the Formation of Whig Ideology." *The Historical Journal* 26 (1983): 773–800.

Ashe, St. George. *A Sermon Preach'd to the Societies for Reformation of Manners . . .* London, 1717.

Astell, Mary. *The Case of Moderation and Occasional Conformity.* London, 1705.

Augustine. *The City of God.* Tr. Marcus Dods. New York: Modern Library, 1950.

Backscheider, Paula. *Daniel Defoe: His Life.* Baltimore: The Johns Hopkins University Press, 1989.

Bahlman, Dudley. *The Moral Revolution of 1688.* New Haven: Yale University Press, 1957.

Balog, Frank D. "The Scottish Enlightenment and the Liberal Political Tradition." In *Confronting the Constitution.* Ed. Allan Bloom. Washington, DC: American Enterprise Institute, 1990.

Barber, Benjamin. *Strong Democracy: Participatory Politics for a New Age.* Berkeley: University of California Press, 1984.

Barnes, Joshua. *The Good Old Way: or Three Brief Discourses Tending to the Promotion of Religion.* London, 1703.

Baron, Hans. *The Crisis of the Early Italian Renaissance.* Revised one-volume edition. Princeton: Princeton University Press, 1966.

Bedford, Arthur. *A Sermon Preached to the Societies for Reformation of Manners...* London, 1734.

Bellah, Robert N., et al. *Habits of the Heart: Individualism and Commitment in American Life.* Berkeley: University of California Press, 1985.

Bennett, G. V. "Conflict in the Churches." In *Britain after the Glorious Revolution, 1689–1714.* Ed. Geoffrey Holmes. London: Macmillan, 1969.

   The Tory Crisis in Church and State, 1688–1730. Oxford: Clarendon Press, 1975.

Berkeley, George. *Alciphron, or the Minute Philosopher* (1732). In *Works.* Eds. A. A. Luce and T. E. Jessop. London: Thomas Nelson and Sons Ltd., 1950.

Berriman, William. *Family-Religion Recommended...* London, 1735.

Berry, Christopher J. *The Idea of a Democratic Community.* New York: St. Martin's Press, 1989.

Bisset, William. *Plain English: A Sermon Preach'd to the Societies for the Reformation of Manners.* London, 1704.

Bloom, Edward A. and Lillian D. Bloom. *Joseph Addison's Sociable Animal in the Market Place, on the Hustings, in the Pulpit.* Providence: Brown University Press, 1971.

Bluet, George. *An Enquiry Whether a General Practice of Virtue Tends to the Wealth or Poverty, Benefit or Disadvantage of a People.* London, 1725.

Bolingbroke, Henry St. John, Viscount. *Historical Writings.* Ed. Isaac Kramnick. Chicago: University of Chicago Press, 1972.

   Letter to Sir William Windham. London, 1753.

   The Works of Lord Bolingbroke. 4 v. London: Henry Bohn, 1844. Reprint. New York: A. M. Kelley, 1967.

Bonadeo, Alfredo. "Corruption, Conflict, and Power in the Works and Times of Niccolo Machiavelli." *University of California Publications in Modern Philology* 108. Berkeley: University of California, 1973.

Bray, Thomas. *For God or for Satan: Being A Sermon Preach'd to the Societies for Reformation of Manners...* London, 1709.

   A Short Account of the Several Kinds of Societies... for carrying on the Reformation of Manners. London, 1700.

Brewer, John. *Party Ideology and Popular Politics at the Accession of George III.* Cambridge University Press, 1976.

   The Sinews of Power: War, Money and the English State, 1688–1783. New York: Alfred A. Knopf, 1989.

Bristow, Edward. *Vice and Vigilance: Purity Movements in Britain since 1700.* Dublin: Gill and Macmillan, 1977.

British Journal. 21 January 1727–19 June 1729.

Brooks, Colin. "The Country Persuasion and Political Responsibility in England in the 1690s." *Parliaments, Estates and Representation* 4 (1984): 135–46.

Browning, Reed. *Political and Constitutional Ideas of the Court Whigs.* Baton Rouge: Louisiana State University Press, 1982.

Budziszewski, J. *The Nearest Coast of Darkness: A Vindication of the Politics of Virtues.* Ithaca: Cornell University Press, 1988.

The Resurrection of Nature: Political Theory and the Human Character. Ithaca: Cornell University Press, 1986.

Bulloch, J. M. *Thomas Gordon, the "Independent Whig."* Aberdeen: At the University Press. Reprinted from *Aberdeen University Library Bulletin* 3 (1917): 598–612, 733–49.

Burnet, Gilbert. *Charitable Reproof. A Sermon Preached to the Societies for Reformation of Manners...* London, 1700.

A Discourse of the Pastoral Care. 3rd ed. London, 1713.

Burrow, Robert. *Civil Society and Government Vindicated from the Charge of being Founded on, and Preserv'd by, Dishonest Arts...* London, 1723.

Burtt, Shelley. "The Good Citizen's Psyche: On the Psychology of Civic Virtue." *Polity* 23 (1990): 23–38.

"The Virtue of Authority: Illiberalism and the Concern for Order in the Ideology of the Societies for Reformation of Manners, 1690–1740." Unpublished paper, 1982.

Calamy, Edward. *A Sermon Preach'd to the Societies for Reformation of Manners...* London, 1699.

Calvin, John. *Institutes of the Christian Religion* (1559). Tr. John Allen. Grand Rapids, MI: Eerdmans Publishing Company, 1949.

Campbell, Archibald. *An Enquiry into the Original of Moral Virtue.* London, 1728.

Carswell, John. *The South Sea Bubble.* Stanford: Stanford University Press, 1960.

Carter, Jennifer. "The Revolution and the Constitution." In *Britain after the Glorious Revolution, 1689–1714.* Ed. Geoffrey Holmes. London: Macmillan, 1967.

Chandler, Edward. *A Sermon Preach'd to the Societies for Reformation of Manners...* London, 1724.

Civil Security, Not Conscience, Concerned in the Bill Concerning Occasional Conformity. London, 1702.

Clark, J. C. D. *English Society, 1688–1832: Ideology, Social Structure and Political Practice during the Ancien Regime.* Cambridge University Press, 1985.

Cobden, Edward. *The Duty and Reward of Turning Others to Righteousness. A Sermon Preach'd to the Societies for Reformation of Manners...* London, 1736.

Cochran, Clarke. *Character, Community, and Politics.* University, AL: University of Alabama Press, 1982.

Colley, Linda. *In Defiance of Oligarchy: The Tory Party, 1714–60.* Cambridge University Press, 1982.

Collinson, Patrick. *The Elizabethan Puritan Movement.* London: Jonathan Cape, 1967.

Colman, John. *John Locke's Moral Philosophy*. Edinburgh: Edinburgh University Press, 1983.

Colnett, William. *A Sermon Preach'd to the Societies for Reformation of Manners...* London, 1711.

Coxe, Thomas. *A Sermon Preach'd at the Assizes held at Bedford...* Oxford, 1730.

Cragg, G. R. *From Puritanism to the Age of Reason.* Cambridge University Press, 1950.

Curtis, T. C. and Speck, W. A. "The Societies for Reformation of Manners: A Case Study in the Theory and Practice of Moral Reform." *Literature and History* 3 (1976): 45–64.

Daily Gazetteer. 30 June 1735–8 April 1736.

Davenant, Charles. *The Political and Commercial Works.* 4 v. London, 1771.

Deane, Herbert A. *The Political and Social Ideas of St. Augustine.* New York: Columbia University Press, 1963.

Defoe, Daniel. *An Essay upon Projects.* London, 1697.

  The Poor Man's Plea to all the Proclamations, Declarations, Acts of Parliament, etc.... for a Reformation of Manners (1698). London, 1703.

  Reformation of Manners, A Satyr. London, 1702.

  Les Soupirs de la Grand Britaigne: Or, the Groans of Great Britain... London, 1713.

Denne, John. *The Duty of Doing All Things to the Glory of God. A Sermon Preach'd to the Societies for Reformation of Manners.* London, 1730.

Dennis, John. *Vice and Luxury Publick Mischiefs; or, Remarks on... The Fable of the Bees.* London, 1724.

Dickinson, H. T. *Bolingbroke.* London: Constable, 1970.

  Liberty and Property: Political Ideology in Eighteenth-Century Britain. New York: Holmes and Meier Publishers, 1977.

  "The Politics of Bernard Mandeville." In *Mandeville Studies: New Explorations in the Art and Thought of Bernard Mandeville.* Ed. Irwin Primer. The Hague: Martinus Nijhoff, 1975.

  Walpole and the Whig Supremacy. London: The English Universities Press, 1973.

Dickson, P. G. M. *The Financial Revolution in England.* London: Macmillan, 1967.

Disney, John. *An Address to Grand Juries, Constables, and Church Wardens.* London, 1710.

  A View of Antient Laws against Immorality and Profaneness. Cambridge, 1729.

Dongworth, Richard. *The Necessity of Reformation: An Assizes Sermon.* London, 1708.

Downie, J. A. *Jonathan Swift, Political Writer.* London: Routledge and Kegan Paul, 1984.

Drew, Robert. *A Sermon Preach'd to the Societies for Reformation of Manners...* London, 1735.

Dunn, John. "The Politics of Locke in England and America in the Eighteenth Century." In *John Locke, Problems and Perspectives: A Collection of New Essays.* Ed. John W. Yolton. Cambridge University Press, 1969.

Earl, D. C. *The Moral and Political Tradition of Rome.* Ithaca: Cornell University Press, 1967.

The Political Thought of Sallust. Cambridge University Press, 1961.

Ehrenpreis, Irvin. *Swift. The Man, His Works and the Age.* v. 2. Cambridge: Harvard University Press, 1967.

Elkin, Stephen L. *City and Regime in the American Republic.* Chicago: University of Chicago Press, 1987.

Ellis, E. L. "William III and the Politicians." In *Britain after the Glorious Revolution, 1689–1714.* Ed. Geoffrey Holmes. London: Macmillan, 1969.

Esprit, Jacques. *The Deceitfulness of Human Virtues* (1678). Tr. William Beauvoir. London, 1706.

An Essay on Conjugal Infidelity. London, [1727].

Every, George. *The High Church Party, 1688–1718.* London: Society for the Promotion of Christian Knowledge, 1956.

Ewald, William Bragg. *Rogues, Royalty and Reporters: The Age of Queen Anne through Its Newspapers.* Westport, CT: Greenwood Press, 1978.

Faulkner, Robert. *Richard Hooker and the Politics of a Christian England.* Berkeley: University of California Press, 1981.

Fiddes, Richard. *A General Treatise of Morality.* London, 1724.

Fieldhouse, H. N. "Bolingbroke and the Idea of Non-party Government." *History* 23 (1938): 41–56.

Fiering, Norman. *Jonathan Edwards's Moral Thought and Its British Context.* Chapel Hill, NC: University of North Carolina Press, 1981.

Fink, Z. S. *The Classical Republicans.* Chicago: Northwestern University Press, 1945.

Fletcher, Andrew. *Selected Political Writings and Speeches.* Ed. David Daiches. Edinburgh: Scottish Academic Press, 1979.

Foord, Archibald. *His Majesty's Opposition, 1714–1830.* Oxford: Clarendon Press, 1964.

Forbes, Duncan. *Hume's Philosophical Politics.* Cambridge University Press, 1975.

Fowler, Edward. *A Sermon Preach'd to the Societies for Reformation of Manners.* London, 1699.

Freeman, Samuel. *A Sermon Preach'd at the Assizes, held at Northampton.* London, 1690.

Galston, William. "Liberal Virtues." *American Political Science Review* 82 (1988): 1277–90.

Gibson, Edmund. *Codex Juris Ecclesiastici Anglicani.* London, 1713.

A Sermon Preached to the Societies for Reformation of Manners. 2d ed. London, 1723.

Gilbert, Felix. *Machiavelli and Guicciardini.* Princeton: Princeton University Press, 1965.

Goldsmith, M. M. *Private Vices, Public Benefits: Bernard Mandeville's Social and Political Thought.* Cambridge University Press, 1985.

Goodale, Jesse. "Pocock's Neo-Harringtonians: A Reconsideration." *History of Political Thought* 1 (1980): 237–60.

[Grant, Francis. Lord Cullen.] *A Brief Account of the Nature, Rise, and Progress of the Societies, for Reformation of Manners &c.* Edinburgh, 1700.

Grean, Stanley. *Shaftesbury's Philosophy of Religion and Ethics.* Athens, OH: Ohio University Press, 1967.

Grove, Henry. *Spectator* No. 588. 1 September 1714.

Gunn, J. A. W. *Beyond Liberty and Property: The Process of Self-Recognition in Eighteenth-Century Political Thought.* Kingston and Montreal: McGill-Queen's University Press, 1983.

——— *Factions No More: Attitudes to Party in Government and Opposition in Eighteenth-Century England. Extracts from Contemporary Sources.* London: Frank Cass, 1971.

——— *Politics and the Public Interest in the Seventeenth Century.* London: Routledge and Kegan Paul, 1969.

Gutmann, Amy. "Communitarian Critics of Liberalism." *Philosophy and Public Affairs* 14 (1985): 308–22.

Hamilton, Alexander, et al. *The Federalist Papers.* New York: New American Library, 1961.

Hanson, Laurence. *Government and the Press, 1695–1763.* London: Humphrey Milford, 1936.

Hare, Francis. *A Sermon Preached to the Societies for Reformation of Manners.* London, 1731.

Harrington, James. *The Political Works.* Ed. J. G. A. Pocock. Cambridge University Press, 1977.

Hart, Jeffrey. *Viscount Bolingbroke: Tory Humanist.* London: Routledge and Kegan Paul, 1965.

Hauerwas, Stanley. *A Community of Character: Toward a Constructive Christian Social Ethic.* Notre Dame: University of Notre Dame Press, 1981.

Hayek, F. A. "Dr. Bernard Mandeville." *Proceedings of the British Academy* 52 (1966): 125–41.

Hayley, Thomas. *A Sermon Preach'd to the Societies for Reformation of Manners...* London, 1718.

Henley, John. *The Sermon that shou'd have been Preach'd before the Societies for Reformation of Manners.* London, 1732.

Herzog, Don. "Some Questions for Republicans." *Political Theory* 14 (1986): 473–93.

Hexter, J. H. *On Historians.* Cambridge: Harvard University Press, 1979.

Heynes, Matthew. *A Sermon for Reformation of Manners, Preach'd... at the Assizes.* London, 1701.

Hirsch, Fred. *Social Limits to Growth.* Cambridge: Harvard University Press, 1976.

Hirsch, H. N. "The Threnody of Liberalism: Constitutional Liberty and the Renewal of Community." *Political Theory* 14: 423–50.

Hirschman, Albert O. *The Passions and the Interests: Political Arguments for Capitalism before Its Triumph.* Princeton: Princeton University Press, 1977.

Hole, Matthew. *The True Reformation of Manners; or the Nature and Qualifications of True Zeal.* Oxford, 1699.

Holmes, Geoffrey. *British Politics in the Age of Anne.* London: Macmillan, 1967.

The Trial of Doctor Sacheverell. London: Eyre Methuen, 1973.

Holmes, Stephen. "The Permanent Structure of Antiliberal Thought." In *Liberalism and the Moral Life.* Ed. Nancy L. Rosenblum. Cambridge: Harvard University Press, 1989.

Hooker, Richard. *Works.* 3 v. Oxford: Clarendon Press, 1793.

Höpfl, Harro. *The Christian Polity of John Calvin.* Cambridge University Press, 1982.

Horne, Thomas. "Politics in a Corrupt Society: William Arnall's Defense of Robert Walpole." *Journal of the History of Ideas* 41 (1980): 601–14.

Horwitz, Henry. *Parliament, Policy and Politics in the Reign of William III.* Manchester: Manchester University Press, 1977.

Hume, David. *Essays, Moral, Political and Literary* (1741). Ed. Eugene F. Miller. Indianapolis: LibertyClassics, 1985.

Hutcheson, Francis. *Illustrations: on the Moral Sense* (1728). Ed. Bernard Peach. Cambridge: Harvard University Press, 1971.

An Inquiry into the Original of our Ideas of Beauty and Virtue; in Two Treatises. In Which the Principles of... Shaftesbury are... Defended against... the Fable of the Bees. London, 1725.

Letters in the *Dublin Journal,* 1726. In *Reflections upon Laughter and Remarks upon the Fable of the Bees.* Glasgow, 1750.

Letters in the *London Journal,* 14 and 21 November 1724.

Ibbot, Benjamin. *The Nature and Extent of the Office of the Civil Magistrate.* London, 1720.

Isaacs, Tina. "The Anglican Hierarchy and the Reformation of Manners, 1688–1738." *Journal of Ecclesiastical History* 33 (1982): 391–411.

"Moral Crime, Moral Reform, and the State in Early Eighteenth-Century England: A Study of Piety and Politics." Unpublished Ph.D. dissertation, University of Rochester, 1980.

Jackman, Sydney Wayne. *Man of Mercury: An Appreciation of the Mind of Henry St. John, Viscount Bolingbroke.* London: Pall Mall Publishers, 1965.

Jacob, M. C. *The Newtonians and the English Revolution, 1688–1720.* Hassocks, Sussex: Harvester Press, 1976.

Jones, J. R. *Country and Court in England, 1658–1714.* Cambridge: Harvard University Press, 1978.

The First Whigs: The Politics of the Exclusion Crisis, 1678–83. Oxford: Oxford University Press, 1961.

The Revolution of 1688 in England. New York: W. W. Norton and Company, 1972.

Kateb, George. "Democratic Individuality and the Meaning of Rights." In *Liberalism and the Moral Life.* Ed. Nancy L. Rosenblum. Cambridge: Harvard University Press, 1989.

Kemp, Betty. *King and Commons, 1660–1832* (1957). Reprint. Westport, CT: Greenwood Press, 1984.

Kenyon, J. P. *Revolution Principles: The Philosophy of Party, 1689–1720.* Cambridge University Press, 1977.

Kohl, Benjamin and Ronald Witt. *The Earthly Republic: Italian Humanists on Government and Society.* Philadelphia: University of Pennsylvania Press, 1978.

Kramnick, Isaac. *Bolingbroke and His Circle: The Politics of Nostalgia in the Age of Walpole.* Cambridge: Harvard University Press, 1968.

"The 'Great National Discussion': The Discourse of Politics in 1787." *William and Mary Quarterly.* 3rd ser. 45 (1988): 3–32.

Republicanism and Bourgeois Radicalism: Political Ideology in Late Eighteenth-Century England and America. Ithaca: Cornell University Press, 1990.

"Republican Revisionism Revisited." *American Historical Review* 87 (1982): 595–628.

Lamont, William. *Godly Rule: Politics and Religion, 1603–1660.* London: Macmillan, 1969.

Langford, Paul. *The Excise Crisis: Society and Politics in the Age of Walpole.* Oxford: Clarendon Press, 1975.

A Polite and Commercial People: England, 1727–1785. Oxford: Clarendon Press, 1989.

Laprade, William Thomas. *Public Opinion and Politics in Eighteenth-Century England to the Fall of Walpole.* London: Macmillan, 1936. Reprint. New York: Octagon Books, 1977.

Law, William. *Remarks upon the Fable of the Bees* (1724). Cambridge: Macmillan, 1844.

Leslie, Charles. *Cassandra. (But I Hope Not) Telling What Will Come of It. Number II . . .* London, 1704.

The New Association. 3d ed. London, 1702.

The New Association. Part II. London, 1703.

Liberty and the Craftsman: A Project for Improving the Country Journal. London, 1730.

Little, David. *Religion, Order, and Law: A Study in Pre-Revolutionary England.* New York: Harper and Row, 1969.

Lock, J. P. *Swift's Tory Politics.* London: Duckworth, 1983.

London Journal. 2 January 1731–28 June 1735.

Lowman, Moses. *A Sermon Preached to the Societies for Reformation of Manners at Salter's-Hall . . .* London, 1720.

Macedo, Stephen. *Liberal Virtues: Citizenship, Virtue, and Community in Liberal Constitutionalism.* Oxford: Clarendon Press, 1990.

Machiavelli. *The Prince and the Discourses.* New York: Modern Library, 1950.

MacIntyre, Alasdair. *After Virtue: A Study in Moral Theory.* Notre Dame: University of Notre Dame Press, 1981.

Mandeville, Bernard. *An Enquiry into the Origin of Honour, and the Usefulness of Christianity in War* (1732). London: Frank Carr, 1971.

The Fable of the Bees and *Fable of the Bees, Part II* (1723; 1729). Ed. F. B. Kaye. 2 v. Oxford: Clarendon Press, 1924.

Free Thoughts on Religion, the Church, and National Happiness (1720). Delmar, NY: Scholars' Facsimiles and Reprints, 1981.

A Letter to Dion (1732). Ed. Bonamy Dobrée. Liverpool: University Press of Liverpool, 1954.

The Mischiefs that ought justly to be apprehended from a Whig Government (1714). Los Angeles: William Andrews Clark Memorial Library, 1975.

A Modest Defence of Publick Stews (1724). Los Angeles: William Andrews Clark Memorial Library, 1973.

A Treatise of the Hypochondriack and Hysterick Diseases (1711). Delmar, NY: Scholars' Facsimiles and Reprints, 1976.

The Virgin Unmask'd (1710). Delmar, NY: Scholars' Facsimiles and Reprints, 1975.

Mansfield, Harvey. *Statesmanship and Party Government: A Study of Burke and Bolingbroke*. Chicago: University of Chicago Press, 1965.

Maxwell, J. C. "Ethics and Politics in Mandeville." *Philosophy* 26 (1951): 242–52.

McAdoo, H. R. *The Structure of Caroline Moral Theology*. London: Longmans, Green and Co., 1949.

McGee, J. Sears. *The Godly Man in Stuart England: Anglicans, Puritans, and the Two Tables, 1620–1670*. New Haven: Yale University Press, 1976.

Meilaender, Gilbert C. *The Theory and Practice of Virtue*. Notre Dame: University of Notre Dame Press, 1984.

Melanchthon, Philip. *Selected Writings*. Ed. E. E. Flack and Lowell Satre. Tr. C. L. Hill. Minneapolis, MN: Augsburg Publishing House, 1962.

The Memorial of the Church of England. London, 1705.

Mendus, Susan. *Toleration and the Limits of Liberalism*. Atlantic Highlands, NJ: Humanities Press International, 1989.

Michelman, Frank. "Law's Republic." *Yale Law Journal* 97 (1988): 1493–538.

More, Hannah. *Works*. London: T. Caddell, 1830.

Moyle, Walter. *An Essay upon the Constitution of the Roman Government* (1726). In *Two English Republican Tracts*. Ed. Caroline Robbins. Cambridge University Press, 1969.

Newman, Thomas. *Reformation, or Mockery . . . A Sermon Preach'd to the Societies for Reformation of Manners at Salter's Hall . . .* London, 1729.

Nokes, David. *Jonathan Swift*. Oxford: Oxford University Press, 1985.

Occasional Paper Upon the Subject of Religion . . . London, 1735.

Onuf, Peter S. "Reflections on the Founding: Constitutional Historiography in Bicentennial Perspective." *William and Mary Quarterly*. 3rd ser. 46 (1989): 341–75.

Owen, J. B. *The Eighteenth Century, 1714–1815*. New York: W. W. Norton and Company, 1974.

"The Survival of Country Attitudes in the Eighteenth-Century House of Commons." In *Britain and the Netherlands, Volume 4: Metropolis, Dominion and Province*. The Hague: Martinus Nijhoff, 1971.

Ozment, Steven E. *The Reformation in the Cities*. New Haven: Yale University Press, 1975.

Pagden, Anthony. "Introduction." In *The Languages of Political Theory in Early Modern Europe*. Ed. Anthony Pagden. Cambridge University Press, 1987.

Penn, Thomas. *A Sermon Preach'd Before the Societies for Reformation of Manners...* London, 1708.

Pennington, Donald and Keith Thomas, eds. *Puritans and Revolutionaries.* Oxford: Clarendon Press, 1978.

Perry, Ruth. *The Celebrated Mary Astell: An Early English Feminist.* Chicago: University of Chicago Press, 1986.

Phillipson, Nicholas. "Adam Smith as Civic Moralist." In *Wealth and Virtue: The Shaping of Political Economy in the Scottish Enlightenment.* Eds. Istvan Hont and Michael Ignatieff. Cambridge University Press, 1983.

"The Scottish Enlightenment." In *The Enlightenment in National Context.* Eds. Roy Porter and Mikulas Teich. Cambridge University Press, 1981.

Pieper, Josef. *The Four Cardinal Virtues* (1954). Notre Dame: University of Notre Dame Press, 1966.

Pincoffs, Edmund L. *Quandries and Virtues: Against Reductivism in Ethics.* Lawrence: University Press of Kansas, 1986.

Pitkin, Hanna. "Justice: On Relating Public to Private." *Political Theory* 9 (1981): 327–52.

Plumb, J. H. *The Growth of Political Stability in England, 1660–1730.* London: Macmillan, 1967.

Sir Robert Walpole: The King's Minister. Boston: Houghton Mifflin Company, 1961.

Pocock, J. G. A. "Cambridge Paradigms and Scotch Philosophers: A Study of the Relations between the Civic Humanist and the Civil Jurisprudential Interpretation of Eighteenth-Century Social Thought." In *Wealth and Virtue: The Shaping of Political Economy in the Scottish Enlightenment.* Eds. Istvan Hont and Michael Ignatieff. Cambridge University Press, 1983.

"Early Modern Capitalism: The Augustan Perception." In *Feudalism, Capitalism and Beyond.* Eds. Eugene Kamenka and R. S. Neale. Canberra: Australian National University Press, 1975.

The Machiavellian Moment: Florentine Political Thought and the Atlantic Republican Tradition. Princeton: Princeton University Press, 1975.

"*The Machiavellian Moment* Revisited: A Study in History and Ideology." *Journal of Modern History* 53 (1981): 49–72.

Politics, Language and Time: Essays on Political Thought and History. New York: Atheneum, 1973.

"The Problem of Political Thought in the Eighteenth Century: Patriotism and Politeness." *Theoretische Geschiedenis* 9 (1982): 3–23.

"Virtue and Commerce in the Eighteenth Century." *Journal of Interdisciplinary History* 3 (1972): 119–34.

Virtue, Commerce, and History: Essays on Political Thought and History, Chiefly in the Eighteenth Century. Cambridge University Press, 1985.

Proposals for a National Reformation of Manners... London, 1695.

[Ralph, James.] *The Case of Authors by Profession or Trade, Stated.* London, 1758.

Rawson, Joseph. *Righteousness the Exaltation, and Sin the Reproach of a People. In a Sermon Preach'd at the Lent Assizes.* London, 1714.

Raz, Joseph. "Autonomy, Toleration, and the Harm Principle." In *Justifying Toleration: Conceptual and Historical Perspectives.* Ed. Susan Mendus. Cambridge University Press, 1988.

"Facing Diversity: The Case of Epistemic Abstinence." *Philosophy and Public Affairs* 19 (1990): 3–46.

Realey, Charles B. "The *London Journal* and Its Authors, 1720–23." *Humanistic Studies* 5 (3). In *Bulletin of University of Kansas* 36 (1935): 1–38.

Redwood, John. *Reason, Ridicule and Religion: The Age of Enlightenment in England, 1660–1750.* Cambridge: Harvard University Press, 1976.

Reflections on the Moral State of a Nation. London, 1701.

A Representation of the State of the Societies for Reformation of Manners, Humbly Offered to his Majesty. London, 1715.

Robbins, Caroline. *The Eighteenth-Century Commonwealthman.* Cambridge: Harvard University Press, 1959.

Robertson, John. "The Scottish Enlightenment at the Limits of the Civic Tradition." In *Wealth and Virtue: The Shaping of Political Economy in the Scottish Enlightenment.* Eds. Istvan Hont and Michael Ignatieff. Cambridge University Press, 1983.

Rogers, Nicholas. "Popular Jacobitism in Provincial Context: Eighteenth-Century Bristol and Norwich." In *The Jacobite Challenge.* Eds. Eveline Cruickshanks and Jeremy Black. Edinburgh: John Donald Publishers, 1988.

Rogers, Timothy. *A Sermon Preach'd to the Societies for Reformation of Manners . . .* London, 1701.

Rousseau, Jean-Jacques. *On the Social Contract.* Ed. Roger D. Masters. Tr. Judith R. Masters. New York: St. Martin's Press, 1978.

Sacheverell, Henry. *The Communication of Sin. A Sermon Preach'd at the Assizes held at Derby.* London, 1709.

Salkever, Stephen. *Finding the Mean: Theory and Practice in Aristotelian Political Philosophy.* Princeton: Princeton University Press, 1990.

Sandel, Michael J. "Mortality and the Liberal Ideal." *The New Republic.* May 7, 1984.

Schama, Simon. *Citizens: A Chronicle of the French Revolution.* New York: Alfred A. Knopf, 1989.

Schwoerer, Lois. "The Bill of Rights: Epitome of the Revolution of 1688–89." In *Three British Revolutions, 1641, 1688, 1776.* Ed. J. G. A. Pocock. Princeton: Princeton University Press, 1980.

"No Standing Armies!" The Antiarmy Ideology in Seventeenth-Century England. Baltimore: The Johns Hopkins University Press, 1974.

Shaftesbury, Anthony Ashley Cooper, Third Earl of. *Characteristics of Men, Manners, Opinions, Times, etc.* (1711). Reprint. Ed. John M. Robertson. Gloucester, MA: Peter Smith, 1963.

Shalhope, Robert E. "Republicanism and Early American Historiography." *William and Mary Quarterly.* 3rd ser. 39 (1982): 334–56.

"Toward a Republican Synthesis: The Emergence of an Understanding of Republicanism in American Historiography." *William and Mary Quarterly.* 3rd ser. 29 (1972): 49–80.

Shapiro, Ian. *Political Criticism.* Berkeley: University of California Press, 1990.

Short, K. R. M. "The English Indemnity Acts, 1726–1867." *Church History* 42 (1973): 366–76.

Sinopoli, Richard C. "Liberalism, Republicanism and the Constitution." *Polity* 19 (1987): 331–52.

Skinner, Quentin. *The Foundations of Modern Political Thought, Volume I: The Renaissance.* Cambridge University Press, 1978.

    "The Idea of Negative Liberty: Philosophical and Historical Perspectives." In *Philosophy in History: Essays on the Historiography of Philosophy.* Eds. Richard Rorty, J. B. Scheewind and Quentin Skinner. Cambridge University Press, 1984.

    Machiavelli. Oxford: Oxford University Press, 1981.

    "The Principles and Practice of Opposition: The Case of Bolingbroke versus Walpole." In *Historical Perspectives: Studies in English Thought and Society.* Ed. Neil McKendrick. London: Europa Publications, 1974.

Smalbroke, Richard. *Reformation Necessary to prevent our Ruine. A Sermon Preach'd to the Societies for Reformation of Manners...* London, 1728.

Smith, Adam. *An Inquiry into the Nature and Causes of the Wealth of Nations* (1776). New York: Modern Library, 1937.

    The Theory of Moral Sentiments (1759). Indianapolis, IN: LibertyClassics, 1976.

Smith, Rogers M. *Liberalism and American Constitutional Law.* Cambridge: Harvard University Press, 1985.

Smith, Samuel. *A Sermon Preach'd to the Societies for Reformation of Manners...* London, 1738.

Smyth, George. *A Sermon Preach'd at Salter's-Hall to the Societies for Reformation of Manners.* London, 1727.

Spademan, John. *A Sermon Preach'd November 14, 1698 and Now Publish'd at the Request of the Societies for Reformation of Manners.* London, 1699.

Speck, W. A. "Bernard Mandeville and the Middlesex Grand Jury." *Eighteenth-Century Studies* 11: 362–74.

    Stability and Strife: England, 1714–1760. Cambridge: Harvard University Press, 1977.

    Tory and Whig: The Struggle in the Constituencies, 1701–1715. London: Macmillan, 1970.

Spitz, Elaine. "Citizenship and Liberal Institutions." In *Liberals on Liberalism.* Ed. Alfonse J. Damico. Totowa, NJ: Rowman and Littlefield, 1986.

Stanhope, George. *The Duty of Juries. A Sermon Preach'd at the Lent-Assizes, holden at Maidstone, in Kent...* London, 1701.

    The Duty of Rebuking. A Sermon Preach'd at Bow-Church... Before... the Lord-Mayor and Aldermen...and the Societies for Reformation of Manners... London, 1703.

Steele, Richard. *Spectator* No. 75. 26 May 1711.

Stephen, Leslie. *History of English Thought in the Eighteenth Century* (1876). v. 1. New York: Harcourt, Brace and World, Inc., 1962.

[Stephens, Edward.] *The Beginning and Progress of a Needful and Hopeful Reformation in England.* London, 1691.

A Plain Relation of the Late Action at Sea . . . with Reflections thereupon and upon the Present State of the Nation. London, 1690.

A Seasonable and Necessary Admonition to the Gentlemen of the First Society for Reformation of Manners. [London?],[1700?].

Stromberg, R. N. *Religious Liberalism in Eighteenth-Century England.* Oxford: Oxford University Press, 1954.

Sullivan, William. *Reconstructing Public Philosophy.* Berkeley: University of California Press, 1986.

Sunstein, Cass. "Beyond the Republican Revival." *Yale Law Journal* 97 (1988): 1539–90.

Sutherland, James. *Daniel Defoe: A Critical Study.* Cambridge: Harvard University Press, 1971.

Swift, Jonathan. *A Project for the Advancement of Religion and the Reformation of Manners.* London, 1709.

Sydney, Algernon. *Discourses on Government* (1698). In *Works.* London, 1772.

Sykes, Norman. *Church and State in England in the Eighteenth Century.* Cambridge University Press, 1934.

Taylor, Charles. "Cross-Purposes: The Liberal-Communitarian Debate." In *Liberalism and the Moral life.* Ed. Nancy L. Rosenblum. Cambridge: Harvard University Press, 1989.

Thompson, Martyn P. "The Reception of Locke's *Two Treatises of Government,* 1690–1705." *Political Studies* 24 (1976): 184–91.

Thorold, John. *A Short Examination of the Notions Advanc'd in a (Late) Book, Intituled, The Fable of the Bees.* London, 1726.

Tillotson, John. Archbishop of Canterbury. *Works.* London, 1701.

Tocqueville, Alexis de. *Democracy in America* (1835, 1840). Ed. J. P. Mayer. New York: Doubleday and Company, 1969.

Todd, Margo. *Christian Humanism and the Puritan Social Order.* Cambridge University Press, 1987.

Trenchard, John and Thomas Gordon. *Cato's Letters* (1733). 4 v. 3d ed. Facsimile reprint. 2 v. New York: Russell and Russell, 1969.

Troeltsch, Ernst. *The Social Teaching of the Christian Churches.* 2 v. New York: Harper and Row, 1960.

Troughear, Thomas. *The Magistrate's Duty to Honour God, Set Forth in a Sermon Preach'd at Southampton.* Oxford, 1733.

Tutchin, John. *England's Happiness Consider'd, In Some Expedients.* London, 1705.

Varey, Simon, ed. *Bolingbroke: Contributions to The Craftsman.* Oxford: Clarendon Press, 1982.

Henry St. John, Viscount Bolingbroke. Boston: Twayne Publishers, 1984.

Vereker, Charles. *Eighteenth-Century Optimism.* Liverpool: Liverpool University Press, 1967.

Wallace, James D. *Virtues and Vices.* Ithaca: Cornell University Press, 1978.

Wallach, John R. "Liberals, Communitarians and the Tasks of Political Theory." *Political Theory* 15 (1987): 581–611.

Walzer, Michael. *Radical Principles: Reflections of an Unreconstructed Democrat.* New York: Basic Books, 1980.

The Revolution of the Saints: A Study in the Origin of Radical Politics. New York: Atheneum, 1965.

Watkins, Renée. *Humanism and Liberty: Writings on Freedom in Fifteenth-Century Florence.* Columbia: University of South Carolina Press, 1978.

Waugh, John. *A Sermon Preach'd to the Societies for Reformation of Manners.* London, 1714.

Will, George. *Statecraft as Soulcraft.* New York: Simon and Schuster, 1983.

Williams, Daniel. *A Sermon Preach'd at Salter's-Hall to the Societies for Reformation of Manners...* London, 1698.

Wilson, John. *Pulpit in Parliament: Puritanism during the English Civil War, 1640– 48.* Princeton: Princeton University Press, 1969.

Wood, Gordon S. *The Creation of the American Republic, 1776–1787.* New York: W. W. Norton and Company, 1969.

Woodward, Josiah. *An Account of the Progress of Reformation of Manners...* London, 1704.

The Judgement of the Rev. Dr. Henry Sacheverell, concerning the Societies for Reformation of Manners... London, 1711.

A Short Disswasive from the Sin of Uncleanness. London, 1701.

Wrightson, K. E. "The Puritan Reformation of Manners with Special Reference to the Counties of Lancashire and Essex, 1640–1660." Unpublished Ph.D. dissertation, Cambridge University, 1974.

[Yonge, William.] *Sedition and Defamation Display'd: In a Letter to the Author of the Craftsman.* London, 1731.

Yorke, Philip. *The Life and Correspondence of Philip Yorke, Earl of Hardwicke, Lord High Chancellor of Great Britain.* 2 v. Cambridge University Press, 1913.

Index

Addison, Joseph, 13, 33, 112n8, 140
Alliance Between Church and State (Warburton), 40
Anglican Church: on the consequences of sin, 45–6, 50–1; on the good state, 41–2; political theology of, 39–40, 53–4, 55, 57; on role of civil magistrate, 53–6; special political status of, 27, 40; two wings of, 19 (*see also* High Church Anglicans; Low Church Anglicans)
anti-Trinitarian views, 21n15, 25n21
Aquinas, *see* Thomas Aquinas, Saint
Aristotle, 6, 54, 64, 66, 95n15
Arnall, William [pseuds. Roger Manley; Francis Walsingham]: career of, 111, 114; on civic virtue, 112, 118–19, 120, 125, 127, 155, 161; on corruption, 114, 115–18, 121, 122, 127; on the good citizen, 125, 127; as a Walpole defender, 93, 111, 112–16, 117
Astell, Mary, 5n9
Augustan era: moral reform in, 46–8; partisan politics in, 16, 17, 19, 155, 158; social structure of, 32, 151
Augustine, Saint, 133, 134

Berkeley, George, 131n10
Bolingbroke, Henry St. John, Viscount: on the balanced constitution, 89, 90, 91, 92, 94, 97, 98, 112, 118, 153, 156; career of, 87; on civic virtue, 76–7, 89, 93, 94, 105, 118, 125, 153–4, 155, 156; on corruption, 36, 97, 98, 99–101, 102, 109, 110, 161; and the Country opposition, 87, 88, 90, 91, 102, 109, 118, 119, 153;

on the good citizen, 92, 94, 112, 125, 126, 153; on a natural aristocracy, 103, 104; on patriotism, 5n9, 33, 103–5, 106, 107, 108, 109; on public finance, 69, 100–1, 102; and the republican tradition, 67, 88, 89, 90, 91, 92, 93, 94, 95, 96, 106, 153–4, 156; on the spirit of liberty, 93, 94, 96, 100, 102, 103; and the transformation of virtue, 68, 88–9, 109, 111, 156; on the virtuous monarch, 95, 96, 104; on Walpole and his Whig ministry, 36, 87–8, 89–90, 93, 97, 98, 100, 101, 102, 103, 111, 120–1, 122, 153, 156
British Journal, 68n12, 111, 113n9, 114, 115
Browning, Reed, 116, 117n21

Calvin, John, on church discipline, 47
Catiline Conspiracy (Sallust), 69n15, 99
Cato, see *Cato's Letters*
Cato's Letters (Trenchard and Gordon): on civic virtue, 10–11, 35, 36, 73, 74, 76, 77–82, 83–4, 85, 86, 89, 109, 126–7, 128, 154, 155, 156, 157, 161, 162–4; on civic virtue of the magistrate, 77–8, 80, 85; on corruption, 81–3; and egoistic psychology, 36, 75, 76, 84, 85, 89, 149; on the good citizen, 74, 79–80, 84, 127, 161, 163; on political liberty, 70–3, 74, 79, 83, 85, 93; and privately oriented civic virtue, 10–11, 35, 83–4; publication of, 67, 68; and republican thought, 35, 36, 67, 81–2, 83–4, 93, 95n15; and the role of the patriot, 84, 85; on the

179